BIOGRAPHY: *A User's Guide*

BIOGRAPHY
A User's Guide

CARL ROLLYSON

Ivan R. Dee
CHICAGO 2008

BIOGRAPHY: A USER'S GUIDE. Copyright © 2008 by Carl Rollyson.
All rights reserved, including the right to reproduce this book or portions
thereof in any form. For information, address: Ivan R. Dee, Publisher, 1332
North Halsted Street, Chicago 60622, a member of the Rowman & Littlefield
Publishing Group. Manufactured in the United States of America and printed
on acid-free paper.

www.ivanrdee.com

Library of Congress Cataloging-in-Publication Data:
Rollyson, Carl E. (Carl Edmund)
    Biography, a user's guide / Carl Rollyson.
        p. cm.
    Includes bibliographical references and index.
    ISBN-13: 978-1-56663-780-0 (cloth : alk. paper)
    ISBN-10: 1-56663-780-5 (cloth : alk. paper)
    1. Biography as a literary form. I. Title.
CT21.R585 2008
808'.06692—dc22   2007044873

Contents

vi Contents

Introduction

FOR YEARS I have had it in mind to write a quirky encyclopedia of biography. It would be written not in the objective prose that flattens out most reference books. My project would be the life and opinions of one man, a practicing biographer. I would address "readers"—anyone interested in the subject of biography and biographers, and not just scholars or other experts. I would confect a work suitable for dipping into, one that can be read in a minute or an hour, by the bedside or propped against another book or other suitable support during a meal. Some of my topics would be conventional (Boswell and Johnson, for example) and others idiosyncratic and autobiographical (see Biography and the Academic Disciplines). While no aspect of biography would go untouched, the arrangement of the book—the topic headings, for example—would be arbitrary in so far as they would reflect one man's tastes and biases. In other words, I would do for biography what Samuel Johnson's dictionary did for the English language: expand the reader's sense of the subject without forsaking the personal predilections of the book's author.

The point of this book is to show that biography has many more dimensions than readers can grasp from reading book reviews and academic tomes on the subject. My hope is that my work has at least half the wit of David Thomson's entertaining *Biographical Dictionary of Film*. Thomson is comprehensive and concise, acerbic and amusing, and even when I disagree with him, I admire his brio, which challenges my own views because his are articulated with such conviction. Where I depart from the Thomson technique is my effort to include the voices of other biographers and critics, commenting on the topics of this book, especially where attitudes differ sharply—one school of writers regarding biography as a legitimate form of criticism while another sees next to no need for biography as a way to study writers. What I propose is to foster debate, not to offer the smoothed-over tone of encyclopedic works.

To add to the idiosyncratic nature of this work, I have included examples of my own reviews of biographies. Thus in the entry on political biography, I describe the genre, but I also include discussion of specific biographies that illustrate the different types of political biography that continue to be published. I do the same for subjects such as royal biography and religious biography. As I argue in my entry on reviews, reviewers seldom have much to say about biography; instead they provide a plot summary, concentrating on the biography's subject while ignoring what contribution to biography the book at hand may be making.

Reference books are usually the work of several authors because no individual can command an expertise in all areas of a subject. At the same time editors enforce a sort of bland uniformity, resulting in reference books that lack a "voice" or guiding spirit. I have tried to overcome both problems—to be comprehensive while maintaining a consistent point of view—by concerning myself mainly with English and American biography and biographers, my focus of study for the past thirty years. But because the writings of the classical world have influenced both English and American biography, I have included entries on Plutarch and Suetonius. Without Plutarch, for example, there could have been no Samuel Johnson, let alone a Boswell.

By the same token, I have also included a small number of European biographers who have had an important influence on English and American biography and who have been available in English translation for several generations. Sainte-Beuve, for example, must be included in any discussion of modern biography, like other figures such as André Maurois.

I also hope that this book will serve as a kind of Hall of Fame for biographers. I have emphasized pre-twentieth-century biographers who have stood the test of time or who have been unjustly neglected of late. But I also include figures such as Leon Edel and Richard Ellmann because critics have accorded them such high praise. Other twentieth- and twenty-first-century biographers are covered in my entry on innovations in biography, but I have not attempted to survey the entire range of important contemporary biographers, a task that could easily be the subject of another book.* Indeed, Steven Seraphin has edited two volumes on twentieth-century biographers for the Dictionary of Literary Biography series.

One feature of this volume that I believe is unique is an account of the novelists who have treated the subject of biography and biographers. These fictions of the biographer's trade seem especially vital because they reveal the nature of the biographical enterprise in ways that biographers themselves tend not to address. The focus of biography is on the subject, not the biographer, yet half the story of a biography is, of course, who is telling the story. And novelists are particularly adept at probing the nexus between biographer and subject. There is a sense in which one can learn more about biography from reading certain novels than from the biographies and biographers themselves.

For a truly random, serendipitous experience, just begin reading alphabetically. For readers with specific interests and hobbyhorses, I recommend rifling through the contents pages or checking the index. Either way, I hope this conglomeration provides the same pleasure people experience while perusing library shelves, coming across titles that spark curiosity. Readers may skip the parts that hold no interest or come back to certain topics later when they have time to digest lengthier pieces.

---

*But as my index shows, this book makes frequent references to the work of contemporary biographers.

Consider then, reader, that you have a menu in hand to be consumed as you please. There is no course you must ingest. Read a line or two, and if it palls, move on to the next item. There is no need to suffer a boring moment and no need to consider the author's feelings. This is a miscellany that is meant to be fondled—rudely or with tender care—as your heart desires.

BIOGRAPHY: *A User's Guide*

Academic Biography

Biography as a discipline of study has never had an important place in higher education. By the late nineteenth century Carlyle's Great Man theory of biography was under attack, especially by historians who believed that the shaping of society could not be adequately explained through the lives and careers of individual figures, no matter how important. The "new critics" also rejected the myth of the Romantic artist, preferring to concentrate on the work of art itself, forsaking any attempt to explain it in terms of the writer's life.

Deconstruction, which has also attacked the authority of the author, would seem to allow little room for the study of biography, though attempts have been made to reconcile "the death of the author" with some kind of "postmodern" study of literature. Neither term, "deconstruction" or "postmodern," has ever made much sense to me, even though academic careers have been built on elaborate discussions of such concepts.

Feminist biographers have partially turned the tide back toward biography by emphasizing the personality of the historian and biographer. To the feminist critic, it makes a good deal of difference whether a man or woman writes a biography. The issue of gender bias has thus generated considerable scholarship and revisionism, so that women historians and biographers have pointed out how much is omitted in accounts of writers such as F. Scott Fitzgerald and Vladimir Nabokov when the work of their wives is neglected. The very concept of a literary career has been redefined in biographies such as Brenda Maddox's biography of James Joyce's wife, *Nora: The Real Life of Molly Bloom.*

Even so, this development in biography has had little impact on the academic establishment. The one outstanding exception is Ambrose White Vernon, who established departments of biography at Carleton College (1920–1924) and at Dartmouth (1924–1967). Vernon's curriculum emphasized rigorous attention to archival research as a kind of antidote to the nineteenth-century emphasis on laudatory accounts of the great men of history. Historical figures were ₃ now subjected to critical questions.

Few examples of biography as an academic discipline remain. New York University established a master's program in biography, but it quickly languished when its two senior professors retired and the English Department resisted hiring replacements to continue graduate study in biography.

SEE ALSO New Critics.

FURTHER READING: For an article reflecting Vernon's academic approach to biography, see Arthur M. Wilson, "The Humanistic Bases of Biographical Interpretation," *English Institute Annual* (1942). For an argument on behalf of biography in an academic setting, see Elizabeth Young-Breuhl, "The Complexities and Rewards of Biography," *Chronicle of Higher Education*, vol. 36, no. 17, pp. B1–2.

Access

You need a burning desire to write about the subject, and you must calculate what resources you will have even if certain people won't talk to you and certain archives (if there are archives) are closed to you. Your proposal defines the issues for you: What kind of biography is it going to be? How much cooperation do you need? With some subjects I've needed little or none. On the other hand, for my biography of Jill Craigie I would never have gone forward without her husband's permission to go through her papers (all in her home). Apart from her private papers, there just wouldn't have been enough material for me to rely on. Even in this case, though, I made it clear I wasn't seeking approval (authorization), just access.

SEE ALSO Authorized Biography; Unauthorized Biography.

Advances

Most publishers offer biographers some type of advance against royalties. The size of the advance depends on the biographer's reputation and sales performance, though poor sales have not hindered me (and I presume other biographers) from finding publishers. A good book proposal can certainly stimulate publishers to offer advances that sales probably will not justify. I've never been an editor or publisher, so I do not understand what looks to me like a fantasy world—especially in regard to literary biographies. They may be prestige items, making the publisher seem serious, but they rarely recoup the publisher's or the biographer's investment.

W. W. Norton, for example, paid $40,000 for world rights to the biography of Susan Sontag that my wife and I wrote. This is a respectable but by no means high figure—except for me. Most of my advances have been in the $30,000 range, with one as low as $10,000. It is not unusual for a biographer to receive $100,000 or more, though I would guess that most biographers fall into my range or lower. Norton, I am sure, did not believe it would make back its investment in the U.S. market. It did an initial printing of 10,000 copies and then a second printing of 2,500. The biography is still in print—a tribute to Norton since most publishers do not keep biographies in print very long. Like most books, biographies have short shelf lives.

SEE ALSO Sales.

American Biography

American biography begins with Cotton Mather's *Magnalia Christi Americana* (1702). This classic work of Puritan biography is a kind of hagiography, extolling the lives of New England's governing officials and interpreting their good works as part of a divine plan, an "errand into the wilderness," leading to the founding of a "New Jerusalem." Mather carefully censored the work, omitting personal details and his subjects' flaws. A somewhat more developed sense of biography is evident in Jonathan Edwards's *An Account of the Life of the Late Reverend David Brainerd* (1749), which concentrates on Brainerd's spiritual development. Even so, Edwards's emphasis is on the exemplary pattern of his subject's life.

Not until the early nineteenth century did biography emerge as a widely read genre. Of course, the founding of the American republic inspired many biographies of American presidents and other important political figures, as well as frontier heroes such as Davy Crockett and Daniel Boone. Biography no longer had a specifically religious focus, yet the notion that the genre should elevate lives as virtuous examples remained the guiding force in the literature of the new nation.

Although American critics praised Boswell's biography of Johnson, in practice biographers did not take a "warts and all" approach to their subjects. Instead biographies were written as patriotic paeans to greatness. Few important American literary figures essayed biography. Exceptions are Washington Irving's multi-volume life of Washington and Nathaniel Hawthorne's campaign biography of his friend, Franklin Pierce. Neither of these biographies, however, made an important contribution to the national literature or the development of biography.

By the time Lincoln ran for office, campaign biographies had become quite common. William Dean Howells, for example, wrote a campaign biography for Lincoln, but, like other efforts in this genre, he made little attempt to do original research or present a balanced picture of the subject. The obvious aim of the book was to get a man elected to office.

Two biographers, however, stand out in nineteenth-century America: Jared Sparks and James Parton. Both did considerable original research and began to establish the biographer as an independent figure capable of writing the lives of prominent Americans with some degree of candor. By the end of the century, important literary figures like Walt Whitman and Mark Twain appointed authorized biographers, Horace Traubel and Alfred Bigelow Paine, respectively, who did not notably advance the genre in literary terms but rather emulated Boswell's dogged collection of the myriad details upon which modern biographies of these subjects depend.

Scholarly biographies of American literary and political figures become prevalent by the mid-twentieth century, but until the advent of biographers such as Justin Kaplan, Richard Ellmann, and Leon Edel, biography as a genre received little attention from critics. By the mid-1960s biography had developed its own culture, so to speak, becoming the province not merely of journalists and other writers appealing to a popular audience but also of academics like Kenneth Silverman. Silverman's career—ranging from a Pulitzer Prize–winning biography of Cotton Mather to a well-received biography of Edgar Allan Poe to a ground-breaking biography of Harry Houdini—illustrates the growth of the genre, which now crosses the line between readers of popular and scholarly books.

FURTHER READING: See Scott E. Casper's *Constructing American Lives: Biography and Culture in Nineteenth-Century America* (1991) for excellent discussions of the development of the genre and of Parton and Sparks, in particular, and Steven Serafin, ed., *American Literary Biographers. First Series* (1991). In "Producing American Selves: The Form of American Biography," in *Contesting the Subject: Essays in Postmodern Theory and Practice of Biography and Biographical Criticism*, edited by William H. Epstein (1991), Rob Wilson contends that American autobiography and biography propagate the "mytheme" of self-invention from Benjamin Franklin to Ralph Waldo Emerson to Ronald Reagan. Examining biographies of William Carlos Williams, Langston Hughes, Wallace Stevens, and Emily Dickinson, Wilson argues that American biographers have used "dead metaphors and entrenched language" to establish a "rhetoric of consensus" about the naked self emerging into a new world, sanctioning the liberal ideology of individualism and optimistic, capitalist values. "There remains a need for the nuts-and-bolts biographer not only to challenge the ideological content of his/her life-study but also to resist the latent ideology of the form itself—as Mailer has done in *The Executioner's Song.*"

Appearances

Several reviewers faulted Daniel Mark Epstein for dwelling on Edna St. Vincent Millay's physical appearance. I was floored when one reviewer said that the photographs in Epstein's biography proved that Millay wasn't beautiful. Photographs hardly tell the whole story. Epstein is evoking what Millay looked like in person. Reviewers assume he is gushing over Millay. But is he? There is ample evidence that Millay did turn men and women on. And it seems to me that in a biography, the story of a life, such matters matter. I remember being criticized for discussing Lillian Hellman's lack of beauty, with one reviewer even saying I emphasized that aspect of Hellman because my standard of beauty was Marilyn Monroe! Well, a few years ago, in a PBS *American Masters* documentary about Hellman, the first several minutes consisted of interviews with people such as Kitty Carlisle Hart who said things like "You know, Lillian was no oil painting." Her looks were part of the story. But reviewers somehow think such attention is unseemly and chastise biographers like Ann Waldron for discussing the way Eudora Welty looked.

Archives

Several European countries, such as Finland, Germany, and Britain, have repositories specifically dedicated to the subject of biography and life-writing. In the United States the term most often used for such collections is "oral history." Columbia University's library, for example, has extensive oral histories, many dealing with literary history. The late Roger Straus, one of the founders of the publishing firm Farrar, Straus and Giroux, gave several recorded interviews deposited there.

The New York Public Library contains the records of many publishers and magazines, including Farrar, Straus, *The New Yorker*, and *Collier's*. Other notable archives include the Library of Congress in Washington, D.C., the Harry Ransom Research Center of the University of Texas at Austin, Harvard University's Houghton Library, Yale University's Beinecke Library, the Huntington Library in Pasadena, California, and the Fales Library at New York University— to mention only the collections that are most often cited in biographers' acknowledgments.

Aubrey, John (1626–1697)

Aubrey's work, *Brief Lives*, was not published until 1813. Basically an antiquarian, Aubrey was a great collector of anecdotes and observations about famous people. He was indefatigable and, before Boswell, perhaps the most persistent biographer when it came to acquiring information. Aubrey had a vast circle of friends and left remarkable observations about John Milton, Thomas Hobbes, and Ben Jonson, for example. Thus Aubrey reported that Hobbes would "drinke to excesse to have the benefit of Vomiting." Physical appearances might be noted: Sir John Denham's eyes were "goose-gray." Aubrey produced 462 brief lives, some as short as a page. He can be considered one of the first oral historians. Unlike Boswell, Aubrey did not claim to pursue a rigorous method. Clearly he reported rumor and gossip, not just verifiable data.

FURTHER READING: Aubrey has been the subject of a biography by the distinguished novelist, Anthony Powell, *John Aubrey and His*

Friends (1948), and important discussions of Aubrey also appear in Donald A. Stauffer's *English Biography Before 1700* (1930), Lytton Strachey's *Portraits in Miniature and Other Essays* (1931), and Richard D. Altick's *Lives and Leters: A History of Literary Biography in England and America* (1966).

Authorized Biography

This kind of biography is written with the full cooperation of the subject or of the subject's literary estate, his family, and friends. Often the authorized biographer is a disciple or close friend—as in the case of James Anthony Froude, Carlyle's authorized biographer. Gore Vidal sought out Fred Kaplan after admiring his biography of Henry James.

I mention Froude and Kaplan because both biographers ran into trouble—the first because Carlyle's family and friends felt that in his book he did an injustice to his mentor, portraying the Carlyle marriage as fraught with acrimony and misunderstanding. The attack on the biographer became public, and Froude even had to endure a book specifically aimed at undermining his credibility. Froude ably defended himself in a short book he planned for posthumous publication, and posterity has fully vindicated him. Indeed, A. O. J. Cockshut, writing in *Truth to Life*, a study of nineteenth-century biography, believes Froude to have written the greatest biography in English literary history.

Kaplan fell afoul of Vidal after his subject realized that he could not control his biographer. Essentially Vidal wanted to vet the book, and Kaplan stood by their agreement that he was to have a free hand. Vidal suffered a form of buyer's remorse, which he tried to obfuscate by claiming he had chosen the wrong biographer—meaning to sign up Justin Kaplan, not Fred. But that claim was ridiculous and easily disproved, as Kaplan has shown.

Bernard Crick, George Orwell's authorized biographer, contended with similar interference from Orwell's second wife, Sonia. It is not an uncommon problem, since there is an obvious conflict between the demands of biographical research and the sentiments of the subject's family and friends. There is all the difference in the world between knowing someone as a friend, lover, spouse, or relative and studying that same person as a subject. Norman Sherry, Graham Greene's authorized biographer, bluntly states in his biography that Greene's friends will not recognize the man they knew. Like so many of us, Greene could seem like a different person to different people. Biographers must take this kaleidoscopic effect into account.

But what is truly extraordinary is that literary people often react to biography in the most stupid way. They can read novels replete with the complexity of human character, yet when the subject is known to them, they believe the biographer has gotten it wrong if his portrayal does not match their experience of the man or woman they knew.

Authorized biographers wary of buyer's remorse sometimes stipulate in writing that the subject or the subject's estate has no power to change, censor, or otherwise adulterate the biography. Martin Duberman insisted on such an agreement with Paul Robeson's son, who asked Duberman to write a biography of his father. Duberman was wise since in fact he did encounter objections from Paul Robeson, Jr.

Biographers, authorized or not, usually take the feelings of the subject's intimates into account. Carlos Baker, for example, was scrupulous about showing drafts of his biography to those close to Ernest Hemingway. Baker's archive at Princeton University shows how careful he was about consulting his interviewees and correcting errors they identified in his narrative. My archive at the University of Tulsa will show to what extent I was able to emulate Baker's example.

I have done as much in my biographies, whether they have been authorized or not. In some cases, though, it can be dangerous to show a manuscript to anyone who might object and perhaps delay publication. Thus my wife and I refused requests from Susan Sontag's representatives to examine our biography of her. And I rejected, as well, a request from Norman Mailer's agent to read my manuscript before I was granted permission to quote from Mailer's work.

I objected to this request and Mailer, to his credit, overruled his agent and granted me permission without asking to see any portion of my biography.

In two instances I have worked on biographies that had a kind of authorization. I began my Rebecca West biography without knowing anyone close to her, except for my London agent, who had been her editor at the *Sunday Telegraph*. Through him I was able to meet Alan Maclean, West's editor at Macmillan, and then through Maclean I made contact with West's heir and literary executor, Norman Macleod. After meeting with Macleod, I proceeded with his blessing—a boon, since several people who had refused me interviews were now suddenly available.

I never attempted to secure a written agreement from Macleod—to use an old-fashioned term, I had a gentleman's agreement with him. In effect he gave me both his full cooperation and his promise not to interfere, though I never put the case to him in precisely that way. To my delight he never made any demands, and though I showed the full manuscript to him, he raised no objections while pointing out a few errors that I then corrected.

My other foray into "authorized" biography came about when I contacted Michael Foot, whom I had interviewed for my Rebecca West biography, about the possibility of writing a biography of his recently deceased wife, Jill Craigie. A fan of my book on Rebecca—as was his wife—Michael welcomed my approach and clinched the deal when he exclaimed, "It's your book." In fact he did not mean it. As soon as the book was drafted, he was appalled that my view of him—particularly in relation to Jill—was not his own, and he demanded changes, even though he had enthusiastically endorsed my view that I should have a free hand, no matter what. But Foot became increasingly hostile as family members and friends objected to parts of my book, particularly to an episode describing Michael's infidelity.

FURTHER READING: I explore the ramifications of authorized biographies in *A Higher Form of Cannibalism* (2005) and in the forthcoming *Adventures of an Outlaw: A Biographer at Work.* Two other excellent studies of authorized biography are Ian Hamilton, *Keeper of the Flame* and Michael Millgate, *Testamentary Acts.* See also Eric Jacob's essay in *The Literary Biography,* ed. Dale Salwak (1996).

CRITIQUE: The recent Stephen Spender biography exemplifies the pitfalls of authorized biography:

Bear in mind that John Sutherland's *Stephen Spender: A Literary Life* (2005) is an Establishment biography. Sutherland, Lord Northcliffe Professor of Modern English Literature at University College London, writes in his acknowledgments:

> My main debt in writing this biography is to Lady Spender. She authorized the book and allowed unfettered access to her husband's literary and personal papers, the bulk of which are in the estate's private keeping. She has also contributed, often in the spirit of a co-author, to the writing of the work.

Not since Anne Stevenson's admission that Olwyn Hughes wrote part of her biography of Sylvia Plath have I read such a confession of cowardice. After such bowing and scraping, what can it mean when Sutherland then observes that Lady Spender "at no point . . . imposed restraint." Why use handcuffs when the biographer has already turned the key in his cell door and politely handed it over to the jailer? I guess I shouldn't be surprised at Professor Sutherland's inability to grasp the enormity of his defeat, since he is the author of a newspaper article titled "The Age of Blackwash," in which unauthorized biographers are excoriated. Sutherland clearly sees himself on the side of the angels.

In 1992, Lady Spender ambushed her husband's unauthorized biographer, Hugh David, in the *Times Literary Supplement* a week before David's biography appeared. She called for a code of conduct for biographers who had, in her view, gotten out of hand. No biography should be written without the subject's approval: she wanted it written into the law. She also wanted biographers to have two lists of acknowledgments, one that indicated which interviewees approved of the biographer and another that did not.

There were other shackles—so many that David Leeming, Spender's second biographer, felt compelled to quote from a "Talk of the Town" *New Yorker* piece reporting that the hysterical attack on David had diminished the "considerable sympathy for the Spenders." Lady Spender's "absurd suggestion that the subject always knows better than the biographer, is so self-righteous that opinion is now drifting the other way."

Sutherland pretends none of this happened. Hugh David appears at a few points in the biography, only to be hammered once again. It is quite true that David received "scathing reviews," but they were of the "how dare he!" kind that the literary establishment has no trouble rounding up when an interloper writes about one of their own. Hilary Spurling, herself a whitewasher of Sonia Orwell, gave the David book a good thrashing, and heavyweights like Frank Kermode and Isaiah Berlin inveighed against David even before his book reached print.

Yet seven years on, when Leeming published his biography, he reports that Frank Kermode "essentially blamed Natasha Spender." Kermode is reported to have said, "When things go wrong, she does the worrying, and Stephen goes on in his usual passive way." But David Plante saw the Spenders quite differently, suggesting that Stephen used Natasha "as a shield for his own anger." Stephen would say, "Oh, Natasha's very upset," but really (Plante insisted), "he's the one who's making her upset."

So which is it? Surely the authorized biographer ought to help us out? Nothing doing. Professor Sutherland is silent about the husband/wife dynamic. And this reticence is what is wrong with this biographer—for all his precious access. He never thinks through the implications of Spender's behavior, or explores why, for example, Spender got quite so upset about Hugh David.

The sly Leeming notes, "unfortunately the whole row gives credence to Spender's often-expressed self-criticism that he was overly concerned with the opinions of others about his life and work."

Give me one of Leeming's sentences for every ten Sutherland writes. Give me even Hugh David, whose biography is no masterpiece but is certainly better than what the reviewers reviled. These two are not superior to Sutherland, by any means, but they are essential to clearing the air around the stuffy authorized biographer.

The Spenders made fools of themselves in protesting too much; even worse, they brought out the literary establishment's forces to crush Hugh David. Ted Hughes & Co. organized a kill-the-book campaign against the publisher (Heinemann). Whatever his merits as a poet, Hughes deserves his ill repute as a foe not merely of Plath biographers but of the genre itself. Hughes proposed a mass protest of writers, calling it "pack pressure on any publisher who did what Heinemann did."

When Heinemann refused to withdraw David's book, the Spenders enlisted the aid of the Society of Authors, whose chairman, Anthony Sampson—"disgusted" by David's book—tried to implement Natasha Spender's penal code for biographers. Although there was much discussion, Sutherland reports, the society's "'code of practice' proposal came to nothing." How could it? When Martha Gellhorn tried a similar tactic against me, by ringing up the Authors Guild, she was immediately told that the Guild could not possibly take sides against an author.

The funny thing about Stephen Spender is that he was always bringing up other writers' lives, spilling the beans, always telling you about how Henry James seduced His Majesty's horse guards (Leeming heard about that one from Spender, who heard it from Hugh Walpole) or regaling listeners about Hemingway's comic vulgarity. And like his friend Christopher Isherwood, Spender could not resist putting real people in his poems and novels. Indeed, his first novel was rejected as libelous.

Compared to this kind of frolic with people's lives, I must say Hugh David hardly seems an object worthy of scorn. "You are taking my life and misinterpreting it and getting facts wrong"—this is the case against David—but the same case can be made against Spender.

And indeed it was. As Martha Gellhorn wrote to me, she was fed up and had decided to expose Spender's lies about Hemingway, her ex-husband, which she did in a hilarious but withering attack on Spender and Lillian Hellman in the *Paris Review*. She called her piece "Close Encounters of the Apocryphal Kind" and was outraged when the pusillanimous George Plimpton, fearing Spender's reaction, refused to use the title. Gellhorn's evisceration of both parties is so unanswerable that Sutherland simply gives ground, not contesting the fictitiousness of what Spender said about Hemingway.

Sutherland tries to muffle his embarrassment for his subject by calling Spender's recollections "some throwaway remarks" in a *Paris Review* interview. But that journal does not publish "throwaway remarks." Indeed, interviewees have routinely vetted their own *Paris Review* interviews, making them, in effect, into autobiographies. Spender put a brave face on his prevarications, replying to Gellhorn with "some asperity" and "heavy sarcasm," to use Sutherland's words. But in private (and here the authorized biographer can proudly parade his treasures), Spender meditated in his journal, "Was anything he recalled about Hemingway reliable?"

From such passages it is clear that Spender had second thoughts about his recollections, but what does his biographer make of his subject's behavior? Spender—whether Natasha or Stephen—has the last word, which is fine in autobiography but not so fine in biography. Sutherland has written a Victorian biography—very strong on facts but obfuscated by the sanctity accorded his subject.

Meryle Secrest provides a more honest account of authorized biography in *Shoot the Widow* (2007). For her biography of Sir Kenneth Clark, the august art historian, she ostensibly had her subject's cooperation. Say what you like, Clark's son Alan told Secrest. As I know from my own painful experience, living figures and their families rarely mean it when they endorse openness. They admire your work, what you have done with some *other* subject, but then they discover that you have got it all wrong when it comes to themselves!

Kenneth Clark tried to control everything—even paying some of Secrest's interviewees on the sly. Such acts lead biographical subjects to believe they have their chroniclers in their pockets. After I stayed with Labour party leader Michael Foot while doing his wife's biography, I learned that something along these lines was said about me. But as Secrest illustrates, inevitably there is a parting of ways when the biographer asserts his or her independence.

How do biographers get into such fixes? Secrest explains: We want access. We are agreeable. We seem like good friends, but to write a credible life we have to get the goods, engaging not in cover-ups but in revelations. Subjects as sophisticated as Sir Kenneth Clark might be assumed to know the score: in the end, the biographer cannot be controlled. Alas, not so. "To hell with you all," Secrest finally had to tell the Clarks. Only then could she write her own book.

Better, it seems to me, to risk the full disclosure of unauthorized biography and the inevitable name-calling (James Joyce called us biografiends) than to capitulate to the kind of propriety that dooms biographical truth.

Autobiography

Twenty years ago, when my agent was circulating my proposal to write a biography of Lillian Hellman, an editor said to her, "Why do we need a biography when she has written so much about her own life?" It was an extraordinary thing to say, especially since Hellman's veracity had been challenged and proven unreliable even before her demise.

The editor's comment, however, reminds me that newspapers, magazines, and publications of all kinds often lump autobiography and biography together. It is a sure sign that all the two genres mean to them is life story. Yet there is all the difference in the world between autobiography and biography, between telling your own story and having someone else on your case.

The autobiographer does not have to be a world-class liar like Lillian Hellman to be a suspect from the biographer's point of view.

The individual simply cannot see himself or herself from all the angles a biographer has to reconnoiter. Indeed, the biography presents such a different perspective on the subject that the subject's friends often say, "That was not the X I knew." And then they leap to the conclusion that the biographer is biased or incompetent.

But there is simply no similarity between knowing a friend, relative, or colleague and making them a subject of study. Norman Sherry, Graham Greene's authorized biographer, declares bluntly in his introduction that the Greene he portrays is not one that his friends will recognize. A deceptive—even deceitful—man, Greene even eludes his biographer's understanding at many points, but at least Sherry has canvased all those points in a way that we simply cannot do, even with our intimates.

To blur the distinction between autobiography and biography is to regard life stories as just so much content devoid of style, point of view, or perspective.

The other aspect of autobiography worth considering in relation to biography is the biographer. Paul Murray Kendall asserts in *The Art of Biography* (1965) that every biography is, in some sense, an autobiography. But Kendall does not go into detail about how that is so. Norman Mailer, on the other hand, has made a signal contribution to our understanding of the nexus between biographer and subject.

Unlike most biographers, Mailer does not hide behind a third-person voice. In his biography of Marilyn Monroe, he is very personal, confessing his biases, expressing his doubts about his qualifications as a biographer, yet treating Monroe as a fellow artist and positing an affinity between them. As I show in *The Lives of Norman Mailer: A Biography* (1991), both he and Monroe are self-invented figures and have craved public exposure and dreamed of a fame that is extra-literary, transcending the usual appeal of authors and movie stars, and aiming for nothing less than a transformation in the consciousnesses of their times.

I read Mailer at an impressionable age. I was turning thirty and reading Gail Sheehy's *Passages,* a book about people who were having midlife crises. I was having one of those crises. I had begun a career as an actor before turning to teaching. Out of graduate school, an assistant professor with a few articles published, I wasn't happy. I wasn't a star. And here was Mailer drooling after Marilyn Monroe and practically saying in so many words that he was unhappy because he couldn't have her and he wasn't a star—not a star by the ambitious lights he had shone on himself. I wrote an article on Mailer's *Marilyn,* which appeared in 1978 in the journal *Biography.*

Then I got a call from a good friend, a former teacher of mine, who was editing a series of bio-bibliographies on popular figures. He wanted to know if I would like to write one on Monroe. Sure! The book was supposed to have a long biographical chapter and then several bibliographical sections—really essays on the various books, movies, works of art, and so forth that were about or had been inspired by Marilyn Monroe. I spent a summer reading countless biographies of Monroe and writing summaries of them. I got bored. I also made a huge discovery: none of Monroe's biographers knew anything about acting. Many of them did not think she was an actress. They saw her as a star who at best strove to become an actress. I saw her as an actress who was a star. Because I had begun as an actor, I felt there was a special bond between us that none of her other biographers had ever felt.

I wrote and visited Monroe biographers, who gave me names and addresses of agents and actors and business associates of Monroe's. And I watched Monroe's movies over and over again, scrutinizing her performances to see whether they were distinctive, whether I could say things about how she prepared for and executed each of her roles. I read psychology, books on acting, books I knew that Monroe had read—such as Mabel Elsworth Todd's *The Thinking Body*—and I read the professional papers of her psychiatrist, Ralph Greenson. It astounded me that Monroe's other biographers had not thought to approach her this way. A few pages in earlier biographies by Fred Guiles and Maurice Zolotow did adumbrate an approach similar to mine, and when I pointed this out to them, they responded enthusiastically, sensing that I would do something new with Monroe by extending and capitalizing on their work. As a result, they were extraordinarily generous with their help and advice.

Thus I was having my vicarious experience and attaching myself to a star. And it was Mailer who had shown how the biographer's deepest needs inform a biography. By way of justifying his choice of Monroe he had said, "put an artist on an artist." I tried to make the equation even more exact: "put an actor on an actor." I give the credit to Mailer because before reading him I had had no particular feeling for Monroe. I had liked her movies, though I had not seen all of them and was certainly not a fan. What engaged me on the deepest, personal level was her idea that she would find her identity through a career as an actress.

Each of my biographies present a facet of myself—or some potential I see realized in the subjects I choose to write about. Lillian Hellman was an obvious choice. Only after I finished the book did I realize there were also some not so obvious reasons why I decided on her. Let's begin with the obvious: I was attracted to her life in the theater. I happen to think it is more difficult to write a great play than a novel or a poem or a short story. Actors usually adore Hellman's plays. They are filled with vivid characters and sharp conflict. Hellman was also a first-class screenwriter—and one of the few to claim single authorship of her scripts. She was active in politics and in her person embodied many of the conflicts in the American sensibility from the depression through the 1960s. And she had written a set of controversial memoirs that cried out for a biographer's investigation.

As a personality I did not think I had much in common with Hellman, yet I found her entirely fascinating and never tired of thinking and writing about her. Much of the joy in working on her, however, had to do with discovering new documents—such as her husband's diaries and various collections of letters in libraries and in private hands. And it was a thrill to interview actors like Walter Matthau and many others in her private life. To gain access to her FBI files was a challenge in itself. And because she had appointed an authorized biographer and did everything possible to thwart anyone else from writing a biography, I took a special pleasure in every new find—as if I were a detective or spy. To do unauthorized biographies is to revel in the illicit.

But I was thunderstruck when I realized the personal basis for doing Lillian Hellman's biography. About a year after it was published, I was interviewing a childhood friend of Martha Gellhorn's for my biography of her. They had grown up together in St. Louis, and years later had had to worry together about whether their sons would be drafted to serve in the Vietnam War. I began to tell her about my worries over Vietnam—that I had been a graduate student in Canada opposed to the war. I had applied for conscientious-objector status. I came to my draft hearing neatly dressed, polite, and respectful. My tone conveyed regret, not rebellion. I spoke the language of a loyal citizen. My draft board was impressed—not with my arguments, I hasten to add, but with my demeanor. They were impressed that I had come from Toronto. They knew that many American men had decided to stay there rather than serve in the armed forces. I stated my principles without prejudice to their own. To this day I do not know what happened. For I did not receive conscientious-objector status, nor was I called to do alternative service. I was simply deactivated—buried, so to speak, in my draft board's files.

When I wrote about Hellman testifying before the House Committee on Un-American Activities, I was reliving my draft board appearance.

I devote a whole chapter to Hellman's appearance before HUAC. It is one of the most vivid things I've ever written. I describe her trip to the hearing room, the size of the room, the cast of characters, and so on. It is like a scene from a play, for I found Hellman's life inherently dramatic and her appearance before HUAC her greatest role.

FURTHER READING: In "Choosing a Life" (*New York Times*, January 13, 1991, pp. 1, 22–23), James Atlas, citing numerous examples (including his own biography of Delmore Schwartz), supports the view that the best biographies are founded on "the biographer's unconsciously realized opportunity for self-expression." Rather than liking the subject, the biographer must be "possessed," fully committed to the strenuous task of discovering and interpreting the evidence. Many biographies fail when the biographer, out of sympathy with the subject, turns against the biographical enterprise, either abandoning the form or attacking the subject.

One of the best studies of writers' autobiographies is *Fabricating Lives: Explorations in American Autobiography* (1991) by Herbert A. Leibowitz. Very few biographers have written their autobiographies. But Michael Holroyd has written two: *Basil Street Blues* (1999) and *Mosaic* (2004). Joan Givner, a biographer of Katherine Anne Porter, has published *The Self-Portrait of a Literary Biographer* (1993), and Meryl Secrest provides the best example of a working biographer's life in *Shoot the Widow* (2007), which is what biographers aim for, she suggests.

Berryman, John (1914–1972)

The poet John Berryman wrote one biography, which remains, especially in terms of its style, a landmark in American biography. In *Stephen Crane: A Critical Biography* (revised edition, 1977), the biographer apologizes for writing a psychological biography because he finds that most works of this kind are not encouraging. The alternative, however, in which the biographer refrains from comment and allows the reader to draw his own conclusions, is ludicrous and would not be tolerated in other disciplines such as geology or physics. Literary questions must come first, but psychological insight informs those questions and has allowed Berryman to come to "tentative but definite conclusions." *See also* Psychobiography.

Biographers in Fiction

Novelists and short-story writers have often featured biographers as major characters and focus on biography as a troubling subject. Below I conduct a chronological tour of a remarkable number of works that take biography as their raison d'être.

1888: In *The Aspern Papers*, Henry James's classic novella, a would-be biographer of Jeffrey Aspern, an early nineteenth-century poet, visits Venice hoping to acquire the correspondence between Aspern and his mistress, Miss Bordereau. Insinuating himself into Miss Bordereau's life, the biographer takes her niece, Miss Tina, into his confidence. But Miss Bordereau catches him searching her desk, and when he returns after a fortnight he finds she has died, and that Miss Tina has fallen in love with him and intimates that only a relative would be permitted to examine the papers. Alarmed at this proposal, the biographer leaves, only to find at his next meeting with Miss Tina that she has destroyed the letters.

1898: In "The Real Right Thing" by Henry James, George Withermore, an inexperienced young journalist and critic, is flattered by an invitation from the widow of the great writer Ashton Doyne to write her recently deceased husband's biography, especially when she gives him complete access to Doyne's papers and puts him to work in his study. Withermore immerses himself in Doyne's archive, encouraged by the almost palpable presence of his subject. Suddenly Withermore feels bereft and senses that Doyne's spirit has departed. Gradually he understands he has misread the scene, and when he has a vision of Doyne at the top of the stairs barring the way back into his room, he understands that his subject has looked upon the biography as a violation of his life. The would-be biographer decides to desist.

1922: In *Jacob's Room* by Virginia Woolf, the life and death (in World War I) of Jacob Flanders is pieced together by a would-be biographer, who struggles with incomplete evidence (sketchy reports of friends, memories, the subject's books and the scenes he visited) to form an image, a credible vision of an elusive individual, an inexplicable past. Considered one of Woolf's first modernist novels, the biographer is (significantly) a woman who refuses to accept the content of stories at face value and forces the reader to think along with her about the implications of another's life.

1922: *Orlando: A Biography* by Virginia Woolf is a spoof of biography. Orlando, the biographical subject, manages to live over three centuries, changing from man to woman, and provoking, in the process, significant questions about the ambiguity of human identity and the extent to which the plodding, fact-oriented biographer can possibly capture the protean quality of an individual's life. Throughout the novel there are comments on the way biographers handle narrative and describe character, on the supple imagination of novelists and the halting, fragmentary compositions of biographers. Biography, Woolf implies, attempts to stabilize itself with the idea of "a single, a real self" and can account for, at most, "six or seven selves." The novel, on the other hand, and most especially her novel, insists on a "great variety of selves," perhaps as many as a thousand.

1930: *Cakes and Ale, or The Skeleton in the Cupboard* is W. Somerset Maugham's tour-de-force treatment of English literary life. The novel's inside view of the making and breaking of writers' reputations also provides insight into the opportunities and constraints of authorized biography. The second wife of Edward Driffield requests that Alroy Kear, a minor novelist, write the biography of her late husband, one of England's most distinguished writers (a fictionalized version of Thomas Hardy). Kear soon realizes that the true story of Driffield's early years cannot be told without including the story of his great love and first wife, Rosie, who calls to mind the great writer's rough beginnings, and is sure to offend the second Mrs. Driffield, who is fiercely protective of her husband's fame.

1933: *Flush: A Biography* by Virginia Woolf is a mock biography of Elizabeth Barrett Browning's spaniel. The dog's consciousness registers the constricted world of the invalid poet with an immediacy of sensory experience uncomplicated by human perception. Flush quite literally noses his mistress's world with a freshness and directness that provides a direct contrast with the highly intellectualized world of Woolf's other mock biography, *Orlando*. Like a biographer, the dog slowly becomes sensitized to the subject's world, absorbing and reflecting Barrett's intensely interior life with an intimacy missing from most conventional biographies.

1938: In Jean-Paul Sartre's *Nausea*, Antoine Roquetin, the biographer of Marquis de Rollebon, grapples in his diary not only with the meaning of his subject's life but with existence itself, concluding that he cannot complete his biography and cannot justify the meaning of another human being's existence any more than his own. Nevertheless the novel provides keen insights into the process of historical research, into the biographer's ambivalence about his subject and his sources, and into the way the biographer's life impinges on his subject, sometimes making the biographer feel he is writing a novel of another's life in compensation for the career he himself cannot pursue. The diary form enhances the immediacy and the rigor of the biographer's thoughts.

1939: *What's Become of Waring* is Anthony Powell's amusing tale of the publishing world focused on efforts to produce a biography of T. T. Waring, one of Judkins & Judkins' star authors. Waring, the author of popular travel books, is reported to have drowned in France. Not much is known about him, yet the publishers intend to capitalize on his recent demise by publishing a biography as quickly as possible. But the Judkins brothers have difficulty agreeing on the writer for the job, and then certain dubious facts about Waring himself come to light, forcing the biographer that the firm finally settles on to consider abandoning the project. Powell's witty exposé of London publishing and the complicated politics of biography make this one of the classic commentaries on the role of biography in the literary world.

1941: In *The Real Life of Sebastian Knight* by Vladimir Nabokov, the narrator is the half brother and biographer of the famous English novelist Sebastian Knight. Nabokov parodies the form of biographies, beginning with an account of the subject's birth, the biographer's primary sources of evidence (including his own memories), and secondary sources while also mimicking the language of biography ("it is known from," "he surely felt," "I cannot say"). Knight's aloofness complicates the biographer's task, making him wonder how well he really knew his brother, and eventually provoking him into believing he has written an autobiography as much as a biography: a story "shaped by the teller, reshaped by the listener, concealed from both by the dead man of the tale."

1948: *Doctor Faustus* by Thomas Mann is a novel written in the form of a biography of a great composer, Adrian Leverkuhn (1885–1940), by his lifelong friend, Serenus Zeitbloom. The narrator/biographer tries to come to terms with his subject's Faustian greatness and creative arrogance, his isolation from humanity, and the paradoxical way in which art both validates and condemns him. Zeitbloom shifts constantly from his present (his growing awareness from 1943 that Germany is losing the war) to the career of Leverkuhn, also contrasting the difference between narrative in novels and in biographies and the handling of human character in the two forms, while insisting not only on the factual accuracy of his account but on his imaginative right to render scenes from his friend's life in which he was not present because he is so attuned to "psychological fact."

1972: Steven Millhauser's *Edwin Mullhouse: The Life and Death of an American Writer, 1943–1954, by Jeffrey Cartright* is a send-up of biography. The novel is divided into "The Early Years," "The Middle Years," "The Late Years." Jeffrey is Edwin's Boswell, not only faithfully recording the minutiae of the writer's life but also creating situations in which he can observe his subject's life and eventually his death. Millhauser captures both the comic and sinister sides of the biographer's devotion to the creative self and the sense in which the subject is the biographer's creation, an extension of his desire to impose a certain order on sometimes trivial, sometimes ambiguous evidence. The very neatness of Jeffrey's mind calls into question his interpretations and the biographer's obsession to invent a coherent self.

1972: In "The Sacred Marriage" in *Marriages and Infidelities* by Joyce Carol Oates, Howard Dean, a diffident college professor and literary critic, writes to the wife of Connell Pearce, a recently deceased poet, about doing a biography. To his surprise she invites him to spend a week examining Pearce's papers. At first taken aback by the widow's friendliness, Dean is charmed by her beauty, and at her instigation they become lovers, which he interprets as a marriage of minds and bodies in the service of his biography, an illusion he is quickly disabused of when he discovers she has invited another scholar to examine the papers. Dean, who has not felt equal to the task of biography, learns (at great cost to himself) just how deeply wedded a biographer can become to his subject.

1976: Carol Shields, *Small Ceremonies*, features a biographer, Judith Gill, working on a biography of writer Susan Moodie, an elusive subject who makes Gill feel like "the enemy," an "invader." Biographers crave "total disclosure," Gill notes, which she regards in herself as an "unhealthy lust for the lives of other people." She also quotes Leon Edel's remark that biography is the "most inexact of the sciences." Gill has attempted a novel but has failed to complete it, and then she is shocked when her friend, a well-known Canadian novelist, Furlong Eberhart, steals her plot. Even worse, another novelist bases his work on her family, though she doubts they will recognize themselves in it. After completing her biography, Gill admits that Moodie remains enigmatic "lost under all the gauze" of her various guises.

Her novelist friend advises that perhaps that is best—in fact, that is the central fact of her life: her desire not to be fully known. Eberhart should know, since he has obfuscated certain crucial facts of his own life. Gill knows because she has done some digging into her friend's past. But because of her own conflicted feelings about the way her family has become grist for the novelist's mill, she decides not to reveal what Eberhart has so carefully concealed. What is perhaps most striking about this novel is the biographer/protaganist who admits that in large measure her subject thwarts her but who nevertheless persists in plying her inexact science.

1979: In Bernard Malamud's *Dubin's Lives*, William Dubin, a biographer of Lincoln, Twain, and Thoreau, finds it difficult to write D. H. Lawrence's passionate short life. Dubin's wife, Kitty, no longer excites him, and nearing sixty he has an affair with the luscious Fanny, a woman in her early twenties. As Dubin's relationship with Fanny deepens and he becomes estranged from Kitty, he feels he has a nature that has been subdued by the lives he has written. He meditates on the complications of biography compared to the complications of his own life. Dubin does not resolve his own problems, and the only clue to his fate at the end of the novel is a bibliography of his work, which includes the publication of his D. H. Lawrence.

1983: *Marbot: A Biography* by Wolfgang Hildesheimer purports to explore the life of Andrew Marbot, an English Romantic. This novel invents letters, journals, and other writings to establish Marbot as the first critic to inquire into the psychological causes of creativity, anticipating the discoveries of psychoanalysis, especially the Oedipus complex, which Marbot acted out with his mother. As much about biography's ability to track the inner motives of the self, this novel brilliantly puts together evidence of Marbot's suicide, even though Marbot did not explicitly reveal his desire to end his life or confess his despair over his inability to paint. Biography is necessary, the novel implies, because self-knowledge—an understanding of the self's deepest motives—is impossible. Only biography, however imperfectly, can objectify the subject.

1984: *The Paper Men* is William Golding's comic novel about Wilfred Barclay, a renowned novelist in decline, and his biographer, Rick L. Tucker, a none-too-fastidious academic who grovels after his subject—even going so far as to dig through Barclay's garbage. Golding revels in this satire of the academic sleuth putatively dedicated to literature, in actuality ambitious and career-driven, attempting to manipulate his subject even as his subject exploits him. This is a wry, sometimes cynical and farcical portrayal of what it takes to become the authorized biographer.

1984: In Penelope Lively's *According to Mark*, Mark Lamming, biographer of Gilbert Strong, embarks on a visit to his long dead subject's granddaughter in Dorset, in order to examine various papers and documents. Happily married and an established writer, Lamming is surprised to find himself falling in love with Carrie, feeling her frank and friendly presence more powerfully than that of her grandfather's more elusive character, until there is a sudden breakthrough (the discovery of a cache of letters) and Carrie suddenly awakens with her own romantic interest. The novel is a superb study of the biographer's psychology, of the interplay between biographical knowledge (how a biographer knows a subject) and how a biographer copes with that knowledge mediated by his own character and present circumstances.

1985: *Flaubert's Parrot* by Julian Barnes is a novel in the form of a meditation on Flaubert's life and work. The narrator, Geoffrey Brathwaite, is not a biographer, but his pursuit of Flaubert is biographical: "Why does the writing make us chase the writer?" he asks. Viewing biography through the metaphor of a trawling net, Brathwaite combs through the major and minor details of Flaubert's life and career, seeking the most intimate contact with his subject and suggesting that "all biographers secretly want to annex and channel the sex-lives of their subjects; you must make your judgment on me as well as on Flaubert."

1988: In *The Truth About Lorin Jones* by Alison Lurie, biographer Polly Alter begins her research believing she knows the truth about Lorin Jones: she was a victim of male chauvinism. A genius, Jones was taken up by art critic Garrett Jones, who married and exploited her, and then by a much younger man, Hugh Cameron, who abandoned her shortly before her early death. The truth, Polly eventually learns, is that Lorin appears in many different guises depending on the personalities and circumstances of those who encountered her. Lurie demonstrates how a biographer acquires information and begins to formulate a narrative sense of the subject's life. Spaced at strategic points are chapters that give fragmentary transcripts of Polly's interviews, encouraging the reader to function, in part, as a biographer, and to assess Polly's interpretive progress.

1989: *Deceits of Time* by Isabel Colegate features Catherine Hillery, a professional biographer who is commissioned to write the life of Neil Campion, a World War I flying ace and Conservative MP who dies in a car crash in 1941. Hillery is puzzled as to why Campion's estate has chosen her as the authorized biographer. She is not an expert in the period and would not seem to have any other particular qualifications for this subject. It is also curious that the estate has waited so long to designate a biographer. Then Hillery learns that a journalist, Alfred Madden, has shown an interest in doing Campion's life. The estate, in other words, has now named a biographer because the unauthorized biographer has forced its hand. Does the estate have something to hide? And is Hillery a safe choice precisely because she is out of her depth? The dilemmas of both the authorized and unauthorized biographer are shrewdly explored, with no party emerging on ethical high ground. When it comes to unraveling Campion's post–World War I politics, including his pro-German sympathies, the biographer discovers not only secrets the Campion family would prefer to keep hidden but also the problematic nature of biography that forces her to consider abandoning her book.

1990: *Possession* by A. S. Byatt is an ingenious appraisal of contemporary biography, a narrative about two scholars (and their rivals) in search of the true nature of the love between two Victorian poets, Randolph Henry Ash and Christabel La Motte, complete with diaries, journals, letters, literary criticism, interviews—in short all the documents, competing scholarly interpretations, and apparatus of modern academic inquiry. Byatt invents not only the poets but their poems, surrounding the story with what might be called the politics and procedure of biography, juxtaposing the different twentieth-century critical terminologies (from Freudian to feminist) with nineteenth-century verse forms and prose.

1990: In *The Players Come Again* by Amanda Cross, Kate Fansler (a literature professor and amateur detective) is engaged to write the first biography of Gabrielle Foxx, wife of the great modernist writer Emmanuel Foxx and the inspiration for his classic novel, *Ariadne*. Committed to honoring the secrets of the three women who have contrived the circumstances in which Fansler discovers Gabrielle's unpublished papers, which turn out to be a novel—also called *Ariadne*, a feminist countermyth to Emmanuelle's work—Fansler decides to edit the novel with a biographical preface, believing that the next generation of scholars should pursue Gabrielle's secret life through her written work. Cross raises important ethical questions about biography as well as revealing much about the biographer's interviewing techniques and examination of written sources.

1991: In *Biography* by Celia Gitelson, biographer Raphael Alter, engaged in a life of the late American poet Maxwell Leibert, becomes so implicated in his subject's life—making love to one of his mistresses, who may also have been Leibert's daughter—that he finds he cannot complete the biography. Alter, a victim of what he calls a "self-imposed autism," rejects the comfort of the biographer's distance from his subject, the appeal of remaining a "bystander," to accept the fact that he has become his subject's "double." Gitelson skillfully interweaves the biographer's and the subject's lives, demonstrating the difference between biographical knowledge of a life that is past and life itself, while also providing an insightful reenactment of biographical research, particularly the biographer's handling of interviews.

1995: Kingsley Amis's comic novel *The Biographer's Mustache* concerns Gordon Scott-Thompson, a journalist who wishes to write the authorized biography of Jimmie Fane, a prolific but now out-of-fashion novelist. Scott-Thompson supposes a biography might stimulate renewed interest in Fane and also gain not only book publication but a lucrative serial in a British newspaper. Amis astutely skewers the contemporary biographer's need to seduce the subject and his friends, but he is just as hard on the biographical subject, who is quite adept at manipulating his biographer. It is difficult to say more without spoiling the enjoyment of the twists and turns of this amusing book. But it does not give much away to say that the biographer learns to dislike his trade, even though it has certain compensations and results in a surprising denouement that says a good deal about contemporary publishing, the literary world, and the biographer's problematic relationship with both. The book's title becomes clear when the biographer shaves off his mustache—a sure sign that he has emasculated his independence.

1995: In Jill Paton Walsh's *A Piece of Justice*, a graduate student, Frances Bullion, is given the dull task of writing a mathematician's biography. Her supervisor, the aptly named Professor Maverack, holds Cambridge's first chair of Biography and is viewed with considerable skepticism by colleagues who doubt that biography is a discipline worthy of university study. It turns out the mathematician did not lead such a quiet life and that his reputation is built on fraud. The indefatigable Fran nearly loses her life because of her unwillingness to write anything less than a candid book. In the end,

Professor Maverack believes his own theory of biography has been vindicated, since Fran has exposed several biographers who have been unwilling to confront the truth. The main thrust of Maverack's treatise on biography is to "deconstruct the self-flattering falsehoods behind which people shelter, and which biographers often collude with."

1998: *The Chimney Sweeper's Boy* by Barbara Vine is a cunning comment on the recent vogue of memoirs of famous authors and other artists by their sons and daughters. When Gerald Candless, a well-regarded novelist (he was once short-listed for the prestigious Booker Prize), dies, one of his daughters, Sarah, agrees to take on the project of writing his life. Although she is expected to concentrate on her own memories, she feels the need to do at least some research on her beloved father's early years. Candless was unusually close to his daughters while treating Ursula, his wife, with an indifference bordering at times on hostility that she is hard put to fathom. Sarah, seeing her work as a labor of love, is astonished to discover how much of his early life her father has invented, including his name and his job history. Astonishingly blind to her mother's suffering, Sarah never realizes how much help her mother could be with the research. The more Sarah functions as a biographer, however, the more apparent it becomes that her father was not the man she took him to be. This novel is a shrewd comment on the limitations of autobiography and the cruel demands of biography, which often lead to retold lives that shock even those closest to the biographical subjects.

1999: In *Losing Nelson* by Barry Unsworth, Charles Cleasby, writing a biography of Admiral Nelson, is troubled by his hero's behavior in Naples in June 1799. Nelson, allied with the king and queen of Naples, allowed the slaughter of hundreds of Republicans—those Neopolitans who supported the French Revolution and briefly established a government when the king and queen fled the occupying French forces. Although most biographers have considered the bloodbath in Naples as the only blot on Nelson's stellar career, others, like Cleasby, have sought to vindicate the admiral, suggesting he was not aware that the king and queen would renege on the agreement that would have given the Republicans the right to flee into exile.

An extravagant admirer of Nelson, Cleasby structures his life around commemorations of Nelson's famous victories. But his work stalls because he cannot find the evidence that would exonerate Nelson. Matters are made worse when his assistant ("Miss Lily") keeps challenging Cleasby, insisting that the biographer cannot create a separate standard for Nelson just because he is a hero. Gradually her skepticism erodes Cleasby's confidence, which then is given a mortal blow when he visits Naples in a final, desperate attempt to extricate his hero from infamy.

Unsworth's novel is a brilliant exploration of what happens when a biographer so identifies with his subject that he loses all perspective. Cleasby refers to himself as Nelson's "other self," his "shadow."

The novel also provides incisive discussions of previous Nelson biographers and their motivations for exalting or debunking his heroism.

2000: *The Biographer's Tale* by A. S. Byatt is narrated by a graduate student suffering from a surfeit of literary theory. Phineas G. Nanson is fed up because no matter the author, literary theory leads to the same conclusions about the indeterminacy of the text. Every literary work is found to be saying the opposite of what it initially purports. The same vocabulary, the same bloodless and abstract analysis becomes tiresome. So Nanson turns to biography as a genre respectful of things, of data, and of the uniqueness of lives.

A great admirer of the biographer Scholes Destry-Scholes, Nanson decides to write the biographer's biography. Soon enough, Nanson realizes how hard it can be to reconstruct a life. Outside of a few papers and public records, there is a remarkable paucity of material about Destry-Scholes. One of Nanson's finds, however, is an incomplete and apparently fragmented manuscript that contains three narratives. Are they meant as three separate projects, or was Destry-Scholes embarking on "an experiment in the nature of biographical narrative"?

All three narratives are presented as documents that both the reader and Nanson can interpret. Thus Byatt, more than any other novelist exploring the nature of biography, plunges into the hermeneutics of the genre. Nanson discovers that parts of the narratives are fiction—and in one case borrowed from yet another work of fiction. What did Destry-Scholes intend by this blurring of fact and fiction? Nanson cannot come to a definitive conclusion, but his quest to understand the elusive nature of biography becomes paramount.

Nanson also shares with many narrators in novels about biography the realization that biography is, in the end, a composite of biographer and subject. The more Nanson attempts to understand Destry-Scholes, the more he begins to reflect upon his own life.

2001: Beryl Bainbridge's *According to Queeney* is a fascinating recreation of the friendship between Samuel Johnson and Mrs. Thrale, seen through the eyes of the latter's daughter, who provides a crisp, unsentimental portrayal of this eighteenth-century liaison and a sidelight not available in James Boswell's classic biography.

When Samuel Johnson died in 1784, the race was on to publish biographies of the poet, biographer, critic, and lexicographer whose personality and prose helped set the literary style of his age. Johnson had attained a towering reputation with his monumental *Dictionary of the English Language* (1755), his edition of Shakespeare (1765), and most of all his multi-volume *Lives of the Poets* (1779–1781), which propounded his theory of biography: "To judge right of an author we must transport ourselves to his time, and examine what were the wants of his contemporaries, and what were his means of supplying them." James Boswell's *Life of Johnson* (1791) presented such a vivid portrayal of the crusty "Doctor"—as he came to be known—such a meticulous account of his conversations, conflicts, and friendships, and such an entertaining extrapolation of the Johnsonian biographical method that other biographers have found it hard to compete. Of course scholars of Johnson and his period have combed other biographies to provide a perspective on Boswell and sometimes a corrective to his ebullient book. But Boswell remains—in tandem with Johnson—the overlord of biography in the English language; that is, no other book or figure has challenged their supremacy.

Perhaps that is what tempted Beryl Bainbridge to write her sly, slim novel. Massive works of scholarship, or even encyclopedic novels, are unlikely to displace—or even budge—Boswell. In this case, quantity cannot overcome quality. Better to produce an elegant foray rather than a set-piece battle plan. But historical novels present a problem: how to reexamine the past—especially such a well-mined period. If the novelist slavishly follows the record, what is the point of writing fiction? If the novelist invents characters and incidents, why should they be taken seriously as interpretation of history? The Hungarian critic George Lukacs thought Sir Walter Scott's novels dealt with the dilemma brilliantly by making major historical figures minor characters and by making minor or invented historical figures major characters. Thus he could provide a narrative of the period, explaining the context in which its principal actors appeared, without hazarding examination of a James Stuart, pretender to the throne of England, who is given a minimal number of words to speak in a novel like *Redgauntlet* (1824). But Scott's invented protagonists are so bland, and patently exist just to provide a kind of neutral sensibility through which history can be filtered, that the imaginative intensity expected of a novel seems lacking. There is too much scenery, too much commentary, and not enough development within his invented characters; that is, they seem to have little inner life.

Bainbridge surmounts these difficulties admirably. Without attacking Boswell directly, she turns to the life of Hester Thrale (1741–1821), a brewer's wife who made it her business to befriend the great man of her age, the man she knew as Mr. Johnson. Although she is an important figure in Johnson studies, having produced

Anecdotes of Johnson (1786) and *Letters to and from Johnson* (1788), her books lack the heft and comprehensiveness of Boswell's. Bainbridge, however, shrewdly draws on a third book, *Thraliana*, which an editor of Mrs. Thrale's diaries published in 1942. That volume includes not only valuable material about Johnson, it also conveys a lively portrayal of Mrs. Thrale's ambivalent relationship with her daughter Queeney. Bainbridge evidently concluded that new light could be shed on Johnson and his period by creating a vivid novel out of Queeney's sensibility, a novel that would allow Queeney to speak for herself, and by doing so add another voice to history. The virtue of Bainbridge's method is that it reopens the Johnson period, so to speak, provoking the urge to reread Boswell, to see Johnson and his circle from yet another challenging perspective.

Perhaps because of the novel's title and the jacket flap's somewhat misleading description, certain hasty reviewers have commented on the novel as if it were narrated by Queeney. The novel does convey her attitudes, but there is a third-person narrator, and Queeney herself may be assessed in her taciturn letters to an inquiring biographer, letters that reveal Queeney as a reluctant witness to history, a witness who prefers the privacy of her own memories and opinions and who fends off the nagging questions of those who would make the lives of poets and other famous figures a public affair.

Boswell's Johnson, the man of great opinions given bluffly, makes his appearance in *According to Queeney* when David Garrick asks him whether it is true that Boswell is writing down Johnson's conversation in a journal, and whether Johnson finds it "intrusive." An untroubled Johnson replies that the journal "will not be accurate, for man's compulsion is to replicate himself. Think of painting—one has only to examine a portrait to see in the sitter a resemblance to the artist." The persistent Garrick wonders, "What if others read it . . . after you are gone? What will you think then?" A spluttering Johnson rejoins: "Why, Sir, I will think nothing, for if the 'gone' you refer to is the grave, I dare say I shall have nothing to think with." This is the Johnson who realized biography's limitations but who also argued in his *Rambler* essay on biography the futility of trying to control the reports of others about oneself. In his own time and afterward, Boswell was criticized for revealing too much about his subject, but Johnson himself—by allowing Boswell to take him down, so to speak—understood that biography is never the whole story, and that every biography is also an autobiography. Thus Bainbridge simultaneously acknowledges and puts Boswell in his place.

Finally, this novel has another point to make: the past—however selective the memory of it must be, however inaccurate biographies may seem—nevertheless persists in the human consciousness and is inescapable. It must be confronted. Queeney would desperately like to annihilate a past that brought her much unhappiness, yet both biography and personal memory are inescapable, Queeney confesses to her correspondent Fanny Burney: "The attention given to the numerous emendations to Mr. Boswell's *Life*, and the spate of reminiscences and contradictions trailing in its wake, constantly resurrect memories I would wish lost in the mists of time. For one so cold of temperament, an affliction my mother laments I inherit from my dead father, it is surprising how my emotions seesaw. I understood as a child that age brings forgetfulness, and am constantly inconvenienced to find that the multiplication of years renders the past more real than the present." Bainbridge's novel is itself immersed in the heat of history and in the cadences of the eighteenth-century prose reproduced so expertly in Queeney's letters. History scorches the human consciousness of even those cooler temperaments like that of Queeney, who tries to deny Johnson's greatness and her mother's attraction to it. The irony of Queeney's letters is that the more she tries to debunk history, the more she is forced to supply her own emendations and contribute to the contradictions inherent in any account that aims to recover the past.

2002: *The City of Your Final Destination* by Peter Cameron concerns a biographer, Omar Razaghi, seeking authorization for his life of the writer Jules Gund. He has written a dissertation on this one-book writer and has received a prestigious grant for an authorized biography. The trouble is that he receives the grant before contacting Gund's executors, who, it turns out, reject Razaghi. His girlfriend urges him to travel to Uruguay to cajole the executors into agreeing to back his project. Omar does so and eventually gains the cooperation of all three executors, yet he forsakes the idea of doing the biography.

This is a compelling book about what it takes to be a biographer. At one point, Omar's girlfriend says one must be ruthless to be a biographer. And Omar, for all sorts of reasons, discovers that he cannot be ruthless, even though he tells one of the executors, "I have the right to write a biography of Jules Gund. You have the right not to cooperate with me. That is my right and that is your right."

2003: *The X President* by Philip Baruth is a novel set in 2055 and narrated by Bill Clinton's authorized biographer. Clinton (always referred to as BC) is 109 and has been rebuilt physically with the equivalent of an internal walker and electrical circuits that keep him surprisingly ambulatory. The plot is pure science fiction, involving time travel (trips back to 1963 and 1995) in an effort to alter past events that have led to a disastrous war that the United States is losing in 2055. The novel includes insightful commentary on the relationship between biographer and subject, the problematic nature of authorized biography, and the way biographical narrative begins to dictate the biographer's choices of wording and interpretation.

2003: *Spiral* by Joseph Geary is a bloodcurdling novel in which biographer Nick Greer forsakes the role of passive compiler of his subject's life and becomes a conspirator, discovering that only through deceit can he unearth the full truth about Frank Spira, a postwar artist who has become the icon of contemporary figurative art.

Greer has been working on a biography of Spira for six years. Just as he is about to complete his masterpiece, he is informed that one of the key figures in his biography, Jacob Grossman, has turned up in New York City after having vanished twenty-six years earlier. Fending off pressures from his agent and editor, who do not wish to delay the appearance of the book, Greer leaves his home in London to interview Grossman, even though the biographer has bankrupted himself during his arduous travels to obtain material for his book and alienated the affections of his wife, who leaves him saying, "You do not know when to stop."

Then Grossman is murdered, and Greer, the last one to see him alive, becomes both a suspect and a material witness. The biographer withholds information from the police, then trades it for a look at Grossman's autopsy report. Eventually Greer burglarizes one of his interviewee's homes and nearly loses his life attempting to unravel the sinister threads of his subject's life.

No novelist before Geary has shown quite such tenacity in revealing the fanaticism of some biographers in their research or how they may become enmeshed in the virtues and vices of their subjects' worlds.

2003: *The Last Gondola: A Mystery of Venice* by Edward Sklepowich, featuring biographer/detective Urbino Macintyre, is reminiscent of James's classic *The Aspern Papers*. Urbino is obsessed with Possle, a fellow American who has befriended the stars of the art and literary worlds. A biography of the reclusive Possle would be a fascinating way to portray the transatlantic cultural world of the twentieth century. But how to contact Possle, now in his nineties, and incommunicado in the Palazzo? To Urbino's surprise, Possle contacts him, and soon a devious game is played out between biographer and subject, each seeking his own secretive agenda. Sklepowich deftly captures the rather crazed mood of the biographer who is not above stealing his subject's possessions or even breaking and entering. As Urbino's close friend, the contessa, points out, biographer and subject are very much alike in their eccentricities and mysterious behavior. This novel ably conveys the notion of biography as a kind of intrigue. As in *The Aspern Papers*, the biographer's best efforts do not yield the cornucopia that seems within his grasp.

2003: In *The Blood Doctor* by Barbara Vine, Martin Nauther, a biographer, investigates the troubling life of his great-grandfather,

Lord Henry Nauther, one of Queen Victoria's physicians (she made him a peer) and an eminent authority on hemophilia.

Martin has inherited Henry's seat in the House of Lords, and like his great-grandfather, Martin's life becomes suffused with a consciousness of blood (his wife has no less than three miscarriages while he is researching his biography). The mysteries that Vine has so exquisitely contrived should not be divulged here, for the joy of this novel is found in her authentic portrayal of the biographer's discoveries.

Martin is suddenly presented with a piece of evidence that simply does not fit his developing view of his great-grandfather (who he suspects is a murderer). Martin learns that Anthony Agnew, the husband of a distant relative, has read a notebook of Henry's that is more revealing than anything Martin has yet found in letters, journals, or interviews. Unfortunately the notebook has been inadvertently thrown into the trash, and Anthony Agnew has suffered a stroke. Will Agnew remember what he read? Even if he does not, though, Agnew's daughter Caroline has told Martin that her father felt so sorry for Henry after reading his notebook that he insisted she put flowers on Henry's grave. Evidently whatever Henry did caused him to experience extraordinary remorse, and the biographer is nonplussed by the intense compassion Anthony Agnew feels for Henry, a man Anthony never met or showed any interest in.

"With all my researches, I know so little of his true nature or his inner life," Martin laments a third of the way through his work on Henry. Yet, in the end, Henry does stand revealed—if not in his innermost being, certainly in the full social, familial, and historical contexts that the best novels and biographies recover.

2004: *Double Vision* by George Garrett focuses on Garrett himself, suffering from an illness that produces double vision, and on Garrett's alter ego, Frank Toomer. Garrett/Toomer are each trying to come to terms with the biography of a deceased writer/friend: Peter Taylor in Garrett's case, and Aubrey Carver in Toomer's. Along the way Garrett, also a biographer, comments on the genre, noting, for example, how Taylor's first biographer fails to incorporate some of the more robust aspects of Taylor the man. Garrett once lived next door to Taylor and discovers from Taylor's biographer many aspects of the man that Garrett did not know or did not fully appreciate. Thus the differences between knowing Taylor as a friend and biographical subject emerge in fascinating scenes, even as Garrett muses about creating a novel about Frank Toomer's efforts to fathom Aubrey Carver.

2006: In *The Thirteenth Tale* by Diane Setterfield, the famous writer Vida Winter invites Margaret Lea, who works in her father's bookshop and has published well-researched pieces on literary authors, to become her biographer. This is surprising to Margaret, who hardly feels qualified for the task. Even worse, how is she to contend with a subject who argues: "My gripe is not with lovers of the truth but with truth herself. What succor, what consolation is there in truth, compared to a story? What good is truth, at midnight, in the dark, when the wind is roaring like a bear in the chimney? What you need are the plump comforts of a story. The soothing, rocking safety of a lie."

Lea knows full well that Winter has misled many interviewers, giving versions of her life that contradict each other. On a visit to Winter, Lea realizes that her subject is dying, which is perhaps a reason why Winter now wants to straighten out her biography. And yet Winter still has trouble leveling with her biographer, and the ever-vigilant biographer—drawn to Winter's story by incidents that remind her of her own life—wonders whether she can ever penetrate the writer's persona.

The contest between biographer and subject is explored in dramatic and fascinating detail in a plot that resembles a tale that might have been confected by one of the Brontës.

2007: *The Great Man* by Kate Christensen: one subject and two biographers circling "like vultures over a dead hyena," comments Teddy, the dead subject's mistress. This kind of unseemly competition indeed happens—though not quite the way Christensen supposes in *The Great Man*.

In order to set her plot in motion, Christensen must situate both biographers at the same starting line. This almost never happens. Biographies and biographers do overlap, but one usually has a head start, even if the latecomer manages to finish first.

Even worse for Christensen's credibility is the fact that anyone knowledgeable about biography or about New York publishing would have to wonder why W. W. Norton would sign Ralph Washington, a neophyte biographer barely thirty, to a contract for a biography of the celebrated painter Oscar Feldman (he died in 2001), a contemporary of the abstract expressionists who remained faithful to figurative art and produced a stunning palette of female nudes. Ralph has no connections to the art world, just an enthusiasm for Feldman's work. (Having published a biography with Norton, I know about the vetting process, the way editors read proposals, and I feel confident in saying Ralph would have been shown the door.)

Henry Burke, in contrast, *has* published a biography, albeit that of a minor poet, and is welcomed by Yale University Press. This scenario is just barely feasible. But a university press routinely sends out biography proposals to experts in the field, and at least one of the outside reviewers would probably have sneered at Burke. These days one blackball is enough to hex a university-press biography.

Perhaps I'm being unfair. After all, Christensen is not writing a primer about how to get a contract for a biography. Still, there is the problem of verisimilitude. Surely this novelist, like any crime writer, must do some research into what really goes on in the world she chooses to depict.

Not that there aren't nice touches in this novel. For example, it begins with a parody of a *New York Times* obit. Feldman is treated in true *Times* fashion, with a Victorian profile. That he had anything like a mistress and two daughters is obliquely suggested in a coy comment about Feldman as a "larger than life figure, by all accounts opinionated, occasionally boisterous, visceral, with insatiable appetites of many kinds." A hankering for ice cream and poker? I'm not sure, however, that the *Times* would venture this far. Some readers may recall the ruckus that followed publication of the *Times* obit

of Susan Sontag—one of the newspaper's more conspicuous air-
brush jobs.

Christensen's biography ends with a wonderful mock *New York
Times* review of the two biographies. I can't say much about the review without giving away some of the juicier ironies of the novel.
My only complaint is that the reviewer, Penny Hightower-Jones,
identified as an art history professor at Rutgers, is far more astute
than most *Times* reviewers, who are quite obtuse when it comes to
understanding how biographies are written and why they turn out
the way they do.

Of course novels must foreshorten and dramatize, but what biographer leaves his interviewee after fewer than five minutes of conversation? This happens repeatedly because, I suspect, Christensen's
biographer is there only to move the plot along, to provoke another
revelation about Oscar that his family and friends are forced to supply almost in spite of themselves. Certainly it is true that once a biographer manages to get witnesses talking, others step forward because they want to put their oar in, but the process is far more
elaborate and devious than this novel allows.

The great novel about biography, one that banks on authentic
insider knowledge, has yet to be written.

Biographical Fiction

SEE Fictionalized Biography.

Biography and the Academic Disciplines

I first suspected that there was something wrong with academic disciplines during my undergraduate "eighteenth-century quarter" at
Michigan State University. I took a survey of eighteenth-century

British history and the novel as well as seminars on eighteenth-century British poetry and continental history. This was my most exciting quarter, as I compared and integrated the courses and got to know my professors, who were themselves quite a study: a gruff, brilliant dialectician whose Brooklynese reminded me of Ralph Kramden; an elegant British lecturer; a dour Pope adept; and a cheerful, flaxen-haired Midwesterner who relished Lovelace's devious entrapment of Clarissa.

I have now written so many biographies that I cannot deal with the disciplines without attaching them to the personalities who pursue them. What struck me during that quarter, however, long before the prospect of writing biography ever occurred to me, was how isolated these courses and professors were from one another. I don't just mean that the content of each course was discrete, or that Alexander Pope never put in an appearance in my history courses, or that literature was taught with very little historical context. Rather, what surprised me was that my professors did not know one another. The History and English departments were on adjacent floors of the same building, and I was delighted that a single set of stairs could take me from one department to another. But when I would mention one of my professors to another, it was clear they had never engaged in significant conversation. I had assumed that what I studied in separate courses they had already integrated. But there was no dialogue between the disciplines. The way I had scripted my undergraduate curriculum had almost nothing to do with the way knowledge was preserved and distributed in the university.

Intent on attending graduate school, I knew I had to choose my discipline. Would it be history or literature? I was attracted to intellectual history (I think because in some way it crossed disciplines), but I knew I would have to master several languages, and my linguistic abilities were not impressive. Literature seemed narrower and, I confess, safer. American Studies was appealing to a disciplinary gadfly, but one of my younger professors—already attuned to a shrinking job market—advised against appearing to be a dilettante. Better to demonstrate that one was a specialist—and this is how, in my first scholarly life, I emerged from the University of Toronto as a Faulknerian.

Yearning for integration, however, I wrote a dissertation on Faulkner's uses of the past. I hit upon this topic after reading many essays about his profound understanding of history, essays that never even mentioned whether Faulkner's interpretation of the past had anything to do with what historians and historiographers meant by historical interpretation. To what extent were Faulkner's characters really thinking like historians? And did the narratives of his novels constitute a reading of history—one that paralleled the history that was studied outside his novels? Was Faulkner offering, in other words, a paradigm of historical interpretation that historians and historiographers would recognize?

It seemed amazing to me that for all the studies of an author "drenched in history," to appropriate Cleanth Brooks's term, not a single critic had asked these questions. I began to realize they had been trained *not* to ask such questions, as if that one flight of stairs between the History and English departments had too many steps and climbing them would leave one winded.

I won't rehearse the findings of my dissertation, except to say that there is a remarkable correlation between Herbert Butterfield's *George the III and the Historians* (1959) and *Absalom, Absalom!* (1936)—and between R. G. Collingwood's *The Idea of History* (1946) and *Go Down Moses* (1942). All four texts are historiographical and present similar paradigms of how history is told and interpreted. Has any university history course, undergraduate or graduate, ever brought such texts together? I pick on the historians because lately, with the advent of the new historicism and cultural studies, English professors can justify teaching just about anything.

What does this recapitulation of my autobiography have to do with the disciplines and the discipline of biography? I'm intent on showing that the disciplines have created almost no space for the biographer, sensing that biography represents an anti-disciplinary or, if you will, an interdisciplinary threat to disciplinary rigor and integrity. To the discipline-bound, biography is corruption; it is an affront to the academically fastidious—a fact brought home to me several years ago during a scholar's talk about his forthcoming biography of Marianne Moore. After his detailed discussion of how he had used the Moore archives, he was asked about the interviewing he had done. He literally turned up his nose at the noxious question. He had done no interviews, he said, dispatching the question with the comment, "They're so messy."

There you have it! Out in the open at last! Biography is grubby! It is the antithesis of a discipline. One is permitted to speak of a body of knowledge, but not of the bodies that produce that knowledge. One is allowed to speak metaphorically, but should one try to be literal, to locate the flesh of ideas and not just to flesh out ideas, the discipline strikes back. New Critics narrow in on the work and decry the intentional fallacy; deconstructionists declaim that there is no author; and new historicists surround authors and texts with cultural data. Only the psychobiographers allow a space for personality, but they do it academically—that is, by making a discipline out of their renegade enterprise.

Imagine if biography were actually at the center of a discipline, if, for example, C. Wright Mills's biography became integral to an understanding of Mills's sociology. How messy! Academics like to gossip as much as anyone else, but what if one took that gossip into the classroom? What if one admitted that what one thinks is inseparable from the whole of what one is? Then it would have to be admitted that the disciplines are no more than a convenience, a helpful shortcut for talking about concepts but inadequate at presenting concepts in their totality. This is surely what D. H. Lawrence meant when he said human beings think with their hands as well as with their brains, and that the novel was the one bright book of life because it did not divide thinking and feeling, the cerebral and the sexual, and so on.

Biography should aspire to that Lawrentian capaciousness, and it should always be an affront to the disciplines, a subversive element that gradually enlarges the disciplines and crosses the boundaries between them. But in fact biography is shunned, even by biographers, who blinker themselves. A case in point is a friend of mine, Michael Wreszin, who has published a biography of Dwight Macdonald. In order to tell you about this biographer, I have to tell a tale out of school, a tale that is not in his biography of Dwight. (Mike always refers to his subject as Dwight, by the way. I've never heard him say Macdonald, and Mike obviously feels quite protective about his subject.) Mike is crusty, argumentative, and engaging, and would not hesitate to criticize Dwight on intellectual or political matters. But parts of Dwight's life are out of bounds for Mike. He draws a line. Why? Because he thinks you can segregate aspects of Dwight the man from what he thought about public issues. In making this distinction, Mike is true to the discipline of history but false to the discipline of biography.

What is it Mike excludes? He discovered that Dwight had affairs with his students. "Not germane to an understanding of why Macdonald was important and why people read him," Mike asserts. Is he right? Mike does not seem to be a prude. I don't think he wants to idealize Macdonald, yet there is a sense in which leaving out this element of Dwight's life creates a world of disembodied ideas and a man with no flesh on him. The obverse of my argument is that biography degrades; it is reductive and deprives ideas of their autonomy. Biography, in short, is irrelevant to the authenticity of a concept. But why the polarity? Why do we have to choose? Isn't it precisely the nexus of thinker and thought that biography should provide?

One can say, for example, that Thoreau is a phony. He spoke about independence and being his own man at Walden Pond, then went home and ate his mother's pies whenever he felt like it. One can also say, whatever the failings or inconsistencies of Thoreau the man, his ideas live and are not impugned by his biography. I have heard both arguments. Similarly, I also know people who now reject Woody Allen's art because they suspect he is a child molester, and people who argue that his personal problems in no way invalidate his films. But of course the dialogue about Allen or Thoreau cannot occur if biographers suppress what they learn.

The discipline of biography consists in including precisely those elements that the disciplines are likely to omit. Have you noticed how angry reviewers are at biographers? Joyce Carol Oates revives the term pathography to deplore the biographer's harping on his or her subject's personal failings and diseases. After he published his biography of Mark Rothko, James Breslin wrote an autobiographical piece for the *New York Times Book Review* in which he said that after completing the book he expected to be punished. These are not isolated instances. I have hundreds of reviews on file, collected for my 1992 study, *Biography: An Annotated Bibliography*, that reveal a record of venom.

It is not surprising. Biographies undress their subjects. When John Updike realized that a biographer was on his case, he hurriedly wrote a memoir, *Self-Consciousness*, so that he could forestall the biography. Indeed, autobiography and the authorized biography are time-honored methods of attempting to derail independent biographies and make them seem illicit and, in our litigious times, even illegal.

I have often joked that I regard myself as an outlaw biographer. By my definition, all biographies are outside the disciplines. Today's biographies are those baggy, unruly monsters that used to be called Victorian novels—the ones that the fussy Henry James deplored and that reviewers grouse about in periodicals like the *Times Book Review*.

As I contend in *A Higher Form of Cannibalism,* biography is raunchy. My fellow biographers by and large resist my point, preferring to think of themselves as noble benefactors of their subjects. Their feelings are terribly hurt when reviewers take after them. For me, bloodied and battle-hardened, biographers and reviewers alike still tend to think of biography as hagiography. I can't tell you how many biographers become disenchanted with their subjects and end up feeling as bitter as their reviewers. It seems to me that the disciplines themselves—the way we are taught to think in categories—cause a great deal of this anger against biography.

The disciplines hide behind coded words. Biography is about investigating those codes. It is about the singular and the subjective. How can one build a discipline on those two words? Biography is anti-jargon and aimed at a general audience. How can one specialize, become part of a coterie, or at least get tenure in an academic department without learning an esoteric lexicon? Academics turning from the disciplines to full-fledged biographies must unlearn much of what graduate school has taught them. It took me ten years to find a new style and six to write my first biography. I found my new voice in my first biography through that messy process of interviewing, when one day, one of my interviewees, Susan Strasberg, said of one of my drafts: "Part of it reads like a treatise, and part of it is in your own voice. Who are you trying to impress? Why don't you trust your own voice?"

This is what biography does. It returns one's voice. It allows one to gain a perspective on the disciplines. I don't regret my training in a discipline or believe that disciplines or departments should be abolished. But I regret that disciplinary training did so little to get me to question the idea of disciplines and to see them for the conveniences and refuges they actually are. Thank God for that stairway connecting the English and History departments, my passageway to and from the disciplines, which I traversed, I now see, because of what was, even then, a biographical impulse.

Biography and Criticism

Since the advent of the New Critics, academics (with certain notable exceptions) have looked askance at biography. Here is a sampling of the critical literature that supports the study of biography: E. M. W. Tillyard and C. S. Lewis, in *The Personal Heresy: A Controversy* (1939), conduct a debate about the biographical element in literature. Lewis contends that very little is learned of the poet's *personality* in his poetry. In literature one looks through a consciousness but not at it. All we need to know about the poet is in the poem. Tillyard does not so much disagree with this position as find it too extreme. He posits the existence of a "mental pattern" in the poet's work that can be deemed part of his personality, and suggests the very concept of style owes something to a recognition of personality in literature. The debate provides a valuable context in which to measure the biographer's handling of literature, though very little is said per se about biographical method.

In "Biography and Criticism—A Misalliance Disputed" (*Critical Inquiry*, March 1975, pp. 479–496), Jacques Barzun argues that biographical and historical knowledge is of primary benefit to the critic, not to the work of art, since it enhances the critic's awareness of the circumstances in which the work was created: "the act of creation does not take place in a vacuum."

In "Some Uses of Biography" (*A Choice of Inheritance: Self and Community from Edmund Burke to Robert Frost*, 1989), David Bromwich argues that there can be no clear separation between biography and criticism, "for a biographical assumption may be implicit in the most abstract critical remark." Taking as examples biographies of Keats, Joyce, and Frost by Walter Jackson Bate, Richard Ellmann, and Lawrance Thompson, respectively, Bromwich demonstrates how new lives of these writers have generated new criticism, stimulating in Frost's case a more complex reading of his poetry. Bromwich also sees certain myths of the poet operating in "successful biographies of an age" which "have as much in common as their biographers rather than as little as their heroes."

In *Using Biography* (1984), William Empson suggests that biography is sometimes useful in understanding the evolution of a writer's work, and that to forbid discussion of an author's intention can result in attributing the wrong motives to a work of literature. Irony, in particular, can often be better appreciated when the critic has a grasp of the writer's biography. Biography is part of the literature student's effort to "empathize" with the writer. Empson employs his biographical method (he explicitly denies he has a "fullblown theory) in chapters on Marvell, Dryden, Fielding, Yeats, Eliot, and Joyce.

In "Biography and Intention," Stanley Fish (*Contesting the Subject: Essays in Postmodern Theory and Practice of Biography and Biographical Criticism*, edited by William H. Epstein, 1991) writes that although the new critics and certain postmodernist theorists have argued that a work of literature cannot be judged by the author's intention, "meaning, intention, and biography are inextricable." Texts, he seeks to demonstrate, are not independent of who the reader thinks the author is, or what the author represents. And this is equally true no matter whether intention is viewed from the perspective of earlier critics who believe "texts read themselves" or later critics who affirm that "texts deconstruct themselves." There are many different ways a text may be approached, but "we cannot at the same time construe them and free ourselves from the considerations of biography."

Ira Grushow, "Biography as Literature" (*Southern Humanities Review*, Spring 1980, pp. 155–160), advocates the study of biography as perhaps the best way of introducing students to literary analysis, appealing to their sense of story, of individuals' effort to "become part of a greater system outside themselves, part of an ongoing march of time." As attention to story values increases, students focus on the biographer, on the choices required in representing a human being in literature, on how "method determines meaning." Comparisons among biographers strengthens the appreciation of style and structure and demonstrates the link between literature and lives that is often not apparent to a student confronted only with a literary text.

In *Novelists in Their Youth* (1990), John Halperin makes a compelling argument for biographical criticism, buttressed by apt quotations from Proust. He suggests that biography makes literature "more accessible, more comprehensible, to wider audiences" by demonstrating the origins of art, and by disposing and dispensing with "some of the myths that have grown up around an author's life" that can distort interpretation. By bringing to bear the historical, psychological, geographical, familial, and social influences on a subject, the biographer can reveal "some of the reasons why the texts produced during the author's maturity came into being."

Francis Noel Lees, "The Keys Are at the Palace: A Note on Criticism and Biography" (*Literary Criticism and Historical Understanding. Selected Papers from the English Institute*, edited by Phillip Damon,

1967), comments on an interpretation of a Rossetti poem, "The Hill Summit," by Sir Maurice Bowra. Bowra's introduction of biographical detail makes the poem "deeper, more resonant, more haunting in tone." Was Bowra reading the poem in the "context of the poet's biography" or "discerning something" in the poem and "adding it to the biography"? While Lees favors the former option, his subtle essay supports, "in principle . . . biographical deduction from a work of literature," and cautions against viewing a work of art as standing free, "absolutely, of its maker and his history."

Biography and Drama

Considerable commentary focuses on the nexus between biography and fiction. As a narrative genre, biography would seem to have the greatest affinity with the novel, since both excel in the creation of characters and scenes through the sensibility of narrators. And yet the biographer has much in common with the dramatist, since biography is a kind of impersonation and the biographer functions as a kind of actor attempting to represent his subject's sensibility. The greatest biography in the English language, Boswell's *Life of Johnson*, consists mainly of dialogue, with Boswell's own comments serving almost like those of a director's notes.

FURTHER READING: In "A Speculative Introduction: Life-Writing as Drama," Evelyn J. Hinz proposes in *Mosaic* (Fall 1987, pp. v–xii) that biography is closer to dramatic form than to fictional narrative. Both drama and biography are scriptlike mimetic forms; "in both cases, art is less an end in itself and more a means of reproduction," a performing of lives. Like directors of plays, biographers are in a position of authority and yet are "at the mercy of their materials," and "great biographers succeed because they adhered to dramatic principles of composition." Hinz concludes: "Although narrative might be closer in a mechanical sense, drama has more in common with the dynamics or spirit of life-writing."

Biography and the Novel

Reviewers routinely praise biographies that are novelistic. This seems to mean that the biography is well written and includes scenes—perhaps even dialogue—and fascinating delineations of personality. Certain biographers—Bernard Crick, for example—distrust the conventions of fiction and warn that the closer the biographer comes to emulating the novelist, the less likely his book is to be valuable as documented history. On the other hand, biographers like Leon Edel and Justin Kaplan aim to make their biographies as "literary" or artistic as possible, using techniques such as flashbacks, disruptions of chronology, and dramatic beginnings and endings that recall fictional devices.

In "The Art of Biography," Virginia Woolf (*The Death of the Moth and Other Essays*, 1942) presented the influential view that biography builds upon "perishable" facts whereas the poet's or novelist's imagination "at its most intense fires out what is perishable in fact" and provides immortal characters. Dickens's Micawber will last longer than Boswell's Johnson, Woolf argues, because the biographer is always tied to a limited number of facts while the novelist is free to invent what cannot be verified or challenged. Nevertheless biography supplies a view of reality, of the rich diversity and unity of human character, that is surpassed only by the greatest artists. Biographers should disclose all facets of their subjects and eschew all forms of censorship, for only in that way can biographies produce "the creative fact; the fertile fact; the fact that suggests and engenders."

Biography and Portrait Painting

Biographers often subtitle short biographies "A Portrait," implying that the narrative aims at a certain economy of presentation, a compactness that may be compared to portraiture, in which the subject's main features, typical expressions, and stances are emphasized rather than a fully detailed accounting of a life.

Charles A. Le Guin, in "The Language of Portraiture" (*Biography* 6 [1983]: 333–341), summarizes the history of criticism linking biographical writing and portrait painting. Since the Renaissance, artists such as Leonardo have been aware of the similarities between the biographer and the portrait painter, using the same kind of language to describe both kinds of art. While critics have recognized differences—biographies tend to portray human character developing in time while paintings provide a static, momentary, spatial view of the subject—the greatest portrait painters and biographers have combined the kinetic and static qualities of their respective arts to render a complex, fully developed view of the self.

In "The Development of the British Literary Portrait Up to Samuel Johnson" (*Proceedings of the British Academy*, vol. 54, 1968, pp. 51–72), David Piper notes that the earliest English literary portrait is of Chaucer, but such portraits did not become prevalent until the seventeenth and eighteenth centuries, when they were preserved by libraries, by other public institutions, and by private hands, and were stimulated by the "growth of critical and biographical studies of great authors." Poets' Corner at Westminster Abbey enhanced interest in the personal figure of the writer as did Pope's assiduous cultivation of his image, produced in no less than "sixty-six primary portrait-types . . . a phenomenal number for a private citizen . . . matched only by royalty." Joshua Reynolds, in his portraits of Samuel Johnson and others, created likenesses with the "most sharp immediacy and individuality yet with the weight and stamina of a profound generalization."

In *Articulate Images: The Sister Arts from Hogarth to Tennyson* (1983), Richard Wendorf summarizes traditional comparisons between portrait painting and biography, noting that the "inherent tension between factual accuracy and imaginative shaping is central to both arts." On the one hand, portrait painters have recognized that biography can capture inner thought and suggest the development of personality over time. On the other hand, painted portraits may seize the subject at a revealing moment, taking in human character instantly in a way that eludes biography. While portraits may thus capture a subject's essence, biographies explore the contours of character. Each art, in other words, has inherent strengths and weaknesses, which writers and painters attempt to remedy by moving toward both spatial and temporal presentations of their subjects.

Boswell, James (1740–1795)

Boswell's *Life of Johnson* (1791) is regarded as the greatest biography in the English language. At the beginning of his biography Boswell sets down his method. Quoting liberally from Johnson's writing on biography, Boswell aims to allow his subject to speak in his own words rather than "melting down my materials." Boswell offers a life, "not a panegyrick," revealing Johnson in his conversation as a great but scarcely a perfect man. His portrait is made up of innumerable details ("minute particulars")—a necessity he believes will reveal human character, which Plutarch (whom Boswell quotes) recognized when he said that a short saying or jest often expressed a man's virtues and vices better than anything else.

The literature on Boswell is vast, and though most of it is laudatory, he has had his detractors. Early on, critics such as Thomas Macaulay treated Boswell as a kind of idiot savant, a buffoon with a fine ear but lacking in any sort of analytical power. Boswell was a human tape recorder, in this view. He had produced a great work of art by accident. His work was a one-off that could not be repeated.

Thomas Carlyle is conspicuous in countering the Macaulay view. In the third volume of his *Miscellaneous Essays*, Carlyle called Boswell's *Life of Johnson* the greatest literary work of the eighteenth century, the product of a genius maligned for his bad qualities which were emphasized over the less conspicuous good in him. The biography's success stems from Boswell's love and reverence for Johnson, his "free insight, his lively talent," and a "childlike Open-mindedness." Biographies such as Boswell's, said Carlyle, are more important than conventional histories based on calendars, registers, and other data which do not yield the "LIFE OF MAN . . . how and what it was; whence it proceeded, whither it was tending." Charges that Boswell purveyed gossip do not trouble Carlyle since he believes that every manifestation of life is worth recording without resort to censorship. Those who fear biographers should hold their tongues rather than complain of what is reported of them.

FURTHER READING: With the discovery of the Boswell papers (the change in Boswell's reputation is well told in Adam Sisman's *Boswell's Presumptuous Task* [2001]), countless academic studies have shown how carefully the biographer structured and revised his masterpiece. Paul Alkon, for example, shows in "Boswellian Time" (*Studies in Burke and His Time*, vol. 14, 1973, pp. 239–256) that as Boswell wrote the biography he gradually shifted from a conception of spatial form (presenting a portrait of Johnson) to a conception of temporal form (presenting a drama) in which duration, the length of time it takes to know the subject, mimics the actual length of the subject's life. Studying drafts of the biography, Alkon concludes that Boswell slowed the book's "psychological tempo" by minimizing external features and descriptions of particular scenes and emphasizing Johnson's persistent presence and voice, thus giving the reader a familiarity with the subject not usually found in biographies.

William C. Dowling, in "Boswell and the Problem of Biography" (*Harvard Studies in English*, vol. 8, 1978), traces the history of Boswell-and-Johnson criticism to show how critics have wrestled with the conception of the biographer as artist, shifting from views of Boswell as a naive reporter (abetted by the biographer's own expressions of naiveté) to studies of his sense of structure and strategy (stimulated by the discovery of his manuscripts). Dowling notes the modern tendency to treat literary works as self-contained wholes, an inclination that excludes biography (which refers to a reality outside itself) from the realm of art. He argues by analogy that like a Greek vase which can hold water and also be viewed as an expression of the "visual imagination," biographies contain facts but also may be perceived as works of art.

Brandes, Georg (1842–1927)

This Danish literary critic wrote biographies of Soren Kierkegaard, Benjamin Disraeli, Goethe, Julius Caesar, and Michelangelo, among others, following in the tradition of the French biographer Sainte-Beuve by analyzing the subject's character and opinions. Brandes believed that literary biographies help situate authors within their historical periods and literary movements. He was greatly influenced by the great French cultural historian Hippolyte Taine, the subject of Brandes's doctoral dissertation. Brandes's importance is discussed in Rene Wellek's *A History of Modern Criticism* (1965), but the most accessible work on Brandes is Bertil Nolin's *Georg Brandes* (1976).

Carlyle, Thomas (1795–1881)

Carlyle's famous essay on biography, first published in 1832, is reprinted in *Victorian Biography: A Collection of Essays from the Period*, edited by Ira Bruce Nadel (1986). A great champion of biography, Carlyle asserts that knowledge is essentially biographical: "Biography is almost the only thing needful." It comprises "Gossip, Egoism, Personal Narrative (miraculous or not), Scandal, Raillery, Slander, and suchlike." Conventional history does not reveal the way human beings have lived, Carlyle says. It is too much taken up with data and dry accounts of events. Fictional works, he insists, are "mimic Biographies," emulating the way people learn about life. The smallest historical fact has more resonance than the "grandest fictitious event" because the former "did actually occur" and was "an element in the system of the All, whereof I too form part."

Carlyle is known for his "great man" theory of history, featured in his history of the French Revolution, a vivid collection of portraits meant to embody his observation that history is the "essence of innumerable biographies." This view of biography influenced other important writers such as Ralph Waldo Emerson, who published *Representative Men*.

Carlyle wrote biographies of Cromwell and Frederick the Great, but perhaps his lasting contribution to the genre is his biography of John Sterling, a close friend. It is often the case with the greatest biographies: the biographer is writing a memoir and therefore able to deal with his subject with a kind of intimacy that is difficult for biographers who have not known their subjects to equal.

Carlyle's other great work of biography is his *Reminiscences*, in which he transforms Jane Carlyle into an idealized heroine whose nobleness of mind and loyalty make his own rather irritable and shabby treatment of her all the more reprehensible. His lyrical tribute to her remains, however, one of the greatest elegiac biographies in the language.

FURTHER READING: Besides Froude's magnificent biography of Carlyle, see Fred Kaplan's excellent *Thomas Carlyle: A Biography* (1983).

Cavendish, Margaret (1623–1673)

The first woman to write autobiography and biography for print, Cavendish was considered colorful and eccentric by her first readers. To modern scholars she has become a far more important writer. The target of much gossip as a social climber, Cavendish wrote in defense of herself and her husband, the Duke of Newcastle, a commander of the royalist forces against Cromwell. Her highly detailed and careful dating of events marks a significant advance in the history of biography. She prided herself on accuracy, titling her autobiography *A True Relation of My Birth, Breeding and Life* (1656).

Cautioned by her husband to avoid personal attacks, the manuscript of her biography, *The Life of the Thrice Noble High and Puissant Prince, William Cavendish, Duke, Marquess, and Earl of Newcastle* (1667), contains handmade deletions in the first edition.

FURTHER READING: See Douglass Grant, *Margaret the First: A Biography of Margaret Cavendish, Duchess of Newcastle* (1957), and Ann Battigelli, *Margaret Cavendish and the Exiles of the Mind* (1998).

Censorship

Biography as a literary genre is largely the product of the eighteenth century and of one seminal work, James Boswell's *Life of Samuel Johnson* (1791). Biographies had appeared earlier, of course, including several by Johnson himself, and the idea of biography extends back to the lives of medieval saints and to Plutarch (46?–120), whose *Parallel Lives* has exerted an enormous influence on the history of biography. But Boswell's innovations revolutionized the genre and made it the target of suppression and censorship. He sought not only to memorialize a great man but also to reveal his flaws. Boswell reported long stretches of Johnson's conversation, noted his mannerisms, and in general gave an intimate picture such as no biography had dared to attempt.

Because Boswell was Johnson's friend, and because Johnson had sanctioned this minute attention to his life and believed in the superiority of biography as a genre, Boswell himself escaped becoming the target of censorship. But biographers since Boswell have had to confront numerous efforts to discourage, censor, and even ban by legal action the appearance of their books. Biographers themselves have colluded in censorship, and their subjects have often destroyed papers and mobilized friends and families to thwart the biographer's investigations.

After Boswell came a retreat from his bolder innovations, which amounted to self-censorship by the biographer. In his *Memoirs of the*

Life of Sir Walter Scott (1837–1838), John Gibson Lockhart explicitly eschewed Boswell's intimate focus. As Scott's son-in-law, Lockhart wished to preserve both a relative's and a great man's dignity, and thus the biographer became, in Ian Hamilton's words, a "keeper of the flame," the one anointed to protect the hero's reputation.

Nineteenth-century biography is replete with examples of this self-censorship. Byron's biographer burned his subject's memoir lest it disgrace his subject. Henry James attempted to fix his own posthumous reputation by burning many of his papers and letters and writing fiction that denigrated the snooping biographer. Thomas Hardy sought to forestall biographers by writing his own but attributing it to the pen of his second wife, Florence Emily Hardy. Mrs. Gaskell, Charlotte Brontë's biographer, ruthlessly suppressed evidence that might show Brontë to be anything other than a conventional nineteenth-century woman. When Thomas Carlyle's biographer, James Anthony Froude, braved this trend against truth and allowed his subject's dark side to show, he was vilified in the press.

The preferred form of biography was not only sanitized, it allowed the biographer virtually no leeway to interpret his or her subject. Instead the biographer presented documents with a narrative that loosely linked them together and gave an account of the subject's times. These multi-volume life-and-times biographies encased their subjects in piety and euphemism.

In *Eminent Victorians* (1918), Lytton Strachey shattered the nineteenth-century tradition of reverence, censorship, and suppression. Instead of a lengthy tome, he wrote essays questioning the probity of public figures such as Cardinal Manning and General Gordon. He skewered his subjects by pointing to telling psychological details. Above all, he offered his own interpretations of events, eschewing long quotations from documents or any deference to authority other than his own.

After Strachey, the twentieth-century biographer has had to ask how much of a subject's private life should be told. No self-respecting biographer can merely cede control to the subject's friends and family. But a subject's papers and the right to quote from the subject's published and unpublished work still reside with families, friends, and literary estates. If a biographer wants full cooperation from them, he or she can seek "authorization." But authorization may require the biographer to adhere to a view of the subject pleasing to a literary executor. Executors can help biographers get publishing contracts; they can also threaten publishers, refuse to make material available to the biographer, and even sue the biographer and publisher over matters of libel, invasion of privacy, and copyright infringement. Even when no legal action is taken, a literary estate can poison the atmosphere in which biographers work—a fact well documented in Janet Malcolm's account of Sylvia Plath's biographers in *The Silent Woman*.

The modern way to censor or suppress an unauthorized biography is to carefully ration or withhold permission to quote from the biographical subject's published and unpublished work. The most famous case involves Ian Hamilton's biography of J. D. Salinger. When Hamilton sent Salinger a manuscript copy of his yet unpublished biography, Salinger took him to court, alleging that Hamilton had infringed Salinger's copyright by quoting certain unpublished letters. In fact Hamilton had quoted a very modest portion of those letters in accord with his understanding of "fair use," the legal doctrine that allows writers to quote from published and unpublished work without securing permission to do so. The judgment against Salinger and his publisher Random House, which forced them to reset the book and eliminate all quotations from unpublished letters, had a chilling effect on the publishing industry. In one instance Louise DeSalvo, author of an unauthorized controversial biography of the novelist Virginia Woolf, was limited to quoting no more than one hundred words from voluminous unpublished writings. As the author of an unauthorized biography of the journalist and novelist Martha Gellhorn, I was threatened with legal action by Gellhorn, and my publisher allowed me to quote nothing from her unpublished papers. Biographers of other controversial figures, such as L. Ron Hubbard, founder of the Church of Scientology, were also taken to court. Margaret Walker, biographer of the novelist Richard Wright, was sued for quoting from letters Wright sent to her. In these two cases biographers prevailed in court, and their books were not suppressed or censored. But the damage was already done, for it made publishers much more wary of publishing unauthorized biographies.

Censorship involving political figures has actually been much less prevalent because the law regards them as public figures, and it is much more difficult for them to sue biographers for invasion of privacy, libel, or copyright infringement. Powerful figures such as the urban planner Robert Moses have tried to stop biographers, but the realm of the politician is so much larger and harder to control that aggressive unauthorized biographers like Robert Caro have been able to gain access to essential evidence. Of course pressure can be brought to bear by powerful families. The Kennedys, for example, attacked William Manchester's biography of John F. Kennedy, making it difficult but not impossible for him to publish his book.

Recent court decisions and a congressional amendment clarifying that fair use applies to unpublished as well as published work has eased the problem of censorship for biographers. But wherever a prominent person's papers are in the hands of an estate with the power of permission to quote from published and unpublished work, the biographer may be in the position of negotiating the truth, of deciding what can be left in or out of a biography to satisfy the keepers of the flame.

SEE ALSO Authorized Biography; Fair Use; Libel; Malcolm, Janet: *The Silent Woman*; Unauthorized Biography.

Chesterton, G. K. (1874–1936)

One of the towering figures of twentieth-century British literature, Chesterton is renowned for his Father Brown detective stories as well as his histories and biographies. Unlike most biographers, he is able to impress his personality and his theories of literature on his subjects, which include Browning, Dickens, Robert Louis Stevenson, and Chaucer. Chesterton is a master at evoking periods of history and the personalities that help to define them. His religious interest prompted him to write biographies of medieval saints Francis of Assisi and Thomas Aquinas.

FURTHER READING: Among the best treatments of Chesterton are Michael Coren's *The Man Who Was G. K. Chesterton* (1989) and Michael Ffinch, *G. K. Chesterton* (1986).

Children's Biography

Some of the best biography is written for children. A case in point is Penelope Niven's *Carl Sandburg: Adventures of a Poet* (2003). Like many other biographies for children, the book is exquisitely illustrated (in this instance by Marc Nadel), and it presents both a chronological and thematic view of its subject. The first chapter, "A World of Words," situates Carl Sandburg in his milieu and in his art:

> Carl August Sandburg was born on a corn-husk mattress in a three-room house in Galesburg, Illinois, soon after midnight on January 6, 1878. The first words drifting into his ears were *"Det är en pojke!"* Swedish for "It is a boy!" Carl was the first son of Clara and August Sandburg, who had left their homes in Sweden as young adults to start new lives in the United States.
> Carl grew up loving words . . .

Niven, the author of a full-length biography, *Carl Sandburg* (1991), has written a beginning chapter for children that is far more compelling than the first paragraphs she wrote for adults. The point is, children's biographies are not just for children! What is childish, or childlike, about what I have quoted? Writing for children should be every bit as good as writing for adults; the reader ought to be plunged into the story of a life through the use of vivid images, sounds, and stark facts.

This biography has another curiously compelling aspect: no photographs. Instead Nadel, an award-winning illustrator, serves virtually as a co-author, creating, for example, a kind of mural for the title spread that pictures Carl Sandburg walking past a warehouse in the turn-of-the century Chicago he wrote about so boldly and pictorially. The building itself is a mural of the objects that define his life: the milk bottles he delivered as a "milk slinger," his soldier's hat and Spanish-American War medal, his guitar, a train of the type he hopped as a hobo, the cover of his children's book *Rootabaga Stories*, and a reproduction of "Fog," his most famous poem, in his own handwriting. This is biography of a high order, biography as an aesthetic object. I cannot think of a better way to introduce anyone to all that biography has to offer than to point out the fine interplay not only between Niven's words and Nadel's pictures but between their evocation of Sandburg and the book's reproduction of his writings— which are themselves bordered by Nadel's illustrations. So-called children's biographies often achieve a richness and unity of effect that are rarely equaled in biographies for adults.

Reading children's biographies also serves as an antidote to the cant one finds every week in book reviews. I'm thinking of those reviewers who are hostile to literary biography, who tiresomely repeat the notion that it is the work that counts, not the artist's life. Tell that to any child who wants to know about his favorite author. As Samuel Johnson remarked in his *Life of Savage*: "The heroes of literary as well as civil history have been very often no less remarkable for what they have suffered than for what they have achieved."

Niven relates in *Carl Sandburg: A Life* that she "came to Carl Sandburg reluctantly." She had little respect for his work and thought of him as "timeworn, glib, chaotic, hardly worth notice in contemporary anthologies." Then she visited his North Carolina home, saw his "writer's workshop," and began what has evidently become a lifelong obsession, beautifully consummated in her children's biography. Although critics often rejoice that so little is known about

Shakespeare's life, leaving them free to wallow in the work, who can tell what a little more biography might do to a reading of the plays and the poetry? A. L. Rowse may have been wrong in his identification of the dark lady of the sonnets, but his critics missed the point: inquiring minds do want to know; his was not a trivial pursuit. Or to put it another way, what would we not give to learn even a few more facts about Shakespeare? The best authors of children's biographies understand this hunger and do not have to apologize to their readers as authors of "adult" biography sometimes do.

Readers looking for innovation in children's biography should consider *Ben Franklin's Almanac: Being a True Account of the Good Gentleman's Life* (2003). Candace Fleming's well-received and wonderfully titled book has an eighteenth-century ring to it, evoking the Age of Reason's mania for improving the mind and the material of everyday life. Fleming felt the conventional, chronological form of biography inhibited her effort to do justice to Franklin's protean personality and awesome achievements. Like Niven, she works the life into a set of themes copiously illustrated in a scrapbook mode that is rather like a child's version of composition. Fleming includes bits of Franklin's prose, etchings, sketches, cartoons, and documents that lend a period flavor, and, of course, are meant to mimic the style of *Poor Richard's Almanac*.

Few biographical subjects are too sophisticated for children to grasp. Or so I tried to show in my children's biography of Picasso (1993):

> He delighted in amusing his friends with simple pictures drawn on tablecloths and napkins on the same days he was creating human figures with exaggerated features (tiny heads and massive bodies) or with whole new anatomies, with animal faces, eyes positioned on one side of the face, and noses pointing in two directions at once—as if to say that modern art should create its own world and the artist should become his own god, presenting art not as a copy of the universe but as original, intact, and self-sufficient. Why not paint a nose pointing in two directions, since art, unlike life, can show the same thing in different ways simultaneously?

For Picasso, art could be created with anything: a pencil, a paintbrush, a piece of rope, grains of sand, a clump of clay, a bit of cloth or wire. He was not afraid to experiment, and no material or subject matter was alien to his art. He believed that art could be equal to any situation; that is what makes him the complete artist.

I could tell that my editor wondered if I was not giving children too much of a workout, but I do not see why young minds should not be stretched. I did not, by the way, blink at the artist's misogynistic cruelty. I described Françoise Gilot as the "one woman he was never able fully to master. In one of his rages he did an unforgivable thing: he crushed a burning cigarette on her cheek, leaving a scar. Gilot did not flinch." "Adult" biographers often make some effort to rationalize or psychologize such actions; I think it is best not to play that game with children.

I favor biographers like Ann Waldron, whose lively biographies *Claude Monet: 1st Impressions* (1991) and *Francisco Goya: 1st Impressions* (1992) remain in print. As other reviewers have noted, she is fun to read for the sheer pleasure of her prose. Profusely illustrated, her books are a bargain compared to the higher-priced and bloated studies produced by art historians. Waldron is also a pioneer, having produced the first biography of Monet for young readers.

But I would be remiss in concluding this entry without acknowledging the contemporary master of biography for children. I first became aware of Newbery Medal–winner Russell Freedman when I watched him give a talk broadcast by C-Span. I was astonished at the depth of his research. Unlike some writers of children's biography, he does not cobble together his narratives from other biographies. I was riveted by his story of visiting Louis Braille's house in France and his many other accounts of firsthand encounters with his sources. I called him up and invited him to speak to my Baruch College class of education students earning degrees that would put them in New York City classrooms. In preparation, I asked them to write biographies of their own, and he treated them as fellow writers, often asking pointed questions about how they planned to begin their books.

Here are two Russell Freedman first paragraphs:

No one had ever seen what Amos Root saw on that September afternoon in 1904. Standing in a cow pasture near Dayton, Ohio, he looked up and watched a flying machine circle in the sky above him. He could see the bold pilot lying face down on the lower wing, staring straight ahead as he steered the craft to a landing in the grass.—*The Wright Brothers: How They Invented the Airplane* (1994)

Eleanor Roosevelt never wanted to be a president's wife. When her husband Franklin won his campaign for the presidency in 1932, she felt deeply troubled. She dreaded the prospect of living in the White House.—*Eleanor Roosevelt: A Life of Discovery* (1993)

Freedman's Eleanor Roosevelt biography is my favorite. Who would not want to know more after that bold first paragraph? But surely "Acrobats of God," the first chapter of *Martha Graham: A Dancer's Life* (1998), opens just as felicitously:

As an ambitious young woman who wanted to create a new kind of dance, Martha Graham spent many hours at New York City's Central Park Zoo. She would sit on a bench across from a lion in its cage and watch the animals pace back and forth, from one side of the cage to the other.

She was fascinated by the elemental power of the lion's great padding steps, by the purity of its movements. Again and again, it took four steps across the cage, turned in "a wonderful way" then took four steps back. "Finally, I learned how to walk that way," Graham recalled. "I learned from the lion the inevitability of return, the shifting of one's body."

Tell me, is there a biographer, writing for adults or children, who can do better than this?

Of course, like other kinds of biography, children's biography also has plenty of inferior performances. In "Series Thinking and the Art of Biography for Children" (*Children's Literature Association Quarterly*, Winter 1989, pp. 187–192), Linda Walvoord Girard enumerates the reasons for the weakness of contemporary biography for children: subjects are idealized, research is minimal, style is choppy, authors are condescending. Many of these faults are attributable to the rigid format of one or another series, mandating that authors treat biography in a reductive, generic way before they have had an opportunity to conceive of a creative approach to a subject. Because of constraints of length and censorship, authors are rarely able to write for children with candor and excitement, though Girard cites several cases of biographers who have written outside the series format and achieved literary distinction.

FURTHER READING: *The Voice of the Narrator in Children's Literature* (1989), edited by Charlotte F. Otten and Gary D. Schmidt.

Contemporary Biography

Reviewers and critics often dismiss contemporary biography, citing the biographer's limited access to data or a lack of perspective. But this is to assume that all biographies must adhere to the same standard and that there is no inherent advantage in writing about a contemporary.

In *Biographers at Work*, for example, editor James Walter argues that although many scholars dismiss the utility of contemporary biography, the biographer is a contemporary witness who can provide a familiarity with the subject that subsequent biographers will not have. For in a sense contemporary figures are part of "our biographies," and it is an illusion to think that someday all the facts will be known. If access is not allowed by the subject of the biography, this may actually be an advantage, since the biographer cannot be co-opted and may learn more by interviewing the subject's closest associates and friends. There is also a unique integrity to contemporary biography in that the subject can "enjoy a right of reply."

SEE ALSO Living Figures.

Definitive Biography

This term is often used to suggest that a particular biography makes previous and subsequent biographies of the subject superfluous. Such a term is bogus and often results in reviews that do not carefully consider what the "definitive" work leaves out: interviews, an adequate acknowledgment of earlier biographies, a pretense concerning access to archives that is not as decisive as the "definitive" biographer suggests, the biographer's relationship with his sources, and perhaps the greatest canard—that definitive biographies are, or should be, "fair and balanced."

CRITIQUE: Can biography ever be definitive? Publishers pretend it can be so. "Now at long last," Robert Dallek's publisher proclaims, "we have the definitive biography of Jack Kennedy."

A publisher's hyperbole is not ordinarily worthy of comment, but reviewers too have hailed this account as conclusive and authoritative. Typical of the cheerleading is Ted Widmer in the *New York Times Book Review*: "Thanks to Dallek's findings, things make sense at an entirely new level." Referring to the biographer's handling of JFK's medical problems, Widmer exclaims, "Suddenly, the most famous celebrity in modern American history is something more vulnerable—a living organism, fighting for survival from the day he was born."

Forgotten is Nigel Hamilton's *JFK: Reckless Youth* (1992), which did a splendid job of revealing that Kennedy's dire ill health began to manifest itself in his childhood and teenage years. Hamilton explored the diagnosis of Addison's disease and the complications from venereal disease that had JFK battling urinary tract infections for most of his life. Only one writer in my Lexis-Nexis survey of more than forty reviews of Dallek's book even mentions Hamilton's groundbreaking biography. What does Dallek present that is not available in previous biographies? The JFK presidential library granted him access to medical records that reveal a more complete and dramatic record of the most overmedicated president in American history. This is valuable material that Dallek skillfully integrates into his narrative, but neither these additional details nor his handling of other aspects of President Kennedy's life constitute anything approaching the term "definitive." That Dallek alone among the numerous Kennedy scholars was granted access to these files raises questions about the kind of biography—if indeed it is a biography—reviewers have extolled.

In fact Dallek does not claim to be definitive. In his extensive notes and acknowledgments he gives full credit to books and articles that are the "indispensable starting point for a biographer." His aim, however, is to make his book the standard one-volume authority on JFK: "My objective has not been to write another debunking book (these have been in ample supply in recent years) but to penetrate the veneer of glamour and charm to reconstruct the real man or as close to it as possible." Note that Dallek does not attack the debunkers. How could he, when his notes section repeatedly cites their work? Ever the gentleman scholar, he uses words like "judicious" and "balanced" in describing his approach. Balance, however, like beauty, is apparently in the eye of the beholder.

Certainly Hamilton did not think of himself as injudicious or unbalanced. He set out to write "a complete life in the English tradition," as he pointed out in his author's note and acknowledgments. His aim was to create a "serious, balanced, and scholarly biography." Yet Hamilton abandoned his three-volume life after encountering opposition from the Kennedy family and impediments placed in his way by the "exquisitely located John F. Kennedy Library at Columbia Point, overlooking Boston Harbor," as the more fortunate Dallek describes the repository in his acknowledgments.

Why did Dallek find favor while Hamilton, the author of a three-volume authorized life of Field Marshal Bernard Montgomery, was turned away? Dallek, author of an acclaimed two-volume biography of Lyndon Johnson, notes, among other reasons for his access, his reputation for evenhandedness. What does this mean? It means that for every negative, he finds a positive. In Hamilton's book, JFK's father appears as a rather scurrilous character. A stock manipulator of genius and a world-class lecher, Joseph Kennedy was also a political schemer who, as U.S. ambassador to Britain, became in effect a Neville Chamberlain adviser and a subverter of his own president's policies. In Dallek's narrative, Joe is an admired athlete, an adored elder brother with an "infectious grin," a "brilliant banker," and "keen observer" of "contemporary American financial practices." In other words, Joe's juicy life is sucked dry by prose that eliminates him as a living character. Here is how Dallek treats Joseph Kennedy's repeated adulteries: "Joe's independence and willingness to defy accepted standards partly expressed itself in compulsive womanizing." It is hardly womanizing at all when put into Dallek's pacifying prose.

Hamilton crafted a biography that reads like an eighteenth-century picaresque novel. His structure is episodic, with inviting chapter subtitles like "A Very Lively Elf" (describing the young JFK) and "Weaving Daydreams" (evoking early signs of the famous JFK wit). Dallek, in contrast, is all business, with sober chapter titles like "The Congressman" and "The Senator." Indeed, Dallek's chapter titles reveal that he is writing not a full-scale biography but a political or intellectual biography with some personal matters thrown in. Jackie Kennedy hardly makes an appearance in this long book.

It needs to be said that beginning with Plutarch, biography takes the measure of the whole man. Plutarch thought it important to note that Coriolanus was a mama's boy. Dallek seems to understand the meaning of biography, but he is so keen to get on with accounts of the Cuban Missile Crisis and other world-shaking events that time and again he shows no curiosity in precisely what he claims at the outset as his interest: to know "the real man." The "real man" is absent, for example, in Dallek's discussion of *Profiles in Courage*. The book was JFK's idea, but its series of narratives was essentially written by a committee of friends and associates, then reshaped by Kennedy, who served more as editor than author. When the book won a Pulitzer Prize, Dallek notes, this event "sparked predictable envy" and generated charges that Kennedy had not written the work that bore his name. It is hard to see balance at work here when the biographer limits his criticism to noting a single motivation after presenting evidence amounting to an indictment of Kennedy's actions just a few pages earlier in the narrative.

Similarly, after detailing JFK's complex medical history (which would have disqualified him from seeking the presidency if the public had known about it), Dallek quotes JFK: "I'm forty-three years old, and I'm the healthiest candidate for President in the United States." Was Kennedy joking? Dallek makes much of JFK's "realism," his willingness to face facts and live without illusions. But JFK's own words seem to pass by the biographer who in the sentence following JFK's boast simply refers to his subject's confidence. To be fair, Dallek later remarks that JFK "enjoyed" overcoming his illnesses. In this instance he finds just the right word to capture his subject's spirited personality, which provided such a vivid contrast with the grim determination of rivals like Richard Nixon.

So many opportunities pass Dallek by. When JFK meets George Wallace, the Alabama governor engages in a tirade against Martin Luther King, Jr., accusing him of womanizing. All Dallek reports about this exchange is that JFK was "not amused." This meeting is recounted in a Pierre Salinger memo given to the biographer by Sheldon Stern, Dallek is careful to explain in the notes. But what did JFK say? To focus on this instance is to reveal an alarming void in this biography: where are the interviews? Dallek mentions speaking to several individuals, but few of them are identified in his acknowledgments, and his notes contain only scattered references to interviews. This unfinished biography is rather like what R. G. Collingwood calls "scissors-and-paste history," a patching together of documents. The patchwork accounts, in part, for the rather leaden feel of Dallek's book.

Almost all of Dallek's details about JFK's sex life come from Seymour Hersh's *The Dark Side of Camelot* (1997), one of those debunking biographies. Although Dallek mentions JFK's meetings with Marilyn Monroe, he does so in such a muted fashion that it is not clear where to place Monroe in order of importance in the president's sex life. Does this omission matter? Not to readers who want a précis of the public man, the politician and statesman, but to those who want to see the "real man," it matters a good deal. The biographer's bibliography lists none of the significant biographies of Monroe by Anthony Summers, Donald Spoto, and Barbara Leaming—all of whom render verdicts on the importance of MM in JFK's life.

Also missing from Dallek's acknowledgments is the kind of engagement with his subject that Hamilton demonstrated when he remarked, "In undertaking this biography, I called upon many distinguished authors and historians who toiled in the field of JFK studies before me." It is this inquiring dialogue with sources—which requires getting up from the library seat and going out on a chase after living history—that Dallek's work lacks. Blessed with his own wealth of archival material, Hamilton nevertheless conducted "fresh interviews with surviving JFK friends and historical witnesses" who "enabled me to round out and balance the vast JFK Library oral history program." The result is a biography that moves at a smart pace even though it is eight hundred pages long, and ends with JFK's first congressional campaign.

To all this Robert Dallek might respond, "But you are demanding a book I did not intend to write." Precisely so. Will Nigel Hamilton please resume his work?

CRITIQUE: What can it mean to call a biography definitive? Why the rush to anoint biographers in this manner? There is always more to learn: new letters and other documents turn up, and fresh interviews can be conducted, not to mention the likely appearance of novel and provocative interpretations. Yet Alistair Cooke hailed David Thompson's *Rosebud: The Story of Orson Welles* (1996) this way: "Definitive and unique. It is impossible to believe that anyone will ever again probe with such patience, eloquence, and insight into the life and work of this fascinating monster."

At that time another contender, Simon Callow, had just produced *Orson Welles: The Road to Xanadu* (1995), the first volume (640 pages) of what promised to be a two-volume biography. The recently published second volume, *Orson Welles: Hello Americans* (2006), covers only six years of Welles's life, taking up the story where Callow left it in volume one, after *Citizen Kane*, and ending in 1947, when the legendary director begins a twenty-year exile from his native land. So now, Callow explains, his biography will have to be completed in a third volume.

Why so many pages? Callow suggests that his approach is the only way to recapture the texture of Welles's life while scraping away the veneer of legend promulgated by his idolaters, especially Peter Bogdanovich. But Callow is not attempting to cut Welles down to size; on the contrary, the biographical subject takes on weight because of Callow's approach.

Texture means, for example, providing a comprehensive view of what went into the making of Welles's botched masterpiece, *The Magnificent Ambersons* (1942), including a full-dress rehearsal of the Booth Tarkington novel Welles adapted first as a radio play and then as a film script.

The legend has it that the studio decimated the film, downsizing a two-hour-plus picture into eighty-eight minutes because it was thought—especially at a time when the world was at war—to be too gloomy. But as Callow shows (relying in part on the work of film scholars), Welles bore considerable responsibility for the mutilation of his work. Instead of staying put and arguing for his vision in the editing room and with RKO studio executives, he was off to Brazil to film another epic, which also ended badly. Welles never took seriously enough his RKO contract stipulating that the studio had the final cut. Instead he thought he could take command of the editing by long-distance telephone and telegram. He kept firing off suggestions for changes (some brilliant, some counterproductive) after the studio began to balk at his film's bulk. Welles knew he had produced a somber film that questioned the value of material progress and America's love of the automobile, but he thought the quality of his work would win audiences anyway. Also, as Callow notes, reinforcing the theme of his biography, the film "perfectly fit into Welles's over-arching fascination with what it is to be an American, a question given some urgency by the war."

But if it fit so perfectly, why didn't Welles stick around? "Perhaps to focus on *The Magnificent Ambersons* to the exclusion of anything else would have been simply too disturbing, too painful," Callow speculates. Another reason, the biographer suggests, is that Welles had ruled out starring in the film (he felt he was too fat for the character he should play), so he had to employ his massive energies elsewhere.

Do these surmises help? I turned to see what that "definitive" biographer, David Thomson, might have to add. Curiously, I could not find his Welles biography mentioned in Callow's second volume—not in the notes, not in the bibliography or in the acknowledgments, even though in *The Road to Xanadu* Callow was scrupulous about recognizing his debt to earlier Welles biographers and scholars, thus satisfying those who view biography as a cumulative and incremental art. Furthermore, Thomson had acknowledged Callow with these words: "I also thank a 'rival,' a man of great generosity and kindness, as well as the author of fine books—Simon Callow."

Thomson is an elegant writer. As his *Biographical Dictionary of Film* demonstrates, he has an economy of phrasing that is every bit as good as Callow's texture. Here is Thomson musing on why Welles chose to film *The Magnificent Ambersons*:

> A great deal of Welles's heart lies in *Ambersons*, and it is a heart that is conventional, nostalgic, romantic, and innately conservative. He was, in his own life, famous and feared as an innovator, a man of new techniques and approaches, an example of startling youth sweeping aside the past. That view was widely held, but it was one he never understood. So he was bewildered that so few recognized his fondness for the spirit of the past. Indeed that past—glowing, perhaps mythic and certainly impossible—was his best corrective to the despair he felt about progress and purpose.

The genius of this passage is then enhanced by a poignant account of Richard Bennett, a has-been matinee idol who Welles said demonstrated the "greatest lyric power of any actor I ever saw" in the important role of Major Amberson:

Welles treated him with love and respect, and gave him an epiphany, the scene in which the dying Major stares into the fire and tries to organize his scattered thoughts on what life is and where it comes from. This scene is in the book, but it is far more affecting in the movie because of its brevity, because of the image—the old white face, in darkness, illuminated by a flickering fire that mimics the sun he talks about—and because of Bennett's face, and his bond with Welles. Bennett could never recollect the lines. So Welles read them to him, off camera, and Bennett repeated them. How Welles adored and worshiped old age and the somber luster of people at their close. There is nothing more moving in American film than the face of the Major and his halting words: "It must be the sun. . . . There wasn't anything here except the sun in the first place. . . . The sun. . . . Earth came out of the sun. We came out of the Earth. . . . So, whatever we are . . ."

Thomson is a mesmerizing writer who knows how to build to a climax and make every detail count. For Welles aficionados, Callow is essential. For the rest of us, Thomson is the ticket.

ONE SYNONYM for the definitive biography is dull; another is dutiful. The biographer is obliged to deal with every aspect of his subject's life and work, and the result can be an ill-proportioned account lacking highlights, a sense of discrimination, or drama. Such tomes become useful reference works but indigestible narratives.

W. A. Speck's subtitle for *Robert Southey* (2006) might have been "an entire biography of an entire man of letters." Since Robert Southey was a poet, novelist, historian, biographer, book reviewer, and playwright, he justified the sobriquet Byron bestowed on him. Actually, however, Southey's greatest achievement, as Speck vouchsafes in the last two pages of his biography, is as a letter writer.

How odd and puzzling it is that the biographer should hold back this claim until the very end of his book, and how disappointing that he does not make better use of his subject's correspondence. Speck quotes one Southey critic, "There he stands, to the life, independent, irritable, generous, tender, kind-hearted, loyal—above all, intensely human." Speck quotes Southey repeatedly, but not to such good effect: rarely does his subject seem as alive as that one critic suggested.

The trouble is that Speck drowns out his subject with so much diurnal reporting. This day-to-day kind of biography blows apart any effort to come to terms with Southey's significance. Thus, for example, Speck announces on page 137 that Southey, a prodigious book reviewer, disparaged five lives of Nelson in the *Quarterly Review*, prompting the publisher John Murray to propose that Southey do the job himself.

But why did Southey dismiss these other books? Instead of providing an explanation, the next fifteen pages follow the calendar of Southey's life before halting for a two-page account of the Nelson biography that Southey finally came to write. From there follows a meager portrayal of what is undoubtedly Southey's most important individual work. No one reads his tedious, book-length poetic epics; at best he is remembered as one of the Lakers who befriended Coleridge and Wordsworth. Of the Nelson biography, Speck observes: "However overdone it might have seemed, Southey's was to become the definitive biography for its generation, and one that is still in print today." Why? He does not say, even though it is rare for a biography to remain in print for so long, and even though subsequent biographers have paid tribute to Southey. Instead Speck quotes Southey's "purple passage on Nelson's death at Trafalgar":

> The most triumphant death is that of the martyr; and the most awful that of the martyred patriot; the most splendid that of the hero in the hour of victory; and if the chariot and the horses of fire had been vouchsafed for Nelson's translation, he could scarcely have departed in a brighter blaze of glory.

The passage may indeed be purple, but this is how many Englishmen regarded Nelson's death, and it is a piece with Nelson himself, who penned his own purple passages in letters and clearly saw himself as a worthy successor to the heroes of ancient Greece and Rome. Southey voiced a nation's sentiments, not only his own. And for a

biographer simply to call Southey's words purple is to display an ignorance of historical context and of the kind of biography Southey
was writing. Southey's cadenced prose was memorable, indeed easily memorized by generations of Englishmen and -women. And
though Southey was chary of describing Nelson's affair with Emma
Hamilton, that he did so at all sets him apart from the Victorian biographers who would soon embalm their subjects in euphemistic
prose.

Discussion of the Nelson biography should have been one of
the big moments in this book. Speck does not even comment on
the fact that Southey (a young radical who supported the French
Revolution and planned to join Coleridge in an American commune that would pursue a quasi-socialist form of government they
called "Pantisocracy") employed narratives such as his biography of
Nelson to move toward a much more conservative and nationalis-
tic position.

If Speck does little to shape his narrative into dramatic units, he
can often encapsulate an episode or theme in his subject's life with
superb economy. Thus he describes Southey's attraction to Mary
Barker, who apparently was a much more lively coadjutor than
Southey's own wife Edith:

> There is certainly a sexual tension in Southey's letters to Mary
> Barker that cannot have been unintentional. "I look upon novel
> reading as being exactly to the mind what rank debauchery is to
> the body," he once observed to her, "over stimulation instead of
> true delight." At the same time, those letters he wrote to both
> Mary and Edith tell them what he wanted them to know. He seems
> to have been trying to control a situation he himself was afraid
> might get out of hand.

This seems admirable in a biography: succinct attention to the nuances and subtext of evidence without unduly pressing a case that
cannot be proved. The trouble, then, is not Speck's writing—at least
not sentence by sentence—but rather that he so often lacks a sense
of timing and pace. His book is not too long; instead he ought to

have had an editor who would suggest, "Cut here, expand there, and for God's sake, build toward those crucial moments in Southey's life." Southey could sparkle, but alas he has been saddled with an all too plodding biographer.

Details

Samuel Johnson said that the petty detail is often the most revealing. It all depends on whether the details are merely a catalog or in the service of a greater story. To me, as a biographer, it was important that Lillian Hellman got into a taxi and put her hand on her lawyer's knee. It said a lot about how she operated. Someone else, I suppose, would call my interest petty or lurid. But to me it wasn't just a pass. Hellman used sex or flirtatiousness as a form of control. She also just enjoyed flirting. I didn't say either of these things, because I had built up a pattern in the book that did not require me to explain.

Eckermann, Johann (1792–1854)

Renowned for his account of his conversations with Goethe, Eckermann is the German Boswell. Like his British counterpart, Eckermann made a study of his friend's conversation, carefully editing his notes and providing a vivid rendition of his subject's style. And like Boswell, Eckermann had his subject's cooperation and brought to the genre of biography an obsession with accuracy and fidelity to precision of expression. Also like Boswell, Eckermann subordinated himself to his subject, carefully monitoring his own role as the great man's disciple. Consequently Goethe, like Johnson, emerges as a rather Olympian figure whom subsequent biographers have felt compelled to deconstruct.

FURTHER READING: Much of the best work on Eckermann is in German. For a study in English, see Avital Ronell, *Dictations: On Haunted Writing* (1986).

Edel, Leon (1907–1997)

Leon Edel published several hundred articles, essays, and reviews, primarily concerned with biographical and literary criticism. Some of Edel's shorter pieces have been collected in *Literary Biography* (1957). His interest in the psychological interpretation of lives is reflected not only in his biographies but also in his critical study *The Psychological Novel* (1955). His innovative five-volume biography of Henry James and his consistent arguments over many years for a sophisticated biographical method contribute to Edel's reputation as one of the foremost literary biographers of the last century.

Edel was an ardent advocate for applying the insights of modern psychology to the study of literature and of writers' lives. No critical account of modern biographical writing would be complete without a discussion of Edel's theory and practice of literary biography, and recent studies and collections of essays on the nature of biography contain contributions by him or about his impact on modern biography.

Throughout his career as a biographer and as a biographical theorist, Edel maintained that biographers must strive for excellence of literary form. A fine biography must have a pleasing aesthetic shape, a concrete delineation of human character, and an economical approach to the biographical subject that reveals the most telling details of a life. In short, modern literary biography must model itself after the novel in order to achieve a vivid and deeply penetrating study of the subject's life.

The biographer should aspire to be an artist, Edel insists. Most important is that the "central myth" of the writer's life is revealed. Edel contends that there is a unified shaping vision by which the creative artist lived, and the biographer must discover and dramatize that vision. Edel has shown that the themes of a writer's life and writing are inevitably intertwined. This does not mean that all creative work is autobiographical, but it does mean, according to Edel, that all art arises from deeply personal feelings: "We know that all literature is a form of disguise, a mask, a fable, a mystery: and behind the mask is the author," he writes in the foreword to *Stuff of Sleep and Dreams* (1982).

Edel's theory of literary biography is best understood by citing an example from his work on Henry James. In his condensed and revised version of the biography (1985), Edel provides a remarkably succinct and insightful summary of one of James's finest and most intricate novels, *The Ambassadors* (1903), which at the same time is a profound revelation of James's own psyche. The novel is told from the point of view of Lambert Strether—in Edel's words, "a middle-aged 'ambassador' sent out" to Europe to retrieve a young American man who has apparently been seduced by the Old World charms of a mature woman. The novel is as much about Strether's acculturation as it is about the young man's presumed debauchery.

Edel focuses on two key scenes that reveal Strether's developing realization that in Europe the young man has had the opportunity to grow and to fulfill himself. At the same time Strether recognizes that he has not himself managed to live life to the fullest. Insulated from the choices Europe has offered this young man, Strether comes to admit that he has never pursued his own desires or developed his own talents. In sum, he has never been free, and his decision is to allow this young man—in many ways Strether's younger self—the liberty to choose his own life.

At the conclusion of his remarks on *The Ambassadors*, Edel notes that "beyond 'technique' and its resourceful experiments, beyond its neat symmetrical design, the care with which it is composed . . . spoke for the central myth of Henry James's life." That myth has to do with leaving America as a young man for the richer life of Europe—not an easy choice for James, who had to struggle with what Edel calls the "authority figures" of his Puritan past. James, in other words, had to reverse the very direction of his family history—the movement from Europe to America—and contend that a return to Europe was in fact a liberating decision. All the terror, the uncertainty, and the anguish, but also the charm, the boldness, and the creativity of James's commitment to a life in Europe are dramatized in the character of Lambert Strether. Edel's own artistry as a biographer is revealed in his use of the word "composed" to speak for both James's novel and his life. The novel is not autobiography in the sense of reproducing the events of James's life, but it is his life in the most profound, psychological sense.

In all his writing on biographical theory, Edel has been careful to point out that he is not psychoanalyzing the writer; that is, Edel is not claiming to know James's innermost thoughts or to be engaging in a scientific analysis of the writer's maladies. Edel is no doctrinaire follower of Sigmund Freud, the founder of modern psychoanalysis. But Edel is impressed with Freud's analyses of the patterns of people's lives and of those crucial moments in which truths about their lives are revealed.

In *Stuff of Sleep and Dreams*, Edel defines his terms. He favors the phrase "literary psychology" to distinguish his method from "other psychologies that are concerned with treating neuroses and pathological conditions of mental health. In other words, literary psychology is criticism and biography divorced from psychotherapy." In the same book, in a chapter titled "The Nature of Psychological Evidence," Edel enumerates the "three postulates" he has taken from psychoanalysis. He believes there is such a thing as the unconscious that manifests itself in human behavior, "in dreams, in imaginings, thoughts." Within this unconscious are "certain suppressed feelings and states of being which sometimes emerge into awareness in the consciously created forms of literature." Finally, "by the process of induction—that is, by examining the mental representation in words of things not present to the senses—we can detect deeper intentions and meanings, valuable both to the biographer and the critic."

Edel insists that the biographer works with facts and with evidence. His biography of James is the distillation of a massive amount

of material on the writer's life and work that includes diaries, journals, notebooks, letters, and various accounts of James's life by himself and by others. As Edel often said, the biographer is not free to
imagine facts, but he is charged with inventing a form that makes the
most profound sense of his subject's life.

It was perhaps inevitable with a great writer like James, who
lived a long, productive life and whose archive continues to grow
with newly discovered letters and other materials, that Edel was
forced to write a lengthy, multi-volume biography. Nevertheless the
size of the James biography would seem to contradict Edel's stric-
tures about precision and economy in the writing of lives. Edel has
tacitly acknowledged this discrepancy between his theory and practice by revising and rewriting his biography twice—in two volumes
in 1977, and then in one volume in 1985. Each time he has done
more than reduce wordage; he has added newly discovered material
and (with the aid of editors) reshaped the entire biography.

In his last edition of the James biography, Edel also responded
to "the changes that have occurred in biographical writing and in social attitudes toward privacy and our sexual lives." It is not that he
has gone in search of James's "sex life," Edel points out, but rather
that he has abandoned "former reticences" and "proprieties" of an
earlier age. He also acknowledges the fact that his earlier edition of
the biography was written "out of respect for surviving members of
the James family, the children of William James."

All these changes that occurred over more than three decades in
Edel's work on Henry James make a fascinating study of how the
writing and discussion of biography have shifted. Edel is one of
several biographers who have taken bolder positions as literary
writers, not just as compilers of facts. He has led the way in speculating on the pattern of James's life and in refusing to be bound by
conventions that other biographers have treated as sacrosanct. For
example, though his life of James is told in chronological fashion,
he has used novelistic devices, such as the flashback and flash forward to earlier and later events in James's life. The implication of
such techniques is that "the facts do not speak for themselves," that

the biographer must be an interpreter of his evidence and create a structure for it.

While Edel has enormous prestige as a biographer, he has not been immune from criticism. He has been accused of too readily adopting the theories of modern psychology and of shifting the emphasis in biography too far toward forms of literature like the novel. Other theorists of biography have insisted on a strictly chronological approach to biography and have eschewed the use of psychological theory. In their view, the employment of fictional techniques and psychological speculation reveals more about the biographer than the subject of the biography. In the main, however, Edel has remained the principal theorist of biography whose arguments have been open to challenge but not to significant refutation.

In *Writing Lives*, Edel discusses many of his fellow biographers, especially predecessors like Lytton Strachey (1880–1932) and André Maurois (1885–1967). His chief criticism of them is their tendency to allow their own personalities to distort the lives they have written about. In a way, Edel's studies of his precursors constitute a reply to his critics. By showing how Strachey, Maurois, and others have erred in this tendency, Edel is critiquing his own practice.

The single most important influence on Edel has surely been Strachey. In *Eminent Victorians* (1918), Strachey wrote pithy and provocative studies of Thomas Arnold, Florence Nightingale, General Charles Gordon, and Cardinal Manning in order to debunk their "eminence." At the same time Strachey was hailed as an artist for his turns of phrase, his economical use of biographical evidence, and his ability to dramatize human personality and history in essay-length form. Edel has not adopted Strachey's satirical style, but he has emulated Strachey's compression of human lives into deft, self-sufficient essays of human character. Indeed, all of Edel's work after the James biography, including his study of the Bloomsbury group, has been predicated on the essay form. In this way he has sought to vindicate his view that biography should be to the point; it should be the crystallization of a life, not a long and tedious—if faithful—chronicle of it.

FURTHER READING: There is a considerable body of critical commentary on Edel's work. See, for example, *Essaying Biography: A Celebration of Leon Edel* (1986), edited by Gloria Fromm, and *Leon Edel and Literary Art* (1988), edited by Lyall Powers.

In *The Art of Biography* (1965), Paul Murray Kendall makes a sustained attack on Edel's violation of chronology. The materials of biography are not "infinitely plastic," Kendall rejoins, and they cannot be used as freely as the novelist uses his. The biographer cannot adopt an omniscient tone or fragment his evidence that actually "ruptures the patterns of life." By doing so, he "loses the sense of life being lived," for his purpose should be to "elicit" the shape of a life, not to refashion it. Kendall cites other biographers who have shared his belief and provides detailed examples of the way Edel has violated these most important principles of biography.

In the introduction to *Golden Codgers: Biographical Speculations* (1973), Richard Ellmann, the masterful biographer of James Joyce, challenges Edel's application of Freud's theories to biography, suggesting a distinction between literary creation and the verbal associations that Freud analyzed. The result of Edel's psychoanalyzing, Ellmann argues, reduces rather than expands a sense of James as author and individual. Ellmann finds that later volumes of the James biography apply Freudian principles less consistently and stringently, sometimes forsaking Freud for insights that derive from an older, eighteenth-century sense of psychology. He finds George Painter's "post-Freudian" psychology more persuasive.

Editorializing

Peter Kurth's Salon essay/interview about his biography of Isadora Duncan is unusually frank, particularly his remarks about how he felt about certain people in his book and how his editor made him tone down some of his judgments. It's an issue biographers must always confront. Do you just tell the story, or do you comment? Some reviewers want the commentary while others dislike what they call "editorializing." Of course, the biographer's focus of research, selection of facts, and structure of his narrative are all implicit examples of editorializing. For the Kurth interview, see: http://archive.salon .com/people/conv/2001/11/12/kurth/index.html

Eighteenth-Century Biography

An early but still valuable study is Mark Longaker's *English Biography in the Eighteenth Century* (1931), a historical and critical survey, with chapters on life-writing before the eighteenth century, the influences that made possible the modern conception of biography, the growth of realism in nonfiction (crime stories and memoirs), the handling of private life in Roger North's biographies, the advance in scholarly methodology and biographical vocabulary, the methods of William Mason in his memoirs of Gray and of Whitehead, Johnson's *Lives of the Poets*, and Boswell's *Life of Johnson*. Each chapter contains a separate bibliography.

Donald A. Stauffer, *The Art of Biography in Eighteenth-Century England* (1941), traces the influence of drama and the novel on biography, the increasing influence of romanticism (producing biographies intensely focused on the individual's sensibility), and popular biographies of journalists and the elaborate, antiquarian researches of scholars—both resulting in enhanced psychological portraiture. Stauffer provides detailed summaries of biographies of a quality just below the most distinguished works of Johnson, Boswell, and North while devoting a separate chapter to the greatest biographies. Throughout, Stauffer includes a discussion of autobiography, stressing that this form of life—writing heavily influenced biography and cannot be sensibly divorced from it. A bibliographical supplement provides an alphabetical listing of the titles Stauffer read, a chronological table of principal biographies, and a description of important works not treated in his text.

Ellmann, Richard (1918–1987)

One of the most renowned biographers of the twentieth century. Unfavorable criticism of Ellmann is rare. In *The Biographer's Art: New Essays* (1989), edited by Jeffrey Meyers, Phillip Herring discusses Herman Gorman's early life of Joyce and Ellmann's theory of biography, concentrating on a chapter in Ellmann's work that exemplifies what Herring calls "biographical license," a speculative reenactment of the subject's life. Examining the critical response to Ellmann's work, Herring takes note of Hugh Kenner's charges that Ellmann relied too much on Joyce's brother Stanislaus, was inaccurate in some respects, relied upon fiction for biographical evidence, and employed an ironic, unsympathetic tone. Nevertheless Herring concludes that Ellmann is one of the two or three greatest biographers of the century and that his work is unlikely to be surpassed by another Joyce biographer.

Naturally, the different approaches of Ellmann and Edel have been compared. Park Honan, in *Author's Lives* (1990), finds Edel "admirably detailed" but "wearisome" because he is not as effective as Ellmann in "making literary criticism seem to advance his biographical 'story.'" Edel relies too much on plot summary and "speculative psychobiographical theory." Commenting on Ellmann's own evaluation of Edel, Honan suggests that Ellmann is "professionally protective, as if he felt Edel had betrayed the guild or the mystery of the craft in slipshod Freudianizing and had failed to realize that a biographer's authority should not be compromised and, furthermore, must be earned and demonstrated through the narrative of a life."

Hilton Kramer (*New York Times Book Review*, February 6, 1972, pp. 1, 32–33) places Edel's work in the first rank with George Painter's biography of Proust and Richard Ellmann's biography of Joyce, and suggests that in the complexity and variety of James's career Edel set himself a far more difficult task. The evocation of James's inner life, his use of psychology, and his opening of new avenues of criticism are Edel's major achievements. Kramer dismisses the often harsh academic criticism of Edel for taking a biographical approach at a time when the academy abjured the personal and historical in its discussion of literature, and he defends Edel from charges of "undue length," concluding that the biography is proportionate to the importance of the subject and necessary to the narrative, novelistic aims of the biography.

In *Whole Lives: The Shapers of Modern Biography* (1988), Reed Whittemore finds Edel's biography of James does not match the newness or novelty of his ideas about the form of biography. He contrasts Edel's idea of the biographer discovering truths hidden by the subject with Ellmann's notion of the biographer as mediator, exploring ideas which the subject had "himself uncovered." Whittemore believes that Edel destroys his disclaimer that the subject cannot be psychoanalyzed "by talking of the biographer in scientific terms as an analyst and saying that the dreams, thoughts, and fancies of the biographee are useful to him just as they would be if the analyst had the biographee on the couch." He finds that Edel's growing psychological perceptiveness in his five-volume life parallels James's own maturation as a psychological novelist.

As I point out in *A Higher Form of Cannibalism?: Adventures in the Art and Politics of Biography* (2005), Ellmann was reluctant to discuss how events and circumstances contrived to restrict his exploration of certain issues. In *Nora*, a biography of Joyce's wife, Brenda Maddox offers a fascinating account of how Joyce's papers were disseminated and often withheld from scholars, pointing out that even Ellmann's biography depends very much on a single source (Joyce's brother Stanislaus), and that in order to publish his biography Ellmann had to engage in considerable self-censorship. The interaction between the biographer and his evidence and the role of literary estates (seldom discussed in biographies) is well ventilated.

FURTHER READING: For a full-length study, see Bernard McGinley's *Joyce's Lives: Uses and Abuses of the Biografiend* (1996).

Empathy

It is probably true that the best biographies empathize with their subject. But would that apply to a biography of Hitler? Would you want to work up sympathy for his poor starving years as a second-rate artist? (That's not just a rhetorical question.) I think there are not really any rules here, only biographers. Lytton Strachey could be pretty merciless on his Victorian subjects, and for him that worked, though of course his approach also has its limitations. He is deliberately debunking the high Victorians, cutting them down to size and sometimes making them smaller than our present age finds justifiable.

I think there is room for a belittling biography. Charlie Chaplin belittles Hitler in his film *The Great Dictator*, and as satire I believe the treatment works. The debunking biography has its place. Biography can create heroes; it can also tear them down. We need both kinds of biography as well as many other kinds. One biography is always a reaction to another. Strachey debunks the Victorians, we can debunk Strachey, and so on. If you want to be empathetic, that's fine, but it's not a model for every biography. E. M. Forster said he loved biographies that tore "great men" to pieces. He had a point, but only a point.

Then too, empathy is in the eye of the beholder. I remember how shocked I was when one of my readers (a British biographer) said that my biography of Rebecca West disproved his theory that you could not write a good biography of a person you disliked. I was amazed. Of all my subjects, I felt closest to Rebecca. There was no dislike at all, none, though I certainly showed she had her faults. How could an intelligent person read my book and be THAT WRONG? I'll answer my own question: it seems to happen all the time, judging by the book reviews I read.

"As to your own experience, with a critic claiming that you didn't like your subject," biographer Roxana Robinson wrote to me, "what else do critics do besides project their own experience onto other people's work?" This, by the way, is Oscar Wilde's view in his famous essay, "The Critic as Artist."

CRITIQUE: The outstanding example of a biography that belittles its subject is Roger Lewis's life of Anthony Burgess. Over the course of more than twenty years, Roger Lewis came to see his literary hero as a fraud—but a magnificent one, whose work is still worth reading not as the oeuvre of a master but as the vulgar output of a versatile writer gamely taking on Napoleon, Joyce, and Shakespeare. Indeed, for Lewis, Burgess took on the whole of the English language and European history, and brooded spectacularly about the future in *A Clockwork Orange*, the novel that became the film that made him famous.

Reading Roger Lewis is rather like reading James Boswell in reverse, so that the biographer becomes not ennobled but exacerbated by his subject. As soon as you realize that Lewis is not about to let up on Burgess, you can relax. Forget about the idea of objectivity, of the biography "fat and worthy-burgherish on the shelf, boastful and sedate" (a quote from Julian Barnes's *Flaubert's Parrot*, which Lewis employs as one of the epigraphs to his book).

Who says biography cannot go negative? Doing so seems fair enough as long as the biographer announces his intention, as Lewis does in his bracing prologue. Still, just about every British reviewer of the book has blasted Lewis. In Britain, it seems, biography is still for the burghers.

Although Lewis's biography goes ballistic, Burgess nonetheless emerges as an outlandishly attractive figure. The biographer captures his subject's robust command of language, his encyclopedic mind, and his maniacal drive to dominate the literary discourse of his time through novels, film scripts, book reviews, television appearances, lecture tours, literary festivals, distinguished professorships, translations, and virtually every other venue a writer can seize hold of in his quest to make himself visible to the world.

In the end, it does not matter how many faults Lewis catalogs—despite Burgess's bogus erudition, his pretensions about his status as a composer, and his hasty pursuit of literary greatness as a decathlon. He remains an appealing, audacious, Dickensian figure, forever decrying the literary establishment that ignores him even as he pockets huge fees for appearances and publications. Burgess provoked high expectations that could never be fulfilled, but he brought to contemporary literature a magnificent horizon.

The question biographers are often asked is one they do not usually answer in their books: Why did you write the biography? But Lewis has the question in mind when he quotes, in another epigraph, Orson Welles's comment to one of his biographers: "I think there's no biography so interesting as the one in which the biographer is present. I think it's a wonderful story, the whole thing: trying to get me . . ." "Get" is the keyword here, implying both an attempt to portray the biographical subject accurately and to snag the suspect, draw up the charge sheet, and determine the number of counts in the indictment.

Like Boswell, Lewis first met his literary lion in distinguished company. Lewis was a student of the biographer Richard Ellmann's at Oxford, when Burgess alighted there in 1985. The illustrious Ellmann, biographer of James Joyce and Oscar Wilde, became for Lewis a wonderful foil to the flamboyant Burgess. Solid citizens will be outraged at Lewis's irreverent depiction of his Ph.D. supervisor. In a squalid house, Ellmann the Eminent makes a "meal of fetching gin and tonics," accompanied by a "plastic tub of what might have been called guacamole." The soft-spoken and diplomatic scholar will not scuffle with his jocular guest: "Tell me, Dick, which white wine did Joyce drink?" Burgess asks. "People come to blows over that," replies the evasive Ellmann.

Lewis's point, I take it, is that he will enter the ring with Burgess. Seldom has a biographer revealed in a biography that he and the subject engage in a kind of duel. This aspect of biography as blood sport is usually dramatized in fiction, or in the biographer's essay in reminiscence (where a few scores are usually settled). Yet out of this conflict between biography and subject comes the story, as Citizen Welles understood so well.

Biographers love to speak of their empathy for their subjects, but friction is required to get the machinery of biographical narrative moving. Like so many good pieces of writing, Lewis's does not depend on his opinions. Reject them and you still have the engines of his perceptions driving you on to marvel at Burgess's mania. "The whole of English Lit. at the moment is being written by Anthony Burgess," the poet Philip Larkin wrote to a friend in 1966. And so it would be until the dynamo ran down in 1993, succumbing to cancer.

The key charge against Anthony Burgess is that he lacked feeling, and so his characters do not live. He is all contrivance, a confection, a counter-jumper whose real name was John Wilson, once upon a time a modest, well-behaved schoolteacher who decided to use literature and a literary life to escape the responsibilities of being a real person. Thus his fiction does not reveal the man, it escapes from him. But in doing so, the literary output becomes, like Las Vegas, a "genuine fake."

It is a romantic idea that we should identify with the biographical subject, a romantic idea that the subject is plumbing his own experience. It is more likely, Lewis proposes, that the subject is consumed in his work and becomes the embodiment of literature—of the tradition he has absorbed. Lewis is a contender, in other words, for the T. S. Eliot Distinguished Professorship in Anti-Romantic Biography, since he has done nothing less than shatter the mold of the genre.

Epistemology

There can be no doubt—as the articles below suggest—that biographical knowledge is problematic. How to enter another's mind? On the other hand, how to know one's own mind? the biographer might reply. No one can see himself or herself in the round, so to speak. Of course, all sorts of data may escape the biographer's grasp. But that is no reason to refute the notion of biography itself. Biographies gain their authority through the cumulative work of generations of scholars and writers. No biography, in itself, can encompass a life, but a life can be made a subject of study—biography by biography—thus providing a form of knowledge that is not available to biographical subjects, or to their friends, associates, and family. Biographers have been all too apologetic about their work, measuring what they do not know against some kind of absolute standard. But there is no such standard, no absolute by which the biographer can be found wanting. Certainly autobiography cannot take the measure of biography, so why should the biographer be viewed as particularly culpable?

FURTHER READING: In *The New Yorker* (April 3, 2000), John Updike notes that novels like A. S. Byatt's *Possession* call into question the materials biographers manipulate: letters and diaries are used to construct factitious narratives, forcing coherence on lives that are far more fragmentary and ambiguous than the conventions of biography could manage.

Similarly, In "Just Published: Minutiae Without Meaning" (*New York Times*, September 7, 1999), Stanley Fish launches a radical attack on biography as a form of knowledge. He argues that biographies are just variations on "contingency." In other words, there is no necessary connection between events in an individual's life and the world at large, but biographers pretend that there is. To make his point, Fish parodies the biographer's first sentence, which usually states where and when the subject (Fish's hypothetical "John Smith") was born. After that, the biography becomes dubious as the gap between facts and what to make of them opens up. Here is Fish's example of a second sentence: "Memories of the Civil War were still strong, and quarrels between partisans often erupted in inns and alehouses of southern Ohio." Fish doubts any convincing relationship could be established between the individual and the historical background. In other words, biographers fake transitions or connections between people and events, creating a story of a life that is entirely arbitrary.

In *An Imaginary Wilderness: Essays on 20th-Century Literature* (1987), Sven Birkerts asserts that biographers cannot know their subjects and refuse to own up to the "problematic status" of biography as a genre. The life of a literary subject takes place in the act of creation that cannot be recaptured by another person. Biographers presume a single, stable self when in fact the subject of a biography may not "feel himself as an integrated, continuous being," and certainly not as the documented, chronological creature of biographies. Amassing testimony and documents comes nowhere near the heart of the subject, and biographies ought to acknowledge their shortcomings.

Evelyn, John (1620–1706)

This noted diarist also produced an important biography, *The Life of Mrs. Godolphin*, a private memorial of his friendship with her that was not published until 1847. Like many great biographies, Evelyn's is also a memoir. It is a particularly affecting work because Margaret Blagge, a maid of honor to the queen, is presented as a kind of saint who died at twenty-five in childbirth, having been married to Sidney Godolphin for only three years. Her virtuous behavior is set against the corruption of Charles II's reign. Evelyn was a kind of protector for her, describing himself as a father, brother, and friend.

FURTHER READING: Geoffrey Keynes, *John Evelyn* (1937), and Gerald W. Marshall, "John Evelyn and the Construction of the Scientific Self," in *The Restoration Mind* (1935).

Evidence

In "The Development, Use and Abuse of Interpretation in Biography" (*English Institute Essays*, 1943), Newman White, a biographer of Byron, emphasizes the importance of intuition in the biographer's discovery of facts, showing how in his own research his reading of

Byron's character led to the discovery of new evidence. While first-hand experience of a subject's travels may be helpful, White persuasively shows how library research can sometimes do as well or better. He shrewdly notes that "excess of interpretation" is often due to a paucity of fact, and he takes issue with André Maurois's emphasis on finding determining themes in a subject's life, which can often lead to facile conclusions about character.

FURTHER READING: Paula Backscheider, *Reflections on Biography* (1999).

SEE ALSO Epistemology.

Fair Use

This doctrine allows biographers, historians, critics, and other writers to quote a modest number of words from their subjects' writings. How modest? A rule of thumb has been to quote no more than three hundred words from a full-length book, a sentence or two from a long letter, a line from a poem or a song. But there is no legal definition of how many words can be quoted. Section 107 of the amended copyright act of 1992 describes four factors which are to be considered when judging fair-use defenses raised against claims of copyright infringement:

(1) the purpose and character of the use, including whether such use is of a commercial nature or is for nonprofit educational purposes;
(2) the nature of the copyrighted work;
(3) the amount and substantiality of the portion used in relation to the copyrighted work as a whole; and
(4) the effect of the use upon the potential market for or value of the copyrighted work.

The fact that a work is unpublished shall not itself bar a finding of fair use if such finding is made upon consideration of all the above factors.

The last sentence is crucial and was added in 1992 because several court cases—especially a suit that J. D. Salinger brought against his biographer, Ian Hamilton—had virtually destroyed the fair-use doctrine in regard to unpublished work; that is, court rulings made it almost impossible for a biographer to quote, or even closely paraphrase, unpublished writing.

Here is how fair use works in practice. A few years ago I received a phone call from a distraught biographer. She had been working amicably with her subject's estate for almost fifteen years, and now, quite suddenly, she had been refused permission to quote from unpublished papers. The literary executor had read a part of her manuscript and apparently had reservations. Even worse, another biographer was waiting in the wings: a certain gentleman who had been plotting for some years to get control of the estate. I got the phone call because a friend had advised this woman that I had confronted a similar situation.

"What should I do?" the phone caller asked. "Neither my agent nor my publisher has been of much help." The biography had been contracted with the understanding that the estate would cooperate, and now the biographer—never having squarely faced the issue of authorization—was in a quandary. Just how much use could she make of unpublished material? Did the estate's prior cooperation give her any warrant for retaining her quotations from unpublished sources? The trouble was that there was nothing in writing, no agreement that in any sense "authorized" the biographer.

I did have some advice for the caller that was based on my own experience with estates and with the subjects of my biographies, which I began working on in the late 1980s, just as my wife, Lisa Paddock, got her law degree and began to explore copyright issues. Our husband-and-wife collaboration was not merely a matter of a writer getting legal advice from his spouse, but rather a close collaboration in the talking out of what became my narratives, which had to over-come the obstacles that biographical subjects and their estates erect to stymie unauthorized biographers. The main weapon, copyright, was not employed to protect the subject's property rights but to en-force censorship on the biographer and to intimidate him or her— perhaps to the point where the biography would be killed. For ex-ample, in a case that finally ended happily for the biographer, Margaret Walker's initial contract with Howard University Press for a biography of Richard Wright was canceled when she was unable to obtain Wright's widow's consent to quote from unpublished mate-rial. Walker was seeking permission to quote from letters that Wright had written to her. Although the letters were Walker's property, she did not own their copyrights. Robert Newman, author of *Cold War Romance: John Melby and Lillian Hellman* (1988), confronted a simi-lar situation. Newman had worked closely with Melby and had re-lied on Hellman's letters to him, which were in Melby's possession. Newman assumed that because Hellman's letters were Melby's prop-erty, Melby could give Newman permission to quote from them. I pointed out to Newman that he would have to seek permission from Hellman's estate. Newman ultimately obtained such permission, but it carried severe restrictions on the amount of material he could quote. As an unauthorized biographer, he did not have the estate's blessing. This episode provides a clear illustration of the way copy-right can be employed in an attempt to limit the scope of an unau-thorized biography. Joan Mellen, who wrote *Hellman and Hammett* (1996) was the first unauthorized biographer to receive unrestricted access to Hellman's papers. Mellen notes Hellman's efforts to prevent the publication of unauthorized biographies but not her estate's to perpetuate those efforts.

Before getting to the advice I gave my caller, here is some back-ground on how biographers work and on the legal climate in which they must face some highly restrictive rules concerning the use of unpublished materials. To start with the obvious: how a biographer works depends very much on his or her attitude toward biography, and this attitude, in turn, influences how he or she deals with legalities. Keep in mind the idea of legality; I will address it later. Here, in capsule form, is a panoply of biographers:

BIOGRAPHER A: He has been the editor and friend of the subject for many years. He has never written a biography, but he is trusted by his subject. Maybe she trusts him because she knows damn well he will never write the biography—so she names him her biographer. Many authorized biographies never get written, instead serving to scare off other potential biographers. When I wrote in 1987 to William Abrahams (Lillian Hellman's anointed one), he replied that he was her "one and *only* authorized biographer." Abrahams died, never producing his biography, though as one of Hellman's literary executors he was in a position to control other biographers' use of Hellman's papers.

BIOGRAPHER B: He is a university professor who develops a special relationship with his subject and with his subject's family. He publishes articles and introductions to books by others and is often quoted in the press, but he never actually produces a biography. The late Carvel Collins, Faulkner's putative biographer and an early candidate for top dog in the manger, comes to mind. Collins first announced his biography in the late 1940s. Decades went by as he created a mystique about his project, implying that he had inside information unavailable to anyone else. When Collins announced that he was deferring publication until Joseph Blotner's authorized biography appeared, he was praised in the *New York Times* for his forbearance. But even after Blotner's book was published in 1974, no Collins biography appeared. Instead Collins continued to lecture and write articles, often pointing out errors in Blotner's official life of Faulkner. When I asked Collins when his biography would appear, Collins said he was still looking for "the figure in the carpet." He retired from the University of Notre Dame and then died without ever delivering on his lifetime promise. Robert Lucid, Norman Mailer's handpicked man, did not deliver either. Lucid never did publish his book, but he did very well by not publishing it. Through

Lucid, Mailer exerted enormous control over how his biography will be written—or, more important, not written. While I was working on my biography of Mailer, I requested a meeting with Lucid. I had met him once after I presented a paper on Mailer at a Modern Language Association meeting, and Lucid had complimented me on my treatment of *Marilyn* and *Of Women and Their Elegance.* I wanted Lucid to know about my plans. We had lunch. Lucid was cordial and thought he could arrange for me to see certain items in Mailer's vast archive, then housed in Manhattan (recently sold to the University of Texas). A year later, when I wrote Lucid asking to see the items we had discussed, he did not reply. For more details on Mailer's attitude toward my biography of him, see the "Afterword" to *The Lives of Norman Mailer: A Biography* (1991).

BIOGRAPHER C: Our phone caller. She proceeds for many years believing she is authorized. She has exclusive access to her subject's papers until that moment when her subject or her subject's estate sees the manuscript, and suddenly she is treated like an interloper.

BIOGRAPHER D: She does not receive authorization, but because of the high quality of her work she often gains the cooperation of her living subjects, or, if they are dead, of their estates, who apparently appreciate the value of dealing with a shrewd, responsible biographer. At least they have some opportunity to influence her. Deirdre Bair, the biographer of Samuel Beckett and Simone De Beauvoir, comes to mind.*

BIOGRAPHER E: The Rollyson/Paddock approach in *Susan Sontag: The Making of an Icon* (2000). We had no "in" with our subject. We

*Even Bair, however, ran into trouble with her Carl Jung biography. Jung's estate objected to several passages in her book and requested the unprecedented privilege of refuting in the text of Bair's biography the passages in question. After mounting a press campaign that aroused concern over her German publisher's effort to compromise one of its own authors, Bair brought enough pressure on her publisher to ensure that her text was not tampered with.

did not ask for authorization. Although we wrote to Sontag asking for an interview, we secured no special access. We did, however, hear from Sontag's agent, Andrew Wiley, who hinted that Sontag might be available for an interview at some later date if we would, as a pre-condition, provide him with details about our sources and methodology. Our vague reply put an end even to minimal cooperation on Sontag's part.

These examples demonstrate that how biographers position themselves has an important bearing on the resolution of legal issues that may arise in the process of writing a biography. I knew, from the start, that there was no way we could obtain permission to quote from Lillian Hellman's unpublished papers. I did what many unauthorized biographers do: paraphrased and quoted only small but lively bits from her unpublished writings. I took a risk, for court decisions of that time (the mid-1980s) severely restricted the fair use of unpublished material. I also gambled that my publisher would not submit my manuscript to lawyers for vetting. I won my bet on that one. The case of Martha Gellhorn, which I will address presently, was another story.

Ian Hamilton's attempt to write a biography of J. D. Salinger marks the juncture where life became truly difficult for biographers. "What a great idea," Hamilton must have thought, "to do Salinger—one of the most private men of letters, a recluse. Everyone will want to read about him." In retrospect, Hamilton's naiveté is comical. He decided he would cover Salinger's life only up to the point when Salinger stopped publishing. As the acclaimed biographer of Robert Lowell, Hamilton probably thought Salinger would somehow relent and at least tolerate the approach of a serious scholar.

As biographers are wont to do, let's enter further into Hamilton's mind-set. Can't you just imagine him thinking: "When Salinger sees how careful I've been, how much respect I have for his work, and how much material I've uncovered that he can't hope to keep private any longer, he will realize there's no stopping me." Just the opposite occurred: Salinger read Hamilton's galleys and filed a suit for copyright infringement. See the first chapter of *In Search of J. D. Salinger* (1988) for the biographer's account of his struggles with his subject.

A court decision resulted in a severe constriction of the fair-use doctrine as it applies to unpublished manuscripts. Salinger was upset about letters written in his youth, which Hamilton both quoted and closely paraphrased. Hamilton's position was that he did not need Salinger's permission since what he quoted was a very small portion of the unpublished material, and his use of paraphrase was within acceptable legal limits. The court disagreed, concluding that Hamilton had merely provided synonyms for Salinger's words—in effect appropriating Salinger's style. It was acceptable to use unpublished material for facts but not to mimic the subject's expression. Hamilton countered that he had quoted and closely paraphrased Salinger in order to convey in the liveliest terms possible his subject's manner. In view of what biographers have done for generations, Hamilton was doing nothing new, but the court found otherwise, and as a result the use of unpublished material by unauthorized biographers became a questionable proposition.

This bald summary of the Salinger case oversimplifies matters, legally speaking. But I am trying to describe its impact on me and on other biographers. I had to watch my every word—even the order of my words—when dealing with unpublished documents from which I had no permission to quote.

That the Salinger decision was immediately used to bludgeon biographers I learned from my own experience. Bill Buford, editor of *Granta* in the 1980s and one of Martha Gellhorn's cronies, wrote on her behalf to Michele Martin, managing editor at Doubleday, my publisher. He noted that Gellhorn had instructed anyone who had any dealings with her to deny me access to interviews and materials such as documents and letters. Then he included the killer sentence: "I do not need to remind you, as you are no doubt aware, of the case between J. D. Salinger and Random House, Inc., that the author retains the copyright in her letters and books and has an absolute right to name and likeness." Another sentence threatened to "enjoin" the publication of my biography. An authorized biographer had been appointed and was already on the case, so to speak.

The copy of Buford's letter that arrived from Doubleday had some handwritten annotations on it. The paragraph about "absolute right to name and likeness" and "intrusion on the privacy of Ms. Gellhorn" was bracketed and labeled "overstated." Another annotation read, "You cannot enjoin an unauthorized biography. Can't quote from letters or unpublished work or copyrighted material. Be careful with paraphrasing." That there might be an authorized biographer at work was news, especially since it did not square with anything Gellhorn had said about her loathing of literary biographies. None of the people I had interviewed had heard of an authorized biographer, and I was troubled only by the suspicion that Gellhorn might be behaving like Lillian Hellman: choosing a man or woman to write the official, uncontested version of her life, or at least to serve as a decoy. In any event, the very suggestion that someone else might be doing a biography only spurred me on.

Doubleday was low key about the letter. I had to write a one-sentence reply stating that I would do nothing to violate Gellhorn's "actionable rights." But when I handed in my manuscript, several months passed without the publisher accepting the biography or evincing any interest in publishing it. My agent then withdrew the book from Doubleday and resold it to St. Martin's Press, which had the manuscript thoroughly vetted by its lawyers.

As to my advice to our distraught phone caller: She had at least two options. First, she could try to work out an arrangement with the estate. This would almost certainly mean compromises, writing a book that would have to please the executors. The virtue of this approach would be that at least some quoted material from unpublished sources could be preserved. The other, unauthorized approach, would preserve more of the biographer's independence—but if lawyers had to vet manuscript, that too would result in compromises, as I had learned in dealing with the St. Martin's Press lawyers.

I advised my phone caller to take the following actions:

• Restrict direct quotation from her subject's unpublished papers to fewer than three hundred words. After the Salinger decision, Beacon Press limited Louise DeSalvo, author of a controversial book on Virginia Woolf that did not have the sanction of Woolf's estate, to one hundred words. St. Martin's lawyers limited me to three hundred words of direct quotation. After an all-day session, a weary counsel gave in to my persistent requests and said, "All right, all right, yes, you can quote Gellhorn's unpublished letter referring to Hemingway's 'hot jungle breath.'"

• Instead of paraphrasing quotations line by line, summarize them for their factuality. Where possible, stitch together published and unpublished sources in the narrative so that the two kinds of evidence will seem—as indeed they often are—inseparable.

• When drawing on long, unpublished letters, do not follow the sequence of any given letter from one paragraph to the next. Take the letter as a whole, analyze it as information, and reorder that information in terms of your narrative, thus truly creating your own organization of the material.

• Be more concise than your unpublished source. From, say, a three-page unpublished letter, squeeze out no more than a paragraph or so for your own narrative.

In the years that have passed since this phone conversation, the law regarding fair use has been somewhat modified. Initially, however, courts in the Second Circuit—which includes New York City, home to most publishers—were obliged to follow the precedent set by the Salinger suit. Journalists, historians, publishers, and biographers continued to have trouble doing their jobs and exercising their First Amendment rights. As a result of their lobbying, in 1992 Congress amended the 1976 Copyright Act by adding to the section concerning fair use a proviso addressing the problem of unpublished work. The long-term effects of this new gloss on the fair-use doctrine remain to be seen. In theory it should ease the minds of unauthorized biographers who need to make some use of their subjects' works, both published and unpublished. We believe it is only because of this relaxation of restrictions that my wife and I were able to get a contract for our unauthorized biography of Susan Sontag—prelude to which was a discussion with our publisher about fair use.

Undoubtedly the burgeoning of electronic publishing has complicated matters. Those who wish to keep abreast of the latest developments regarding fair use may consult a newly formed online copyright law archive produced by the Stanford University library in conjunction with the Council on Library Resources. Those biographers who wish to forge ahead despite the unsettled state of the law should fortify themselves with some knowledge of their own rights and responsibilities.

It helps to bear in mind that in the case that started the current fair-use controversy, *Harper & Row v. Nation Enterprises*, which the U.S. Supreme Court decided in 1985, Justice Sandra Day O'Connor's opinion for the Court specifically indicated that fair use adheres to all rights protected by the 1976 Copyright Act, including the so-called right of first publication. The right of first publication is the author's privilege of being the first to issue his or her writings publicly, and it is this principle that stands in the way of wholesale copying of unpublished material.

In this case the Court found against *The Nation*—rejecting the magazine's defense that its publication of extracts from Gerald Ford's forthcoming autobiography merely made fair use of Ford's explanation of the Nixon pardon, a matter of enormous public interest. *The Nation* may have printed only three hundred words from Ford's lengthy manuscript, but they were the three hundred best words— "the heart of the book," as the Court characterized them. But *The Nation* lost its case not only because it had preempted Ford's right of first publication, causing *Time* to cancel the contract with Ford granting it the exclusive right to print prepublication excerpts, into the bargain, but also because the defendant came into court, as the law so vividly puts it, with "unclean hands." *The Nation* had got hold of the Ford manuscript illicitly. The First Amendment is a permeable shield and does not trump larceny. Biographers should be wary of sources and, wherever possible, acknowledge them explicitly—for the sake of self-protection as well as good manners.

Once an author deposits writings in a publicly accessible archive, however, he or she does surrender complete control over them, and it is the biographer's prerogative to take advantage of this opportunity. As L. Ray Patterson and Stanley W. Lindberg explain: "the author who presents his or her papers to a library obviously does so in the interest of posterity. Having sought posterity, the author should hardly be able to use the law of copyright to manipulate the judgment of posterity." (See their laudable book *The Nature of Copyright: A Law of Users' Rights*, [1991].) Even when others have deposited an author's writings in archives, as in the case of J. D. Salinger, the copyright law does not protect that author's right to privacy. Where Ian Hamilton made his mistake was not so much in using Salinger's letters but in using too much of them, with the result that the court found that Salinger's property rights had been violated. It seems likely that *Salinger v. Random House*, were it tried today under the revised version of the fair-use section of the Copyright Act, would have a different outcome. Salinger does have a First Amendment right to remain silent, which in this context means a right to prevent his works from being published; but this right does not preempt the critic's or the historian's or the biographer's constitutional right to make use of them. This right is guaranteed by the First Amendment, by the 1976 Copyright Law, and by the source of this law, Article I, section 8, clause 8 of the Constitution: "The Congress shall have Power . . . To promote the Progress of Science and useful Arts, by securing for limited Times to Authors and Inventors the exclusive Right to their respective Writings and Discoveries." Copyrights, like trademarks and patents, protect limited monopolies.

The law, as it is currently interpreted, throws biographers back on their own styles, forcing them to make restricted sources their own in much the way a novelist transforms the raw material of life into a new, vibrant fiction. There are drawbacks, of course. Sometimes, as with "hot jungle breath," there is no piquant equivalent. I sacrificed vividness when I could not quote Gellhorn's unique coinages, and I could not appeal to that voyeuristic yearning of readers to have access to juicy chunks of unpublished correspondence.

Reviewers ignored the conditions under which I wrote my biography. They paid no attention to the way the copyright law had partly determined the shape of the book, even though in my prologue and epilogue I discussed unauthorized biography as the frame for the book. Altogether St. Martin's Press had asked me to cut approximately five thousand words. In addition, virtually every page had to be altered, if only in some minor way. The most persistent concern of the lawyers was that I would get too close to Gellhorn's expression, to her manner of saying things—the very thing protected by copyright.

St. Martin's lawyers did such a good job that Gellhorn dropped her allegations of copyright infringement and concentrated on threatening a libel suit before publication, provoking another marathon legal session at my publisher's lawyer's offices. Very little of the text changed that time, and St. Martin's came away from the last skirmish with Gellhorn more convinced than ever of the integrity of my book.

Such experiences have certainly stiffened my resolve as a biographer, and they prompt me to quote an unpublished line from Hemingway. After having divorced Gellhorn, he wrote long, complaining letters about her to his army buddy, General Buck Lanham. I delighted in quoting some of Hem's most colorful phrases, which the lawyers kept insisting must be cut. One particularly painful bit of surgery had to do with a passage in which Hemingway asserted that Gellhorn was an impossible woman who wanted everything to run smoothly all the time. She would not be pleased, he concluded, unless he could hire for thirty-five dollars a month "a butler with the probity of Cardinal Newman and the organizing capacity of Henry Kaiser"—in short, the very qualities necessary to today's biographers.

For another anatomy of different kinds of biography, see Deirdre Bair's "The How-To Biography" in James Walter and Raija Nugent, eds., *Biographers at Work* (1984), a useful discussion of biographies authorized (controlled by the subject, the subject's heirs, or the subject's estate), designated (similar to the authorized biography, except that "no authority over the final published manuscript" is exercised), independent (written without the sanction of the subject or of the heirs and the estate), and bowdlerized (a miscellaneous, tendentious collection of data sometimes found in popular biographies). Bair also offers good advice on copyright issues and examples from her biographical work on living figures.

SEE ALSO Unauthorized Biography.

Feminist Biography

Feminist biography began, it may be argued, with the publication of Nancy Milford's *Zelda* in 1970. Zelda has continued to be an attraction for women biographers (Sally Cline, Kendall Taylor, and Linda Wagner-Martin), all of whom attempt to rehabilitate the image of a woman overshadowed by her husband F. Scott Fitzgerald. All these biographers, to some extent, are examining the plight of women in a patriarchal society, though the extent to which men are to blame receives varying degrees of attention.

In *Lesser Lives* (1972), Diane Johnson does not announce a feminist approach, yet her concentration on the lives of the first Mrs. Merideth, Mary Ellen (the daughter of Thomas Love Peacock), and other "lesser lives" is a rewriting of literary history and a challenge to conventional biography, which usually treats such figures as mere episodes in the lives of major writers. Yet without a fuller accounting of minor figures, history is distorted, the "famous writer" presides at his dinner table, and the context of his life is distorted by total concentration on his remarks, Johnson points out in her preface.

The Challenge of Feminist Biography: Writing the Lives of Modern American Women (1992), edited by Sara Alpern, Joyce Antler, Elisabeth Isabel Perry, and Ingrid Winther Scobie, is a superb collection of essays eloquently presenting the feminist case for a new kind of biography, more personal and more sensitive to women's roles, and

more savvy about the connections between public and private experience in the lives of women and men than has been the norm in
traditional biography.

Recent years have seen several collections about the art of biography in which biographers attempt to explain their methodology,
their attraction to their subjects, and the reasons why biography has
become such a popular genre. This collection ranks at the very top
of such productions for the candor of the biographers' comments,
the high quality of the essays, and the persuasiveness of the argument that feminist biography holds the promise of opening up and
radically transforming biographical conventions.

Each essay contains a succinct description of the biographer's
subject, her research methods and experiences, the autobiographical
elements in the biographer's handling of the subject, her conclusions about her subject, and how the biographer's work contributes
to a feminist agenda. To put it this way, however, is not to suggest a
program—a lockstep vision of what women's history should be or
an attack on traditional biography. In fact several of these biographers discuss their problems with doctrinaire feminists and reject
what they term the tyranny of "politically correct" injunctions; to
the contrary, each biographer's experience is presented as unique
and resistant to codification.

With the exceptions, perhaps, of Freda Kirchway, Mabel Dodge
Luhan, and Helen Gahagan Douglas, many of the biographical subjects presented in this book may seem obscure, but in every case the
biographers convincingly show the importance of their subjects and
thus simultaneously point up the inadequacies of conventional history and biography, which have largely ignored their significance.

As a biographer of Gloria Steinem, an author of several books of
powerful feminist literary criticism, and in her role as Amanda
Cross, detective novelist, Carolyn Heilbrun was a superb choice to
deliver the annual Alexander Lectures at the University of Toronto,
now published as a book, *Women's Lives: The View from the Threshold* (1999). In these direct and engaging lectures we can hear Heilbrun's firm speaking voice—and her pride in how much feminist

criticism has contributed to literary study as well as her recognition that women still find themselves in a state of what she calls "liminality."

Liminality refers to woman in a state of transition. Women seem constantly to be on the threshold, entering a new stage of awareness that makes them more forceful literary voices than earlier women writers could have imagined. And yet, in Heilbrun's account of literary history, women never seem to arrive at the moment of fulfillment.

Heilbrun's lectures cannot be bettered for a concise review of current women's memoirs and fiction and of the classic writers, most notably George Eliot. Occasionally, however, when Heilbrun stumbles in the minefield of academic jargon, her points are weakened or seem almost a parody of themselves and of academic "discourse," to use a term favored by academics. Thus we have sentences that only years in the academy can prepare one to write, let alone appreciate: "Let me pause here to make a quite irrelevant and yet to me significant point about the liminality of current professional female nomenclature." Such locutions aside, this short book remains remarkably accessible to students and scholars at all levels of academic study. Even the general reader with some tolerance for riding the liminality thesis a little too hard will be stimulated and provoked by this trenchant book.

FURTHER READING: Paula Backscheider, *Reflections on Biography* (1999).

Fiction

Using works of fiction as evidence for the life itself is not all that unusual in biographies of writers who are overtly autobiographical in their fiction. In Blake Bailey's biography of Richard Yates, his use of the fiction to narrate the life arises out of many interviews with Yates's friends and family, which allow the biographer to read the fiction in a way someone without access to interviewees and other sources cannot. I'm familiar with this approach, having used it myself at times in my biographies. Certain literary critics abhor this method since they want to keep their literature pure—that is, unsullied by the writer's life.

A friend of mine just published a mystery. A character in it is based on her ex-friend who is also an ex-friend of mine. When I read the mystery, I thought this character was based on a famous writer, not on my ex-friend. I didn't even think of that ex-friend until I raised the issue with the writer of the mystery. Then she pointed out who her model was, and I suddenly realized how well our ex-friend fit the character. To me, the character was fully realized and yet was obviously taken in large part from the writer's life and, in a sense, from mine. But I needed the writer to point that out to me. And this is what literary critics who complain about using fiction in biography never seem to realize. A character can be fully realized in a work of fiction and yet also be taken from life. It does not diminish the fiction to know it is based on fact—though, again, some critics seem to think so when they criticize biographers for tracing real-life sources for characters.

Fictionalized Biography

Why read fictionalized biographies—or watch docudramas, for that matter? I asked the question in a *New York Sun* review of two fine specimens of the genre.

CRITIQUE: Readers and viewers are disturbed when fiction melds with fact. What to trust? I asked this question myself when I read Jerry Stahl's *I, Fatty*, an engaging effort to recreate the rise and fall of Roscoe Arbuckle, one of Hollywood's greatest filmmakers—a term I choose deliberately, because Arbuckle did much more than play the funny fat guy; he wrote and directed as well.

In the novel, Arbuckle takes credit for introducing Buster Keaton to the cinematic art. Is this Fatty, the unreliable narrator, making more of his influence than the facts warrant? Is this Stahl aggrandizing his character? To satisfy my curiosity I turned to Marion Meade's superb *Buster Keaton: Cut to the Chase: A Biography* (1995): "In Keaton's career, there would be only one artistic influence—not Griffith, not Sennett, not Chaplin, but Arbuckle." Reading Meade, I saw that Stahl actually underplays Arbuckle's violent temper—or is it the character, who like every autobiographer cannot see how his story conceals as much as it reveals?

Similarly, is it the bulky Arbuckle (he weighed close to three hundred pounds) or Stahl who does not see that the Arbuckle scandal (he was tried three times—unjustly—for allegedly raping and crushing to death the actress Virginia Rappe) was linked in the public mind with what Meade calls "an undercurrent of kinkiness" in his films?

Stahl does not include Meade's work in his bibliography, so I do not know if he consulted it. It might have done him good to read sentences such as: "A revolution in manners and morals was creating a younger generation whose behavior seemed, to their parents, absolutely depraved." *I, Fatty* sometimes lacks social/historical context, but that is one liability of using a first-person, self-exculpating narrator. "What was said to have happened to Rappe was every mother's nightmare," writes Meade, who then quotes silent-screen actress Lina Basquette, only fifteen when the trials commenced: "My mother snatched the newspapers away from me. Those stories were not proper for me to read."

Like all good fictionalized biographies, Stahl's makes the reader reconsider the facts and speculate about what is missing from the record. How could Arbuckle have allowed himself to become mired in such compromising circumstances? Without placing undue blame on others, the Fatty of this novel shows how: he began life, in his father's eyes, as a criminal, one whose very birth ruined his mother's health.

Novels and films often focus on a single traumatic event—let's call this the Rosebud phenomenon, in honor of *Citizen Kane*, one of the greatest fictionalized biographies. The conceit of Peter Stephan Jungk's novel, *The Perfect American*, a fictionalized biography of Walt Disney, is that the town of Marceline, Missouri, is Walt's Rosebud, the place he would reimagine in his vision of a wholesome America and recreate in nostalgic theme parks like Disneyland. There is a stunning scene in this novel in which Walt must repair the Abraham Lincoln figure—an "electric scarecrow . . . much more lifelike than, say, the wax dolls at Madame Tussaud's. The surface of its rubber cheeks began to sweat and glisten under the heat of the spotlights. All its limbs were movable, the head alone was able to perform eighteen separate movements, the body forty-nine [probably more than our stiffer presidents could manage]." This figure can shift its weight and coordinate gestures in sync with some of Lincoln's memorable words.

I saw this automaton in action thirty-five years ago on a trip to Disneyland, and I did find it a marvel—much more appealing than seeing an actor play the president. Disney believed that technology could bring us nearer to the past, to the world of Marceline, and to American values worth preserving. In the novel he is the only one who can control the Lincoln figure, which is still in development. But then it attacks Walt, and he barely escapes serious injury. Both the grandeur and the transgressive aspects of Disneyism are on display.

Of course no such scene ever took place—or at least I presume not. In this case I did not bother to measure Jungk's fiction against the facts. The book is narrated by Wilhelm Dantine, a disgruntled ex-employee whose life is, he believes, ruined and repossessed by "Uncle Walt," who he says has taken credit for all the drawings and scripts and even ideas that animators like Dantine (Disney liked to call them imagineers) created. So again we have the problem of an unreliable narrator. But to me this novel seems to be about the metaphorical nature of Disney, not so much an effort to fill in gaps in the Disney biographies or to dramatize what is already known about Disney's life.

Several years ago I reviewed Jungk's innovative biography of Franz Werfel, the Austrian author of *The Song of Bernadette*, who was also a Hollywood denizen. The book had an interesting method: at the end of each chapter italicized passages, written in the present tense, showed the biographer interacting with his interviewees, listening to their contradictory or incomplete stories, and marking the changes in time—comparing Prague and the Vienna of the 1990s with those of forty years earlier. In such passages the biographer dramatized biography as a work of history while at the same time identifying the gaps in his knowledge, the areas closed to his investigation, the moments when one interview faltered, the occasions when another interview elicited an energetic, almost hectic counterpoint to the calm, well-ordered narrative of the chapters themselves.

Wilhelm Dantine does much the same in this novel, except that unlike Jungk, the biographer, he is freer to reimagine scenes that others have told him about. In Dantine's hands, biography also becomes an act of revenge, demonstrating that animosity may yield truths just as important as those brought about by the biographer's empathy for his subject. Wilhelm Dantine (WD) becomes his subject's alter ego, the Hyde to Walt Disney's Jekyll.

Many readers remain skeptical of fictionalized biography. After Robert Penn Warren sent William Faulkner *All the King's Men* (based on Huey Long's life), the latter replied that Warren should have thrown it away, except for the novel-within-a-novel, the haunting story of Cass Mastern, an entirely fictional creation who is the subject of narrator Jack Burden's doctoral thesis. Faulkner believed that including historical figures—or even characters drawn on such figures—debased fiction. After all, you can quarrel with Warren's interpretation of Huey Long, but no one other than Faulkner can be an authority on the Snopes family.

In *The Historical Novel* (1963), Georg Lukacs argued that Sir Walter Scott's novels solved the kind of problem Faulkner identified by making major historical figures minor characters while using minor or invented historical figures as major characters. Thus Scott could provide a narrative of the period, explaining the context in which its principal actors appeared, without hazarding examination of, for example, James Stuart, pretender to the throne of England, who is given a minimal number of words to speak in a novel like *Redgauntlet* (1824).

Writers with less reverence for history, who see history itself as a kind of fiction, or who see fiction as the supreme creation capable of subsuming facts for a higher truth, might side with E. L. Doctorow, who when asked if Emma Goldman and Evelyn Nesbit ever met—as they do in *Ragtime*—replied, "They have now." A less playful writer than Doctorow might have handled the question differently: "Look it up."

Far more interesting to me is the interplay between biography and the novel. It is a two-way street. When *New Republic* reviewer Lee Siegel observed that Joyce Carol Oates's *Blonde* was indebted to my biography of Marilyn Monroe, I turned to Oates's pages to see if she mentioned me. Indeed, she did. Like Jerry Stahl, she appends a bibliography and a commentary on her novel. Her way of integrating Monroe's movies as events in her biography, and her dramatization of Monroe's acting not so much as an expression of her subject's personality but as an active shaper of it, agreed with my reading of Monroe's life.

I also saw that in at least one respect Oates had surpassed me. Her evocation of Monroe's childhood is haunting. The novelist creates scenes—more than could be done with fact alone—in which Monroe's harrowing encounters with her violently unstable mother create a disequilibrium. If I were to write my biography of Monroe again, I know that the level of my engagement with Monroe's childhood would be much greater because I have read Oates.

This suggests the point Stahl makes about his character's childhood in *I, Fatty*. The title of his novel evokes *I, Claudius*, one of the greatest of fictionalized biographies. Stahl, by having Arbuckle tell his own story, and Jungk, by injecting a new voice into the Disney saga, emphasize the truth of the truism that biography is never the whole story. But then neither is the novel. You need one to complement the other.

Freud, Sigmund (1856–1939)

Freud's conceptions of the unconscious and of the way individuals imaginatively shape their lives has profoundly affected biographers, writes Richard Ellmann in "Freud and Literary Biography" (*Freud and the Humanities*, edited by Peregrine Horden [1985]): "We live among feelings, to which facts may or may not adhere. Biographers have never felt so free of the necessity of distinguishing fact from fantasy." Yet Freud has taught biographers to be skeptical about their subjects, for modern biographers cannot take as seriously the rational explanations of their subjects or the "autonomy" of the will as nineteenth-century biographers did. The systematizing of Freudianism, however, has led to reductive biographies that resemble one another in their adherence to the same psychology.

FURTHER READING: Peter France and William St. Clair, eds., *Mapping Lives: The Uses of Biography* (2002).

SEE ALSO Psychobiography.

Froude, James Anthony (1818–1894)

Lytton Strachey is usually hailed as the progenitor of modern biography. But that honor should belong to J. A. Froude. Not only did he wrest biography from the insufferable bonds of Victorian reticence, he brought a narrative power to the genre that surpasses even what is generally regarded as the greatest biography in the English language, Boswell's *Life of Johnson*.

Whereas Boswell was a great dramatist, a master of dialogue, Froude was the virtuoso of the analytical monologue, tallying the significant events in his subject's life in a supple prose, which Strachey himself revered. It is hard to see how Strachey could have portrayed with psychological subtlety the dark, repressed side of Victorianism had not Froude offered him an inside look. Even now, no one has surpassed Froude's account of a singular marriage, the fraught union of Thomas Carlyle and Jane Welsh. As Julia Markus points out in *J. Anthony Froude: The Last Great Undiscovered Victorian* (2005), Froude had an innate understanding of women, one he developed by becoming Jane's confidant and not merely the disciple of Thomas Carlyle.

After reading Markus's fine biography, I have come to wonder whether biography is not, in fact, a feminine genre. It is women— and the feminine sensibility in certain men—that make a biographer attuned to what Boswell called "minute particulars." Such things speak to the domestic economy of life that lights up the best passages of his *Life of Johnson*, such as the scene where Boswell visits Johnson in his chambers and describes the great man with hose around his ankles and a wig (too small for his head) askew.

When Thomas Carlyle, like Samuel Johnson, realized that after his death there would be many biographers vying to limn his life, he quickly settled on his disciple Froude, giving him complete access to papers—including his wife's frank letters—that Carlyle otherwise considered burning. Having visited the Carlyles on nearly a daily basis for many years, and in possession of an archive, Froude understood that for revealing what he knew there would be no forgiveness. After Carlyle's death in 1881, Froude edited Carlyle's own *Reminiscences* (1881) and the *Letters and Memorials of Jane Welsh Carlyle* (1883), and wrote a four-volume biography (1882–1884) of Carlyle.

Froude's exposure of the Carlyle marriage, especially of Carlyle's violent nature, brought down the wrath of the Victorian establishment on the biographer's head. As Markus shows, Froude's life was ruined. Entire books were devoted solely to destroying him. Froude— no stranger to controversy since he had published a youthful novel attacking Oxford's Church of England principles and been booted out (and disinherited) as a consequence—nevertheless was aghast at the attacks that persisted for decades and would continue long after his death.

Yet Froude did not tell all he knew about the Carlyles. Only in a posthumously published essay-length monograph, *My Relations with Carlyle* (1903), did he reveal that Carlyle was impotent and that the marriage had never been consummated. With that shocking disclosure, Froude's biography of Carlyle and its unsparing exploration of the frustrations and furies of the marriage suddenly redeemed itself in the minds of some modern readers, even inspiring the work of biographers such as Phyllis Rose in *Parallel Lives: Five Victorian Marriages* (1983).

But impotence, Markus asserts, is not the half of it. She points to certain telling passages in Froude and in Jane Carlyle's letters that suggest Carlyle was a wife-beater. Although Markus never uses such a blunt term, her meaning is clear—as is her excoriation of generations of biographers who have not been willing to confront the full story Froude felt compelled to tell.

Froude himself wanted oblivion and did his best to destroy his papers. His life, early and late, was too painful to contemplate, even though in his last years he was restored to Oxford when he was appointed Regius Professor of Modern History, taking the place of his fiercest critic, E. A. Freeman. The attacks on Froude fomented by Carlyle's family and friends have to this day blunted a true appreciation of perhaps the greatest biography in the English language.

Yet Froude is not studied in the academy, where biography has a small role. English professors would rather teach second-rate novels than first-rate biographies. The very idea that biography is a genre worth studying is absent in the anthologies that dominate the discipline in college classrooms. The modern syllabus has no space for biography, no consciousness of the process by which great books and great authors are created. Instead professors bemuse themselves with "theory" and treat texts as though they were liturgy. Texts for writing classes feature mostly essays by contemporaries thought to be "relevant" for students who are not deemed intelligent enough to accommodate the discipline of history.

The irony is that Froude surpassed his master. Unlike Carlyle, Froude's prose has not dated. As Markus observes, his writing is as fresh today as when he wrote it. Froude is not just the last undiscovered Victorian, he stands for a way of writing about the world that each generation ignores at its peril.

Gaskell, Elizabeth (1810–1865)

Primarily an important novelist, Mrs. Gaskell wrote the life of Charlotte Brontë at the request of Brontë's father, who became disturbed about inaccurate accounts that appeared in obituaries. Gaskell had known Brontë and admired her work, but the biographer was also concerned to defend her subject against accusations that her writings were "coarse," a term that appeared on reviews of the novels, especially *Jane Eyre.*

Jane Eyre's outspokenness troubled Victorian critics, although Jane's candor is exactly what attracted both contemporary readers and later generations of critics. Gaskell shied away from much discussion of Brontë's work, preferring to elucidate her personality from long quotations from Brontë's letters and from Gaskell's recollections of her own relationship with her subject.

Gaskell tended to transform Brontë into a proper Victorian woman, softening her subject's harder edges and her passionate side. Thus Gaskell makes no mention of Brontë's infatuation with her Belgian tutor. For its period, however, Gaskell's sustained discussion of Brontë's private life was a departure from Victorian propriety. Far more than other biographers of her time, Gaskell presented her subject's life as a psychological drama. The biographer's evocation of Brontë's life at Haworth Parsonage is a vivid and indispensable source for later biographers, as is her description of the landscape and geography of the Brontë family's life.

In the end, whatever its limitations—including the suppression of evidence—Gaskell's biography is one of the towering achievements of nineteenth-century biography, one of the few works to be set beside Boswell's *Life of Johnson* as a signal contribution to the genre.

Gay and Lesbian Biography

This kind of biography often takes the form of reexamining the sexuality of famous figures, looking for evidence of homosexuality, for example, that other biographers have dismissed. The resulting biography is almost always speculative and controversial.

CRITIQUE: A case in point is C. A. Tripp's *The Intimate World of Abraham Lincoln* (2005), which reminds me of other great speculative biographies, such as Fawn Brodie's on Thomas Jefferson or Erik Erikson's on Martin Luther. Like his predecessors, Tripp teased out anecdotes and details that other historians either dismissed or passed over without much comment. His book grabbed headlines for its argument that, as Jean Baker puts it in her introduction, "Lincoln's primary erotic response was that of a homosexual."

It is quite easy to find lapses in Tripp's methodological rigor, and it is to his publisher's credit that critical views of Tripp's argument are included in the book. Besides Baker, one of Mary Todd Lincoln's biographers, the historians Michael Burlingame and Michael Chessen both hold the work up to scrutiny. The former provides "A Respectful Dissent," the latter "An Enthusiastic Endorsement"—though he does not ratify Tripp's conclusions but rather hails the therapeutic nature of his effort.

In Chessen's view, Tripp's work has shaken up the Lincoln establishment, much as Annette Gordon's book on Jefferson rocked historians like Joseph Ellis, who disputed her revisionist view of Jefferson's involvement with Sally Hemings. Ellis had to recant when DNA evidence made Gordon's case. Historians, like members of any other academic discipline, form a kind of cabal, a truth Chessen alludes to in coining the term "Orthodox Lincolnistas." It often takes a Gordon (a law professor) or a Tripp (a psychologist) to bring a fresh perspective to hallowed ground.

Part of the strength of Tripp's book is the author's historiography. He spent more than a decade researching Lincoln's life, assessing not only primary sources but also the notable biographies, in the process detecting the points at which Carl Sandberg and Ida Tarbell, for example, seemed aware of Lincoln's homosexual tendencies but chose not to explore them.

Chessen is quite right to say it is not enough to throw obstacles in Tripp's way—to say, for example, that just because Lincoln slept with men means nothing. Men often shared beds in the nineteenth century. But Lincoln slept for four years in the same bed with Joshua Speed, and in the White House he clearly developed an infatuation with a union officer, though neither Tripp nor anyone else can determine just what the nature of their intimacy was. And Tripp highlights other instances of Lincoln's intimacy with men.

Tripp died in May 2003, just two months after completing a draft of his book. So he could not have read Daniel Mark Epstein's suggestive dual biography of Lincoln and Whitman. Like Tripp, Epstein focused on stories that other historians and biographers have discounted. Epstein explored the report that Lincoln was one of Whitman's early readers, though he could find no specific reference to Whitman in any of Lincoln's own writings.

Supposedly Lincoln liked to read Whitman aloud at his law office, but when he brought the book home, Mary Todd Lincoln threw a fit and banished the scandalous book from her house. Epstein notes that Lincoln would probably not have thought of mentioning Whitman in public or in print, given the poet's celebration of homoeroticism. I am surprised that Tripp makes little of this Lincoln-Whitman connection.

Instead he focuses on one of Lincoln's bawdy poems (the president was fond of dirty jokes, especially those of the anal variety), in which a boy marries a boy. Whereas Whitman celebrated the "love of comrades," Tripp notes, Lincoln wrote the "most explicit literary reference to actual homosexual relations in nineteenth-century America." Under pressure from a Chicago publisher, Lincoln's law partner and biographer, William Herndon (a source for both Epstein and Tripp) bowdlerized the poem's penultimate line, altering "Besides your low crotch [big penis] proclaims you a botch" to "Besides your ill shape proclaims you an ape."

Tripp sees the stormy Lincoln-Todd marriage as more evidence of Lincoln's uncomfortable relationship with women. Baker believes Tripp is too hard on Mary; Chessen, that Tripp is not hard enough; other historians, I am sure, would say Mary was volatile enough not to need the added tension of living with a homosexual to ignite her combustible temper. Baker, for all her reservations, believes Tripp does illuminate puzzling aspects of Lincoln's marriage. Mary may well have been aware of her husband's homoeroticism and the gossip it excited, which Lincoln did nothing to counteract.

But Tripp does not say that Lincoln was a homosexual. Rather, he uses the scale of measurement that his mentor Alfred Kinsey invented, to give Lincoln 5 points out of 7—that is, Lincoln was primarily homosexual in orientation but capable of sexual relationships with women.

Historians often deplore gossip, but biographers should not so easily discard it. Why do certain people seem to stimulate certain kinds of gossip? Why did Virginia Woodbury Fox, wife of the assistant secretary of the navy, Gustavus V. Fox, report in her diary this confidence from her friend Letitia McKean, a "player" (as Tripp puts it) in "Washington's fashionable society": "Tish says, 'there is a Bucktail soldier [C. M. Derickson] here devoted to the President, drives with him, and when Mrs. L. is not home, sleeps with him.' What stuff!"

Read the rest of Tripp's chapter on the Lincoln/Derickson liaison and it is difficult not to see the close bond Lincoln formed with this handsome man nearly a decade his junior. Tripp does not claim to know what happened between the sheets, but Mrs. Fox's brief report is not a detail that Plutarch would have omitted.

Tripp did not set out on a gay-pride mission. His book makes clear that he is scornful of activists like Larry Kramer, who see Lincoln as unambiguously homosexual. The word itself did not come into currency until late in the nineteenth century. And as Baker points out, moralists at the time were more concerned with self-pollution (masturbation) than with homosexuality. Both women and men slept together, kissed, and held hands in ways that began to seem inappropriate only several decades after Lincoln's death.

What, then, is Tripp's point? The same as any biographer's: to explore the mystery and complexity of human identity. By any measure, his probing account deserves the deference of even his most skeptical critics.

FURTHER READING: Mary Rhiel and David Suehoff, ed., *The Seductions of Biography* (1996).

Goncourt, Edmond (1822–1896) and Jules (1830–1870)

Renowned for their diaries, which record minute details of scenes and conversations, the Goncourt brothers aimed to capture the spirit of the moment with verbal portraits and impressions, recording both the literary life of Paris and public events such as the 1870 Paris Commune. Although their influence is apparent on later novelists such as André Gide, the Goncourts have also attracted a considerable audience in the English-speaking world.

The brothers also wrote histories and biographies, including studies of Louis XV.

FURTHER READING: Robert Baldick published *The Goncourts* in 1960. Richard Grant published a reliable introduction to their work in *The Goncourt Brothers* (1972).

Gosse, Edmund (1849–1928)

Gosse is best known for a memoir of his father, *The Life of Philip Henry Gosse*, which Henry James among others praised. Like Elizabeth Gaskell's biography of Charlotte Brontë, Gosse's work has been lauded for its psychological realism. Part of its power derives from Gosse's depiction of the father-son relationship, which also captures the shift away from Victorian values to a more modern candor that has now become standard practice in biography. At the time of its publication, Gosse's book received mixed reviews—largely because reviewers were still not accustomed to frankness about intimate matters.

An influential critic, Gosse attacked Victorian biographies, which seemed to him shapeless (often mere compilations of letters with desultory commentary by the biographer) and gargantuan collections of aimless detail. Gosse supplied his own antidote to Victorian amplitude with succinct biographies of *Gray* (1882), *Jeremy Taylor* (1904), *Sir Thomas Browne* (1905), and *Raleigh* (1886). His longer biographies include *Conventry Patmore* (1905) and *Ibsen* (1907). His shorter profile/portraits of Thomas Hardy, Robert Browning, Robert Louis Stevenson, and others were collected in *Portraits from Life* (1991).

Yet Gosse could not entirely free himself from the constraints of Victorian self-censorship. He suppressed considerable intimate material about his friend, the poet Algernon Charles Swinburne. Even Gosse's unpublished *Confidential Papers,* deposited in the British Museum, omitted discussion of Swinburne's sexuality and other controversial issues.

Gosse's approach to biography reveals the limitations of the memoir form. As a man of letters he knew many of the subjects of his biographies and portraits, and as a result he often preserved the secrets of friendship rather than honor the demands of the probing biographer.

FURTHER READING: James D. Woolf, *Edmund Gosse* (1972); Ann Thwaite, *Edmund Gosse: A Literary Landscape* (1984).

Gossip

The term is used quite loosely in reviews of contemporary biography. To certain reviewers, gossip means almost any sort of intimate detail. The Sontag biography I wrote with my wife was called gossipy by a few reviewers, even though the biography stringently omitted the second- and thirdhand reports that usually are considered gossip. The implication of gossip is that it is vicious, unfounded, and therefore unreliable. Or gossip is viewed simply as the result of scandal and controversy.

Yet gossip is also the staple of many biographies because it conveys the reputation and impressions of the biographical subject. The biographer, to be sure, is obligated to investigate the veracity of gossip, but gossip itself is also a kind of barometer that no biographer can ignore if the ramifications of the subject's life are to be comprehensively assessed.

FURTHER READING: The standard text on the subject is Patricia Meyer Spacks, *Gossip* (1985).

Greco-Roman Biography

The origins of biography may be found in the structure of Greek encomiastic works, which idealized their subjects rather than analyzed their characters. Duane Reid Stuart, *Epochs of Greek and Roman Biography* (1967), argues that Socrates, Plato, Aristotle, and other philosophers brought a new rationalism to biography. Greek biography existed to portray "commanding figures" or to purvey "specialized knowledge." At the close of the third century B.C., the Peripatetics formed a professional class of biographers. The Greeks and their "Alexandrian continuators" took a schematic rather than a chronological view of biography, presenting an established character and showing little interest in the modern, psychological treatment of individual development. The Romans favored a "bluff realism" in their biographies, with Tacitus introducing the "judicial tone of real biography" and "discriminative portraiture."

Yet the evidence for a tradition of Greek biography is fragmentary—much of it has been lost, and scholars do not agree on its importance. In *The Development of Greek Biography* (1971), Arnaldo Momigliano subjects the evidence to a searching analysis, often arguing with the findings of previous scholars. Biography—writings about individual lives—seems to have begun in the fifth century B.C. and to have been fostered by Aristotle's belief that the genre could support his philosophical ideas. The Romans continued to make the Greek distinction between biography and history, biography tending to be more anecdotal and encomiastic. Greek biography made no clear distinction between fiction and fact, though certain Greeks such as Aristoxenus developed a new blend of writing: "learned, yet worldly; attentive to ideas, yet gossipy."

Biographers in late antiquity concentrated on actions that revealed character, not a life's history, so that something like a caricature emerged, evoking the essence of a personality, the "myth of the holy man," writes Patricia Cox in *Biography in Late Antiquity* (1983). Biography created an "imaginal place between where the history of a man's life and his biographer's vision meet and mingle." Poetic truth and historical fact merged, for biographers wished to capture a man's "soul-revealing gestures" and "inner radiance."

Group Biography

In "Group Biographies: Challenges and Methods" (*New Directions in Biography*, edited by Anthony M. Friedman [1981]), Margot Peters suggests that group biography may be the best way of analyzing a major figure's relationships with other figures, or of linking minor figures of the same period. Group biography has the virtue of placing greater emphasis on circumstances and the societal connections of individuals. Peters analyzes several group biographies, discussing the virtue of organizing them by time or place, and assesses the future of the genre.

A more academic study by Lawrence Stone, "Prosopography" (*Daedalus*, Winter 1971, pp. 46–79), traces the origins of prosopography (group biography) and the work of historians who have concentrated on "small-group-dynamics" or on the statistical study of mass behavior. He discusses how data are evaluated in both kinds of group biography, and the limitations and achievements of certain practitioners. Stone argues that prosopography is a maturing form, with Americans beginning to surpass the Europeans in the depth, range, and institutionalization of the genre.

CRITIQUE: An example of a recent state-of-the-art group biography is Ronald Bosco and Joel Myerson's *The Emerson Brothers: A Fraternal Biography in Letters* (2005).

"In many ways, our biography is patterned after the 'lives and letters' format made popular in the nineteenth century," the authors write, "in which extensive quotations from the subject's correspondence are woven into a continuous narrative of the subject's life." I immediately thought of Elizabeth Gaskell's classic biography of Charlotte Brontë, in which the subject's letters dominate to such an extent that at times the biographer seems an editor rather than an interpreter of a life.

Gaskell's selections and her diction emphasize the ladylike Charlotte and subtly dampen her subject's passionate nature, transforming her into a Victorian comestible. Bosco and Myerson also domesticate the renowned Ralph Waldo Emerson, making him seem far less radical than the writers of essays such as "The American Scholar."

Their Emerson—called Waldo throughout the narrative—is a man acutely conscious of his family's two-hundred-year history in America. When his older brother, William, decided not to pursue the pulpit—the favored occupation of generations of Emerson males—it was Waldo, an indifferent student at Harvard and a slow developer, who felt called upon to fill William's role. As Bosco and

Myerson observe of his younger siblings, "[W]henever a writer spoke of them [Edward and Charles] in comparison to their older brother Waldo, he, rather than they, suffered by the comparison." Edward and Charles were brilliant phrasemakers and scholars, and had they not been cut down by disease (neither man made it out of his twenties), it is to be wondered what prodigies they might have performed.

Waldo outlived and outperformed his brothers, and perhaps he would have done so even if they had remained beside him. For if Waldo seems in this book more family-bound and tradition-minded than other biographies make him out to be, it also could be argued on the basis of this fraternal biography that he resigned from Boston's Second Church in 1832 (before either Edward or Charles died) precisely because he felt, even more than his brothers, the oppressive pull of the Puritan past.

It took many years for Waldo to evolve into the transcendentalist who saw in himself and in every individual an entire universe. "I feel the centipede in me," he wrote in his journal. Emerson came to feel he could crack open the world's significance by dwelling upon the infinitesimal and the particulates of personality.

We know the Emerson of the poems, essays, and journals, but the letters published in this biography for the first time present not only a man with a different voice but a mind creating itself through the epistolary form. As Bosco and Myerson point out, earlier scholars (biographers included) have tended to concentrate on Emerson as a subject "surrounded by and developed through reference to a cast of increasingly renowned characters." Emerson looks different, his two new biographers emphasize, when seen in relation to his brothers. On February 23, 1827, the twenty-four-year-old Emerson, corresponding with his nineteen-year-old brother Charles, then convalescing in St. Augustine, Florida, observed:

> The river of life with you is yet in its mountain sources bounding & shouting on its way. . . . Vouchsafe then to give to your poor patriarchal exhorting brother some of these sweet waters. Write.

Write. I have heard men say . . . they had rather have ten words viva voce from a man than volumes of letters for getting at his opinion. —I had rather converse with them by the interpreter. Politeness ruins conversation. You get nothing but the scum & surface of opinions. . . . Men's spoken notions are thus nothing but outlines & generally uninviting outlines of a subject, & so general, as to have no traits appropriate & peculiar to the individual. But when a man writes, he divests himself of his manners & all physical imperfections & it is the pure intellect that speaks. There can be no deception here. You get the measure of his soul. Instead of the old verse, "Speak that I may know thee." Brandish your pen therefore, & give me the secret history of that sanctuary you call yourself.

Written like a true biographer! Here Emerson demands from his brother an openness of soul that will correspond with Emerson's own desire to fathom the world. To know more of his brother is to rejuvenate himself. To see life as Charles does is also, for Waldo, a way of seeing. This is why he exclaimed in a journal entry (December 8, 1834), "what poems are many private lives." Like Samuel Johnson, who believed anyone's life well told would make a fascinating biography, Emerson eschewed "vulgar greatness," the kind that makes reviewers crave only biographies about "important" people. These fascinating letters include not only correspondence among the brothers but also between them and their formidable aunt, Mary Moody Emerson (Waldo called her a genius), their mother, the much beloved Ruth Haskins Emerson, and Charles's fiancée, Elizabeth Hoar.

This is really a work of prosopography, a collective biography that shows how central the family grouping was to Emerson and his generation. Emerson discovered a personal appeal in the moral value of a life, played out against one's obligations to the past and present, to the family, and to the self, as exemplified in his step-grandfather, Ezra Ripley, the subject of Waldo's observation that a "man is but a little thing in the midst of [the] great objects of nature," who yet may "abolish all thoughts of magnitude & in his manners equal the majesty of the world." Ronald Bosco and Joel Myerson are to be commended for reviving that singular sense of majesty. Their book presents not only a novel way of reintegrating Emerson into the world out of which he arose, but also an inspiring evocation of biography itself as the way to illuminate the secret sanctuary of the self.

Hagiography.

SEE Latin/Medieval Biography.

Hazlitt, William (1778–1830)

Hazlitt is best known for *The Spirit of the Age*, his sparkling portraits of the literary figures he befriended. Those of Wordsworth and Coleridge, for example, are classics. A critic as well as exemplar of the Romantic sensibility, Hazlitt's candor is remarkable, especially in his self-study *Liber Amoris*, a unique work that defies the conventions of nineteenth-century biography that suppressed the frankness that Boswell had elevated into a signal principle of biography. Hazlitt is unsparing in his account of his infatuation with a servant girl, an affair that appalled his contemporaries and later biographers who found this episode a blot on their subject's reputation.

Hazlitt also wrote a multi-volume admiring biography of Napoleon. He tends to see Bonaparte as an extension of the French Revolution rather than as a reaction against it. Hazlitt's later writing criticizes Wordworth, Coleridge, and others for repudiating their early support of the Revolution. His yoking together of personalities and politics is a harbinger of Carlyle's approach to biography.

FURTHER READING: Robert W. Uphaus's *William Hazlitt* (1985) is a good introduction. One of the best recent biographies is A. C.

Grayling, *The Quarrel of the Age: The Life and Times of William Hazlitt* (2001).

Histories of Biography

Waldo H. Dunn, *English Biography* (1916), begins in the Latin period (690 A.D.), with chapters on English verse lives, sixteenth- and seventeenth-century biography, the eighteenth century, autobiography, "problems and tendencies of the present," and a concluding assessment of biography's status as literature. This survey highlights the most important biographies, recognizing Boswell's dominance but suggesting that Carlyle's *Life of Sterling* may be the perfect biography, an example of "pure biography" conveying the unfolding of a life without the interruptions of critical biography, which seeks to treat the subject's work and career, often to the detriment of a unified picture of human character. Taking Plutarch as a model, Dunn suggests that contemporary biographers have not sufficiently differentiated biography from history, making the individual life, not the times, of paramount importance.

William Roscoe Thayer's *The Art of Biography* (1920) presents three lectures—on biography in antiquity, medieval to modern biography, and biography in the nineteenth century. Thayer favors Plutarch's definition of biography, separating the telling of lives from history. Thayer adopts Carlyle's assertion that biography is an art. Defending Boswell from Macaulay's harsh criticisms, Thayer emphasizes Boswell's artistry, his deft selection of evidence, and his accent on the salient points of Johnson's character. Thayer exaggerates Boswell's accuracy when he likens the biographer's sensibility to a photographic plate. Arguing that the biographer must reach a balance in presenting his subject's virtues and vices, Thayer deplores Froude's biography of Carlyle for its lack of proportion in presenting Carlyle's less appealing traits.

Wilbur Cross, *An Outline of Biography from Plutarch to Strachey* (1924), analyzes the appeal of biography, the curiosity to know how others have negotiated the difficulties of life, the development of the genre from Plutarch to Vasari, Walton, the Victorians, and Strachey, how biography has expanded to meet the requirements of various civilizations and helped establish the profession of letters in England, the superiority of autobiographies and intimate personal narratives and of Boswell's biography of Johnson, how biographers who have no personal acquaintance with the subject proceed, Strachey's fine style and clever use of secondary sources.

Harold Nicolson, *The Development of English Biography* (1928), is a series of lectures tracing the development of English biography from 500 A.D. to the twentieth century. Nicolson develops the concept of "pure biography," which is factual and accurate (a work of verifiable history), concentrates on an individual, and has a "conscious artistic purpose." For most of its history, biography has been "impure," the product of writers who have falsified or censored their evidence, obscured the historical significance of individuals in favor of subjective portraits, and paid insufficient attention to the shape of biographical narrative. Above all, biography should be the province of the skeptical, not the credulous: it is the "preoccupation and solace, not of certainly but of doubt."

André Maurois's *Aspects of Biography* (1929) is a deft, lucid inquiry into the history of biography, identifying the essence of modern biography as the accumulation and interpretation of evidence. Maurois believes biography is an art but must adhere to a chronological and factually accurate portrayal of its subject, emphasizing character development and situating the biographer's point of view as closely as possible to that of his subject. Defending the use of intimate, even seemingly trivial detail, Maurois observes that a life can become "unreal as a result of too much being left out." Using his own biographies of Shelley and Disraeli, the biographer suggests that there is a strong autobiographical component in the biographer's selection of subject and theme.

Edward H. O'Neill, *A History of American Biography 1800–1935* (1935), is a historical and critical survey, concentrating on the most significant works of clerical, literary, political, and scholarly biogra-

phy and on the most important American biographers: Irving, Parton, Sparks, Adams, Paine, and Freeman. Biographies of Lincoln
and Washington are treated in separate chapters. Opening and concluding chapters address definitions of biography and the development of the genre, with special attention to Strachey's influence on
contemporary biographers. Although O'Neill addresses issues of
style, structure, and technique, his survey is primarily content based
and attempts to identify those biographies of literary and public figures that are the best of their kind. O'Neill sees American biography
as having moved from didactic and romantic attitudes to a more
skeptical and inquiring spirit.

Richard D. Altick, *Lives and Letters: A History of Literary Biography in England and America* (1966). After chapters on early English biography and on Johnson and Boswell, Altick concentrates on
the nineteenth and twentieth centuries, in which writers thought in
terms of literary careers and the reading public demanded knowledge about authors. Biographies satisfied the public's desire for a
"sense of participation in the creative act," and many authors—
beginning with the Romantic period—appealed to their readers' curiosity and fashioned their lives as carefully as the plots of novels.
The countervailing tendency—the Victorian quest to censor literary
lives—has gradually diminished as later generations, removed from
the initial controversies over revealing intimacies, have made private
papers accessible. Altick favors biographies that aspire to art, eschewing the Victorian aim of mere compilation in favor of rigorous
scholarly interpretation and speculation.

In *One Mighty Torrent: The Drama of Biography* (1937), Edgar
Johnson, a biographer of Sir Walter Scott and Dickens, provides a
comprehensive history of biography and autobiography from the
sixteenth century to the early twentieth century. Less scholarly than
Altick, Johnson aims to evoke in extensive paraphrase and critical
commentary the major works of biography, noting especially the
strengths and weaknesses of the biographer's narrative design and research, and the historical context in which biographies are written.
Unlike Nicholson, Johnson sees no progress in four hundred years of

biographical writing, though he examines the twentieth-century concern with relating the character of the artist to his work and favors the biographer's integration of Freudian and Marxian methods to provide a richer psychological and social presentation of the subject.

In *The Nature of Biography* (1957), John Garraty presents a succinct account of the development of biography from ancient times to the present. The second part of the book explores the biographer's choice of subject, materials, use of psychology, research techniques, and literary form. As a historian, Garraty draws most examples from his discipline, but his instances of how biographers actually work, and his critical analysis of several biographical texts, make his work an indispensable resource for both the biographer and the scholar of biography. For each of his chapters, Garraty provides an extensive and useful essay on sources.

In *The Art of Biography* (1965), Paul Murray Kendall, a biographer of Richard III and Louis XI, provides an astute critique of modern biography and discusses the history of the genre by focusing on neglected or insufficiently appreciated examples of the best biographical writing. Kendall probes the relationship between fact and interpretation, arguing strongly for a chronological approach to life-writing and vigorously attacking Leon Edel's manipulation of time and evidence in his biography of Henry James. Although biography may aspire to rival the highest art, Kendall believes it is always a "flawed achievement" and that biographers who use fictional techniques distort the way human lives actually unfold. If biography is not of the very highest rank, however, he believes the twentieth century has produced an impressive body of biographical literature.

In *The Nature of Biography* (1978), the biographer Robert Gittings presents a brief but incisive account of the development of biography—concentrating on English biographers, especially Lytton Strachey. Although skeptical of psychoanalytic method, Gittings provides specific examples of biographies that have used Freudian insights to advantage. But the chief contribution of modern psychology, in his view, has been to make the writer more aware of unconscious motives in writing biography. Calling the past fifty years the "golden age of biography," Gittings believes that women have been especially adept at dealing with the complex and contradictory characteristics of their male subjects.

In *Ultimately Fiction: Design in Modern American Literary Biography* (1981), Dennis W. Petrie argues that literary biography must have a design as clearly articulated as novels. In searching chapters on biographies of Faulkner, Fitzgerald, Dreiser, and James, Petrie assesses the extent to which Joseph Blotner, Andrew Turnbull, W. A. Swanberg, and Leon Edel provide compelling, fully realized portraits, combining both a sense of history and psychology. Edel's *James* is the model by which these other biographers are judged and found wanting, though each biography is lauded for qualities that redeem the biographer's efforts to present a persuasive narrative. The first two chapters reveal Petrie's debt to fiction—particularly Steven Millhauser's novel, a mock biography titled *Edwin Mullhouse: The Life and Death of an American Writer, 1943–1954, by Jeffrey Cartright*.

Phyllis Rose, "Fact and Fiction in Biography" (in *Writing of Women: Essays in a Renaissance* [1985]), believes that biography is undergoing a "mimetic shift" similar to what occurred in the novel at the beginning of the twentieth century. Until recently biography, a conservative and elitist genre, has not experimented much with technique and subject matter. Now biographies of neglected women and family biographies have redefined the conception of character and of what constitutes a successful life and a biographical subject: "In biography, the bourgeois-democratic revolution is just beginning." The handling of chronology, characterization, and perspective are changing, Rose claims, citing the innovative contributions of Justin Kaplan's *Walt Whitman* and Norman Mailer's *The Executioner's Song*. Such works have redefined notions of fact and given biographers the freedom to imagine their form. (SEE ALSO Innovative Biographies.)

David Novarr's *The Lines of Life: Theories of Biography, 1880–1970* (1986) provides a close reading of the most important books and articles by forty-nine biographers and critics. Novarr summarizes and critiques their arguments, and his conclusion provides an overview of biography, noting that it has been resistant to "genre theory" because it has been so variously defined as "history, literature, didactic aid to religion or morality." Novarr argues for an open-ended view of biography and attempts to balance opposing views—for example, Kendall's insistence on the "invisibility" of the biographer, who should subordinate himself as strictly as possible to his subject, and Edel's promotion of the biographer's independence, his freedom to manipulate literary form and chronology.

Marc Fumaroli, "From 'Lives' to Biography: The Twilight of Parnassus" (*Diogenes*, Fall 1987, pp. 1–27), describes the development of writing about lives from antiquity to the present. Fumaroli traces biography to the Greek "desire for a complete inventory of the real," a collection of "lives," extended by the Romans into the compilation of legendary lives, and by the Christians into narratives of canonized lives. Now biographies are mass produced; there is potentially a biography for every life, a leveling of the significance of self. Fumaroli compares the English and French traditions of biography, the former tending toward luxuriant disorder and the latter toward severe regularity.

In *Modernizing Lives: Experiments in English Biography 1918–1939* (1987), Ruth Hoberman includes chapters on Lytton Strachey, Geoffrey Scott, David Cecil, Percy Lubbock, A. J. A. Symons, Virginia Woolf, E. M. Forster, and Harold Nicholson. Hoberman explores the "revolt against Victorianism," the influence of the novel on biography, the biographer's rejection of the omniscient point of view in favor of the "mediated biography" (in which the biographer appears as a clearly identifiable character), feminism and biography, psycho- and sociobiography. As A. O. J. Cockshut suggests in his foreword, Hoberman focuses on the "impact of literary modernism on the art of biography." She discusses those biographers who reshaped traditional biography "into a more flexible, more artful form, able to accommodate modern ideas of the self, of time, and of narration."

In *Pure Lives: The Early Biographers* (1988), Reed Whittemore explores early biography, dominated by encomium that did not concentrate on the specifics of an individual's character. Heavily influenced by Aristotle's concept of tragedy, biographers had to find their subjects "superior beings, persons an audience could look up to and be purified by." Chapters on Plutarch; Aelfric; Machiavelli, Cellini, and Vasari; Holinshed and Shakespeare; Johnson and Boswell; and Sterne suggest that early biography was influenced by history, poetry, drama, and autobiography more than it was by avowedly biographical works. Whittemore takes issue with several modern biographies of Johnson by Macaulay, Joseph Wood Krutch, John Wain, and Walter Jackson Bate. Sterne he regards as the transitional figure to the modern age because of his ability to create a more "spacious life" for the self not predicated on the self's public stature or worldly actions.

In *Whole Lives: Shapers of Modern Biography* (1989), Whittemore attempts to pinpoint those biographers—Carlyle, Leslie Stephen, and Sigmund Freud—who have "taken hold" of lives in their entirety, providing a view of the inner, psychological life of their subjects. Carlyle stressed the "essence" of an individual's character, and in the first two volumes of his life of Frederick the Great explored the father-son relationship in a new way. Freud, in his life of Leonardo, suggested the crucial role of the unconscious, of the "real content" of lives masked by their public actions. A concluding chapter surveys American biography, assessing the contributions of popular biographers such as Anne Edwards, Norman Mailer, and Gloria Steinem as well as more scholarly figures like Richard Ellmann and Leon Edel.

Biography is the dominant nonfiction of our age, Nigel Hamilton observes in *Biography: A Brief History* (2007). It pervades all realms of the media. So why is there "no single, accessible introduction to the subject, either for the general reader or the specialist?" Hamilton asks.

Curiously, Hamilton dodges the question, preferring to cite his own credentials and arguing there ought to be a book of the kind he has just written. I quite agree, and though I think he misses a few opportunities to show just how important the genre is, in the main he has done a splendid job in the compass of 327 pages.

But why has it taken so long to produce this primer? Most biographers, in my experience, do not know the history of the genre. They are attracted to biography because of the subject, not because biography per se intrigues them.

There are very few scholars of biography in large part because biography as a subject is not taught in higher education. Biographers are rarely represented in literature anthologies. Aside from a few stars like Edel and Ellmann, academia does not respect or reward biographers. Where are the distinguished chairs in biography? Such honors go to postmodern studies, women's studies—virtually any sort of specialization except biography.

Finally, there is not much of a market for books *about* biography. I once proposed a book to be titled "Biographies for Dummies," but the best efforts of an agent could not convince the publisher of the Dummies series that sales would amount to much.

Biographers are bottom feeders—the lowest of the low. Joyce called them biografiends, and Rudyard Kipling deemed the genre a "higher form of cannibalism." That biography added a new terror to the thought of death is a statement that has been attributed to several writers.

To read a good biography may be fun, but it is generally considered a kind of slumming among the literati. Thus writers like Joyce Carol Oates and John Updike have published dismissive pieces on this scurrilous, if titillating, subliterary entertainment. Of course the Parnassus crowd allow for honorable exceptions and will even, occasionally, permit a biographer to sit at the table, or even write their biographies, provided the biographer remains on the towline.

Hamilton acknowledges this hostility to biography—especially when he describes Janet Malcolm's brief against biographers in *The Silent Woman*. But he does not, for example, even allude to the minor literary industry that has produced dozens of novels featuring biographers as villains.

When did biography—once a rather distinguished genre in the days of Plutarch and Suetonius—descend the literary scale? As soon as the first biographers tried to deal frankly with the private as well as the public lives of their subjects.

Even now the libel and copyright laws are such that biographers are hemmed in and produce tepid narratives for fear of legal action. I know biographers who would like to do contemporary figures but shy away to safe, dead subjects, even though it can be just as hard to joust with literary estates. We who do the work of contemporary biography need to be well versed in the law—or marry a lawyer, as I have done.

What Hamilton never quite concedes is that because biographers have so often worked through a veil of censorship, it has proven difficult for them to write with the freedom of style that any novelist takes for granted.

One of Hamilton's missed opportunities is his treatment of James Anthony Froude, who incurred the wrath of Carlyle's relatives and friends by writing frankly about the great man's troubled marriage. Even so, Froude held back crucial facts—like Carlyle's impotence— while nonetheless creating a penetrating narrative that should stand beside, say, George Eliot's treatment of Dorothea and Casaubon in *Middlemarch*. Hamilton notes Froude's impediments, but he does not seem to grasp the biographer's heroic triumph.

Where Hamilton distinguishes himself is in expanding a sense of biography, which is not just a written narrative but also film, sculpture, painting, and all the arts. It has been a great misfortune for biography, Hamilton points out, that "instead of becoming, like 'history' or 'art' or 'literature,' a premier domain of the humanities and sciences," biography has become "constrained by a focus so narrow that no student could be made sufficiently curious to learn of its history," its "integral role in the shaping of human identity, as well as its varying practice through the ages across different media."

Hamilton has begun to rectify an enormous injustice by showing that biography, in itself, is a form of knowledge, a way of apprehending the world that deserves its own departments and centers of scholarly study.

Someday, perhaps, with more studies like Hamilton's, the empire of biography will finally win the respect it deserves.

History and Biography

Biography is bad history, according to the historian Patrick O'Brien, who asks "Is Political Biography a Good Thing?" (*Biography*, Winter 1996):

> Political biographers succumb all too often to one or other (sometimes to both) of two temptations: either they present their subjects as extraordinary and omnipotent or alternatively as predictable individuals whose characteristics and actions form the basis for generalizations about the governments of the day.

These temptations inevitably result in "exaggerating the role of great men," O'Brien argues.

Furthermore O'Brien finds the use of psychology in political biography virtually worthless. The same "qualities of character and traits of personality" are identified so often that they become "commonplace" and explain nothing. What the biographer finds unique in his subject has more to do with the role he played in a political system, O'Brien argues, and it is precisely that system that biographers ignore in their quest to prove their subjects "made a real difference." Like other forms of biography, then, political biography is actually a retreat from knowledge. O'Brien concludes: "Just as there are scholars of the performing arts who prefer to contemplate actors rather than acting, players rather than plays, so too in history the sheer volume of political biography represents a triumph of form over substance."

In *New Light on Dr. Johnson: Essays on the Occasion of his 250th Birthday* edited by Frederick W. Hilles (1959), James L. Clifford contends that biography must be subjective. Clifford says it has "no standing as history," for the subject's life depends on the "pattern that has been set up in the biographer's mind." But how this is any different from the historian's work puzzles me, since surely the historian must do the same: present the pattern set up in his own mind.

Clifford uses examples from incidents in the life of Johnson, and from his own experience, to illustrate the problems of dealing with conflicting or meager evidence. He argues in "A Biographer Looks at Dr. Johnson" that a biographer should select his material, describe his subject, and evoke the scenes of his life not only in accord with what can be verified but in the light of the biographer's total understanding of his subject's life. In *Necessary Lives: Biographical Reflections* (1990), B. L. Reid contends that biography is a branch of history, not of the fine arts. The biographer's first commitment is to the orderly, chronological, and detailed presentation of facts. That some biographies achieve the status of art is almost incidental. Reid gives a compelling account of his development, from early creative work to literary criticism and then to biography, explaining the biographer's craving for "straight exposition" and for filling out his subject's life "piece by piece." Knowing things as they occurred in the subject's life—this is the "essential biographical satisfaction."

Oscar Handlin, in *Truth in History* (1979), discusses the division between biography and history occasioned by late-nineteenth-century efforts to develop history as a scientific discipline dealing with "large impersonal forces," not "dominant individuals." With no "consistent theory of biography," biographies by historians tended to be gigantic, a compilation of details, situating subjects into their times. In the 1920s the debunkers satirized the cult of the hero in psychological portraits that often demeaned their subjects. Biography attempted to compete with fiction, but it could not offer the intense intimacy of the novel. Erik Erikson introduced new rigor into psychological biography, but his concern with evidence was not as great as the historian's, and Handlin doubts that modern psychology can explain the particularity of individuals in other cultures, other times.

CRITIQUE: My review of H. W. Brands's biography of Woodrow Wilson explores the way historians write biography: If you ask a historian to write a biography, you are more likely to get history. Biography puts characters first while history favors events. Of course, characters and events cannot be easily separated, but one can predominate over the other, depending on the predilections of the narrator. This observation holds true even when the distinguished historian Arthur M. Schlesinger, Jr. (editor of the American Presidents series) gamely tries to graft biography onto history. In his editor's note, he observes:

> Biography offers an easy education in American history, rendering the past more human, more vivid, more intimate, more accessible, more connected to ourselves. Biography reminds us that presidents are not supermen. They are human beings too, worrying about decisions, attending to wives and children, juggling balls in the air, and putting on their pants one leg at a time. Indeed, as Emerson contended, "There is properly no history, only biography."

Quoting Emerson is a scandal—that is, if you are an academic historian. No Ph.D. student would hazard Emersonianisms before a dissertation committee, and beware the untenured professor who would make such an argument for biography. Martin Gilbert, Winston Churchill's authorized biographer, reveals in *In Search of Churchill* that at Oxford his professors never uttered Churchill's name, even though Gilbert's area of study was appeasement.

In one sense, H. W. Brands, author of *Woodrow Wilson*, a part of the American Presidents project, is a Schlesingeronian. The historian, who holds the Glassock Chair at Texas A&M University, writes in direct, vivid prose, and he certainly makes the Wilsonian personality accessible—for example, describing the twenty-eighth president as the son of a preacher who would justify his political program as the will of God. And the historian evinces a biographer's wit when describing President Wilson's effort to oust the Mexican dictator Huerta: "To give God a hand, Wilson stepped up the pressure." When the president's interventionism results in a political mess, Brands describes him as resisting the "temptation to offer Mexico any larger instruction." Thus Wilson's lofty arrogance is summed up in the kind of deft understatement that a good short biography must employ. Wilson's Mexican episode is almost comic—and certainly would be so if Gore Vidal were writing this biography.

Brands fulfills the mission of the American Presidents series in so far as his book is an economical way of presenting history. It is all there neatly told: Wilson's family background; his careers as teacher, university president, reform governor of New Jersey, and president; his institution of the income tax, his capitulation to the momentum of war—and then the spectacular defeat of his quest to bring the United States into the League of Nations.

In another sense, however, this book fails as biography. We learn, for example, about Wilson's first wife only as she lies dying. This may have seemed a good move to the historian who wishes to save space for a discussion of the policies and events that give Wilson his place in history. Brands does present a tidy passage on the marriage, but segregating Ellen inevitably works against the mission of biography because she never emerges as a person, and it is hard to take her seriously given the paltry paragraph afforded her.

For justice to Ellen, turn to Louis Auchincloss's short biography of Wilson in the Penguin Lives series: "Ellen was a cultivated and well-educated woman, a talented amateur painter and a poetry lover, with a fine mind that she nonetheless subjugated to her husband's." The truth is—as you'll discover by reading Frances Saunders's biography of Ellen, which neither biographer, alas, includes in his bibliography—Ellen stretched her husband and made him more receptive to others than his aloof sensibility would otherwise permit. If Ellen had survived, perhaps history would not have been different. Perhaps Wilson would still have lost the Senate fight over the treaty determining the structure of the postwar world. But with Ellen alive, some of Wilson's actions might have been different. At the very least, his advisers would have had greater access to him.

Wilson, an intolerant man, was not served well by his second wife, Edith. While so much is evident in Brands's description of her actions, the historian does not single out Edith, leaving it to the reader to ferret out how she went about exacerbating her husband's tendency to isolate himself from friends and opponents. In Auchincloss's account, however, Edith appears as nothing less than the villainess, for he begins and ends his biography with excoriating accounts of her meddling efforts to put her husband, rather than the country, first as President Wilson suffered his debilitating strokes during the last seventeen months of his second term.

Auchincloss makes Edith a character in a Henry James—or even a Louis Auchincloss—novel. Not only did she disserve her country, ultimately she disserved her husband, cutting him off from his closest friends and associates—people like Colonel House, who wrote that his estrangement from President Wilson was a "tragic mystery." Why did his friend close the door on him? House wondered. "But the key that must unlock the innermost door may still be found," Auchincloss adds in the concluding sentence of his biography: "It may be discovered in the last word that Woodrow Wilson uttered: 'Edith.'"

Auchincloss fulfills biography's mandate: his reading of character rests on Emersonian aperçu that Thomas Hardy rephrased as "Character is fate."

Holmes, Richard (b. 1945)

The celebrated biographer of Shelley and Coleridge, in his highly praised *Footsteps: Adventures of a Romantic Biographer* (1985), Holmes offers a candid, vivid autobiography describing his pursuit of Robert Louis Stevenson, Wordsworth, Mary Wollstonecraft, Shelley, and Gerard de Nerval. Holmes explains both the development of his biographical method and his maturation as a writer, recreating the travels and the times of his subjects, exploring gaps in the evidence, arguing for the biographer's special perspective while conceding the limitations of the biographical narrative form, especially in the case of de Nerval, whose madness seems to thwart the rational, organizing patterns of the biographer.

Innovative Biography

Most biographies have a chronological structure. The biographer is circumspect. Unless he knew the subject, and the biography is also a memoir as in Boswell's *Life of Johnson*, the biographer does not present himself as a character in the narrative. The form of biography, in other words, has changed little over the centuries. Yet there are remarkable exceptions—writers who wish to experiment with the biographical form.

The biographer may begin with a startling incident. Justin Kaplan, for example, began his biography of Walt Whitman with the poet's death, and Leon Edel used flashbacks and other novelistic techniques. A biography of Edna Ferber relates her life backwards! Edmund Morris invented himself as a character in *Dutch*, and even subtitled his authorized biography of President Reagan "A Memoir." The reaction to such departures from custom are often hostile: Morris suffered the worst reviews of his distinguished career as a biographer.

CRITIQUE: Some of the most provocative innovative biographies are described below. A. J. A. Symons's *The Quest for Corvo: An Experiment in Biography* (1934) is a classic "experiment in biography" in that Symons constructs a plot around his efforts as a biographer to fathom the mysterious, sometimes scurrilous life of Frederick Rolfe, who also wrote under the name of Baron Corvo. Symons is scrupulous in taking the reader into his confidence, showing how he became interested in Corvo, how he gained the confidence of his interviewees—sometimes failing to maintain their trust (as in the case of Rolfe's brother)—and openly admitting the gaps in his narrative. At the same time Symons also shows the limitations of this biographical form, since he admits that in certain chapters he has condensed his "quest" for dramatic purposes and in the interests of efficiency.

In *Marilyn* (1972), Norman Mailer has a twofold purpose: to faithfully measure and evaluate the obstacles that bar the biographer's way to a full understanding of his subject's life, and to tentatively suggest a biographical method (a "novel biography") that aims to recreate the whole person while conceding that the search for wholeness is elusive and problematical. Seldom has a biographer been this candid about the hazards of biographical research or confessed so blatantly to his sense of personal connection with his subject.

Some biographies interrupt narrative for conversation between biographical subject and author. In Andrew Field's *Nabokov: His Life in Part* (1977), even the subtitle announces a deviation from usual practice, in which the biographer claims to be writing "a life" or even "the life" of the subject. Field imitates intermittently the Boswellian formula and Nabokov's novels, in which the narrator raises doubts about conventional biography, exposes Nabokov's doubts about Field, and explores the relationship between Nabokov's idea of biography and the biographer's, revealing both the divergences and convergences of the biographer and his living subject. The biographer's effort to show the flux in his conceptions of his subject seems particularly appropriate given the elusive nature of reality in Nabokov's novels and the way his narrators become suspect authorities.

James Gindin's *The English Climate: An Excursion into a Biography of John Galsworthy* (1979) aims for a "fusion of the accidental man, his times, and his conscious artistry, of all the elements that created the work." By interviewing Galsworthy's friends and family, absorbing the "English climate," and showing how he interacts with his interviewees, Gindin reveals and speculates on his own "subjectivity, at almost every point" rather than assuming the "objectivity of myself and others." Consequently he provides a rich atmosphere in which his sources appear with the roundedness of characters in a novel. Of himself and his sources Gindin concludes: "We were, in miniature, recreating a past I had come to learn about, and I was also learning that the past is not entirely isolated within a moment on an historical continuum."

In *Saul Bellow: Drumlin Woodchuck* (1980), Mark Harris provides a running commentary on his effort to write an unauthorized biography of Saul Bellow. Harris's conceit is that Bellow's distrust of him has prompted the biographer to examine his own motives and to realize why the artist resists Harris's effort to make him into a monument. Harris also comments on his interviewees, sizing them up for reliability and at the same time explaining his own developing understanding of Bellow, corresponding with his subject years before deciding to do a biography, then meeting him several times and trying to make sense of his ambiguous responses. As Harris describes this evolving but somewhat mystifying relationship, he intersperses passages from Bellow's novel *Humboldt's Gift*, providing a parallel between the characters of Charles Citrine and Humboldt, and Harris and Bellow.

In *The Family Idiot: Gustave Flaubert, 1821–1857* (1981), Jean-Paul Sartre reads Flaubert from the inside to understand what words meant to the creator of the modern novel, and to examine the "prehistory" of his subject, generating speculation even where almost no evidence exists, as for much of Flaubert's childhood. Sartre elides difficulties with extravagant statements such as "A life—a life is a childhood with all the stops pulled out, as we know." To make a point Sartre will resort to philosophical pronouncements, repeated interpretations of the same facts from different perspectives, or appeals to sources outside the evidence at hand—to Margaret Mead, for example, who has "demonstrated how in certain societies the adult's aggressiveness depends upon the way he was fed in the cradle."

The first chapter of Elinor Langer's unusual biography *Josephine Herbst: The Story She Could Never Tell* (1984) explains how the biographer became interested in her subject and decided to write a biography. Langer does not merely reveal her intensely personal feelings about Herbst, she also alerts readers to her biases against biography (it normally asserts a kind of impersonal objectivity) and charts the changes in her own views as she researched and wrote her book, making Herbst into a kind of double of herself ("A mysterious kinship linked me with this female stranger as if not only our blood but the cells of our marrow were somehow matched"). The book is exemplary of Langer's definition of biography: "the story of one life as seen by another."

David Thomson's *Warren Beatty and Desert Eyes: A Life and a Story* (1987) verges on the silly and self-conscious. Thomson nevertheless manages to explore provocative issues about the biographies of contemporary figures, suggesting that accounts of living subjects can capture more of the disorderly and neurotic aspects of a career, the muddle of work in progress—especially of film stars who "change before our eyes." Thomson tries to capture this instability of personality by counterpoint, juxtaposing a biography of Beatty with a story that derives from the biographer's thinking about the Hollywood out of which his subject develops.

Ian Hamilton in *In Search of J. D. Salinger* (1988) includes himself as a character in his narrative, explaining his youthful enthusiasm for Salinger, showing his fluctuating feelings about his subject, how his interviewees responded to him, debating with himself the merits of an unauthorized biography (comparing his research on Salinger with his authorized biography of Robert Lowell), and describing the court battle with Salinger over quoting from unpublished letters. A provocative look at the politics of biography, of how the biographer goes about dealing with a variety of sources who make claims on the character of his narrative as the biographer struggles to keep intact his own vision of the subject.

In Peter Ackroyd's *Dickens* (1990), the biographical narrative is interrupted six times. In the first interruption, Ackroyd asks, "But what if it were possible, after all, for Charles Dickens to enter one of his novels." Then Ackroyd creates a colloquy between Dickens and Little Dorritt. In the second interruption, Ackroyd accosts his subject. In the third, Ackroyd's previous biographical subjects (Chatterton, T. S. Eliot, and Oscar Wilde) engage Dickens in a discussion of literature. The fourth presents an outing of Dickens's characters from different novels. In the fifth, Ackroyd interrogates Dickens about the extent to which he can know himself any better than the biographer does. In the sixth, Ackroyd interviews himself about his misgivings and his hopes for the biography. These interpolations, it seems to me, are intriguing—a refreshing way to reconceive Dickens as an author whose characters share the same universe as he does. But most critics chastised Ackroyd and found his inventiveness self-indulgent.

In *Coleridge: Early Visions* (1990), Richard Holmes has tried to experiment, to set Coleridge "*talking,*" rendering as many episodes as possible through his "flights of phrase and metaphor"—a "romantic monologue"; and providing footnotes—not to document or expand on the text but to "initiate another level of speculation, a third perspective—besides those of Coleridge and his narrator." This "downstage voice" represents a sort of "gloss" on the narrative, which in itself reflects the dominion of the subject over his biographer.

In *Clear Pond: The Reconstruction of a Life* (1991), Roger Mitchell, a poet, explores the Adirondacks, where he grew up, and how he became interested in the life of an "ordinary person," Israel Johnson. Mitchell's narrative tells how he first learned about this early settler through brief references to him in a few documents such as county survey records, a journal, and property deeds. The vagaries of research, the effort to reimagine nineteenth-century landscape, gaps in the evidence, and speculations on Johnson's motivations and actions make this a compelling demonstration of how a biography takes shape in the mind of a writer who begins as neither a historian nor a biographer.

In the preface to John Worthen's, *D. H. Lawrence: The Early Years, 1885–1912* (1991), Worthen, David Ellis, and Mark Kinkead-Weekes announce a "new kind of biography": each author will cover a period of Lawrence's life. Acting as one another's "research assistants," they have "challenged the half-conscious tendency of every biographer to turn a blind eye to inconvenient items of evidence and argued out fundamental positions." They reject the "idea of a personal core or center, an 'essential self,'" as a dubious proposition that Lawrence himself questioned. They hope to avoid the "genetic fallacy," the explanation in terms of origins, which "always implies determinism." Instead they welcome a "necessary tension between a continuous and a continuously changing Lawrence," more faithful to the "actualities and unexpectedness of life." No single view, they conclude, can be definitive.

Daisy Bates in the Desert: A Woman's Life Among the Aborigines (1994) is Julia Blackburn's evocative biographical meditation on an Irishwoman who spent most of her life among the Australian aborigines, documenting their lives and reinventing her own.

Bates (1860–1951) was a self-trained anthropologist who kept journals of her daily life in the bush and wrote newspaper articles and a book about her experiences. She was also a self-invented figure, telling outlandish tales about her own background.

Blackburn does her best to sort fact from fiction, but she also uses her subject's prevarications to evoke the legend Bates clearly wanted to make of her life. Blackburn is far more daring than most biographers. Although she relies on diaries and journals, she casts much of her narrative in a first-person voice—as if to present Daisy unmediated by the biographer's speculations. Of course the narrative itself is one huge conjecture as to what it felt like to live as Daisy Bates day to day.

The first-person narrative works because it is sandwiched between Blackburn's meditations on Bates. The biographer thus emphasizes the gaps in the evidence that her imagination must fill. At times Blackburn compares herself to her subject—something biographers rarely do in their narratives. Yet Blackburn rightly implies that this is the biographer's quest: to fuse with his or her subject without losing the critical distance needed for a narrative of another person's life.

Such experiments in biography can be pretentious and unconvincing—a biographer's dodging of the data or a cover for a lack of it. Blackburn writes too well and has researched her subject too thoroughly to be guilty of these faults. Instead she reveals biography as a form always concerned with fact but always struggling to transcend particularities to capture the whole person.

Rare and Commonplace Flowers: The Story of Elizabeth Bishop and Lota de Macedo Soares (2002), by Carmen Oliveira, begins with an epigraph from Titus Livius: "*Scribitur ad narrandum, non ad probandum,*" translated as "One writes to narrate, not to prove." Has she used the story of poet Elizabeth Bishop and her lover Lota de Macedo Soares, a self-taught Brazilian architect, as the scaffolding for what Truman Capote called a "nonfiction novel"? A bestseller in Brazil, this dual biography does indeed read like a work of fiction, which means, in this case, dramatic scenes, dialogue, flashbacks and flash forwards, shifting of tense from past to present, and a lively narrator who treats her two principal subjects as characters trying to work out their individual destinies through their devotion to each other.

The biographer never pretends that she is not dealing with intractable reality; the gaps in the story are not elided by transitions that skip over what the biographer does not know. Instead Oliveira's speculations provide a deeper understanding of her subjects and their milieu even if the "facts" are not ascertainable, as when Bishop encounters Lilli Correia de Araújo:

> Perhaps because of the massive walls of Lilli's house, perhaps because of Lilli's calm voice, perhaps because of the blue of the sky; perhaps because of the fundamental reality of the mountains; perhaps because of the languid sensation conveyed to her by the town with its hills from another century to be climbed without hurrying; perhaps because of all this at once, Bishop uncharacteristically gave in to an impulse. She bought a big eighteenth-century house that was falling to pieces.

In such passages the full experience of Bishop's life comes hurtling toward us—subdued only slightly by all those perhaps.

I think Oliveira also means something else when she suggests her intention is to narrate, not to prove. By not including notes to her biography—you know, those references keyed to page numbers at the back of the book that make your eyes swim—she has eschewed the biographer's always somewhat bogus claim to have documented reality. Biography is not the sum of its documentation; a story always goes beyond its sources.

In *Like a Fiery Elephant: The Story of B. S. Johnson* (2004), winner of the Samuel Johnson Prize for Biography, Jonathan Coe has written an unconventional biography of an unconventional writer.

152   BIOGRAPHY: *A User's Guide*

Coe surmounts the difficulties of getting to know Johnson and his work by making the reader a kind of collaborator or interlocutor. The biography reads like a jocular conversation—or a story by Henry James, with the "industrious biographer" recounting how he foraged through his subject's papers. Coe refers to "our hero," about whom "you will be pleased to learn" that after a period of struggle Johnson achieved literary, if not popular, recognition.

Unlike Johnson's unconventional novels, Coe's unusual biography is not that daunting. After his chatty introduction, he provides a chapter with brief but lucid descriptions of Johnson's novels and of how they related to his life. Only then does the biographer begin to provide a chronological account of his subject's life.

But the conversational tone continues, with the biographer pointing out when evidence is scarce. He also lets Johnson tell part of the story by including extracts from Johnson's journals, fiction, and journalism. The result is a remarkable sense of intimacy—a bond that is formed not only between reader and subject but also between reader and biographer. Coe tosses in asides about his own career as a novelist, though in judicious fashion. He earns the reader's confidence by sharing the difficulties of researching and writing a biography, including those first confusing days as the biographer begins to sift through his subject's papers, seeking something that will make Johnson "come alive."

Why shouldn't a writer as unorthodox as Philip K. Dick merit a quirky biography? This seems to be the question that Emmanuelle Carrère poses in *I Am Alive and You Are Dead: A Journey into the Mind of Philip K. Dick* (2004). But Carrère's book has already proven too odd for some critics. He dispenses with notes, bibliography, and even photographs of his subject (though the biographer describes a few snapshots, and the jacket cover has an image of Dick in dark sunglasses). These omissions are not the result of laziness or disregard for the conventions of biography—indeed the biographer is scrupulous about revealing those instances where he has no evidence and cannot enter his subject's consciousness. Rather, the absence of such trappings constitutes an acknowledgment that *au fond* biography is a work of the interpretive imagination.

I was disappointed to see that the book had no index, but then I began to think about what indexes do to books: they chop them up into data. Isn't there a powerful reason why novels have no indexes? Wouldn't an index be useful in *Wuthering Heights*, for example: "Heathcliff, mysterious origins of." But an index violates the imaginative flow and rearranges the narrative universe. Carrère does not want you to carve his book up into information bits, or to use it to gaze at pictures. He wants to create the experience of a novel while playing by the rules of biographical narrative.

The biographer's narrative is meant to put Dick back together, not sunder him apart as the paraphernalia of biography too often does—just as Dick's own novels claim to be recovering a part of reality that no one other than the author himself seems to acknowledge.

If you like your biography straight up, *King of the Jews* (2005) is not for you. Nick Tosches's book is more anti-biography than biography. He doubts that we can know much about the past. His title is ironic. There was no King of the Jews, no Jesus. The passage in Josephus, for example, that would seem to affirm Christ's existence is, Tosches insists, a later addition, a backdating of the check, so to speak, a lie repeated so often that it is taken for truth.

Thus Arnold Rothstein, purported fixer of the 1919 World Series, backer of Broadway plays, befriender of Lucky Luciano and other gangsters, a descendant of a family that got its start in the infamous Five Points, the original of Meyer Wolfsheim in *The Great Gatsby* and of Nathan Detroit in *Guys and Dolls*, cannot—any more than Jesus or Yahweh—be separated from his myth.

Tosches calls biographers like David Pietrusza (*Rothstein*, 2003) "earnest"—meaning, I presume, sincere but also rather simple minded, since they take the idea of history and biography seriously. To Tosches, there are facts established by depositions and autopsies, what the subject says about himself, what contemporaries say about him—but little else for the biographer/historian to go on.

Tosches's scorn for historian/biographers is presented anecdotally. He mentions, for example, a wage schedule for Italian immigrants discussed in a book by "a man with a PhD whom *The New*

York Times's praised as presenting his data 'with scholarly precision.'" Doing his own critical thinking, Tosches decides the schedule is the "stuff of folklore and fantasy." He writes the learned author asking for the source of the schedule but receives no reply. Then he sees this fictitious document quoted in yet another book and concludes that the "lie repeated becomes history; its precision praised." This is the refrain of his book.

What is Tosches's solution to this problem? *King of the Jews* includes lots of documents—especially depositions about Rothstein's death—which make for rather dull reading but which also emphasize Tosches's unwillingness to engage in the pretenses of biographers and historians:

> When I set out to write this book, I was intrigued by the figure of Arnold Rothstein. I still am. But as I researched more deeply, I came to see that the picture of him that history gave us was wrong. Was I to offer a different picture? Was I to take a man's life and make of it an exercise in interpretation? Was I to claim to have arrived at the "truth"? Was I to fabricate a "riveting portrait" by hiding one aspect of him and presenting another, without ever knowing—who could?—which aspects of him held weight and meaning for him, in his life, as he lived it? This would be to compound the misknowing that already was.

Of course Tosches has a point, but it is rather like the child's discovery that there is no Easter Bunny. Well then, and what else might not be true? The adolescent skeptic concludes, "I'm going to give up my plans to major in history. It is, as Henry Ford told us, bunk."

And not only is history bunk, but so are its principal figures. In Tosches's world, for example, all American presidents—whether it is FDR or Richard Nixon—share the title "the late great." There is not much to choose between them, which is perhaps why Tosches refuses to criticize his subject.

Rothstein was a man who practiced rather than preached, paid no lip service but simply paid. If his power is to be judged as having been criminal, then what harsher judgment have we reserved for the far deadlier, more ruinous, and malfeasant corporate and political powers that increasingly oppress and rob us with the blandest of smiles and most vacuous of blandishments?

Rothstein an honest crook? Better than FDR? Has Tosches forgotten that Rothstein blandly called himself a businessman? And are the opening words of *King of the Jews* then only ironic?

> Once upon a time, when New York City lived and breathed, there was a man marked for death, like us all.
>
> His name was Arnold Rothstein, and he himself was the only God he worshipped, and he was a great and sinful man.

Does Tosches believe in sin? Where does the irony of his prose end?

Heaping scorn on historians and biographers and politicians is an old sport. Done well, as in Josephine Tey's *The Daughter of Time*, which exposes the stupidity of the tales historians have told about Richard III, it is instructive and therapeutic, if not reliable history. And certainly Tosches, a stylish and very funny writer, manages his riffs on a single note about as well as any writer I know.

But to say that biographies and histories distort is such a truism that the intellectual underpinnings of this work—what is it exactly?—do not sink very deep. I wanted to know more about Rothstein. I wanted interpretation.

FURTHER READING: Paula Backscheider, *Reflections on Biography* (1999).

SEE ALSO Feminist Biography.

Intellectual Biography

Intellectual biography is essentially the history of a mind. This form of biography assumes that ideas are separable from a full account of the subject's life, so that the subject's personality comes into play only in so far as the intellectual biographer feels that temperament informs ideas and positions. The advantage of intellectual biography is that it eschews any concern with the mundane and avoids an interruption in the chronological but strictly analytical discussion of a subject's mental life.

Yet in *Reinhold Niebuhr: A Biography* (1985), Richard Fox argues that intellectual biography should correct historians' tendencies to treat "ideas as free-floating essences evolving in proud disregard for mere social reality." Historians compensate for this tendency by restating intellectual, social, and cultural debates whereas the "real challenge is to put ideas in their full biographical and communal context." Fox sees individuality not as something apart from social conditions but rather as an expression of them. Citing T. S. Eliot, he suggests that the individual should be viewed in an intellectual biography as the fruit of tradition.

Fox's definition of intellectual biography comes close to obliterating it. How can the biographer explore the nexus between "social conditions" and ideas without coming close to producing a full-scale biography?

CRITIQUE: Intellectual biography in the wrong hands offers only the husk of a man. It strips the subject's thoughts from the thinker. It flays the flesh, leaving the body of thought barren of its maker. Nicholas Capaldi, author of *John Stuart Mill: A Biography* (2004), acknowledges that a full-fledged biography is the only way to do justice to John Stuart Mill. After reading his preface, I had high hopes that he would not only deliver the best biography of Mill yet but perhaps a robust example of the genre.

Biography, in the right hands, is a uniquely integrative medium. Here the biographer has an opportunity to rectify the piecemeal readings of Mill, which in Capaldi's words focus on "isolated aspects of his work." Owing to the nature of his genre, a biographer can more fully describe the scope of Mill's sources, explaining how the philosopher drew on both the rationalism of the eighteenth century and the romanticism of the nineteenth.

Capaldi notes shrewdly that Mill himself, in his *Autobiography*, emphasized that a life narrative could best trace the "successive phases of any mind which was always pressing forward, equally ready to learn and to unlearn either from his own thoughts or from those of others." Mill had in mind his relationship with his own father, the rather austere James Mill, who thought society and the individual could be constructed on exclusively rational principles, a conviction that his son spent a lifetime modifying by investigating the role of feeling in Wordsworth, Coleridge, Carlyle, and other foes of what Capaldi calls "the Enlightenment project."

Best of all, Capaldi shows why Mill's own autobiography, for all its brilliance, will not do—precisely because it has inhibited others from constructing an alternative life narrative. The subject's interests, Capaldi points out, are not "necessarily the interests of a reader or biographer who is trying to see Mill against the backdrop of nineteenth-century social, moral, economic, religious, cultural, and philosophical developments."

Previous biographers, whom Capaldi is careful to cite and to draw upon, failed to account adequately for the Romantic strain in Mill's writing—indeed, the biographer ends his book claiming that Mill is the "greatest of the English Romantics." His predecessors' failure to explore Mill's Romantic side fully also leads Capaldi to criticize them for devaluing the role that Mill's wife, Harriet Taylor, played in strengthening and developing the philosopher's belief in the autonomy of the individual.

Autonomy, the biographer argues, is the key to Mill's philosophy. Where other critics see inconsistency in Mill's writings—suggesting, for example, that he was unclear on his support for democracy—this biography sees a philosophical and temperamental unity of feeling and thought. Mill could be for or against labor unions, for instance, depending on whether he thought unions would promote or restrict the individual's autonomy. He had reservations about certain democratic institutions because, like Tocqueville (one of Mill's sources), he feared the tyranny of the majority.

The biographer rescues the philosopher from the clutches of Fabian socialists and the left in general, noting that Mill believed in a strong military and an interventionist foreign policy, and was opposed to central planning. He favored profit-sharing for workers and a market economy, and argued against violent revolutions, which he believed were built on hate.

But Mill was no conservative. He attacked the Tory party and the landowning class in England, and he brought upon himself the wrath of both conservatives and liberals for his outspoken advocacy of votes for women and women's rights in general. When attacked in Parliament for having written that the Conservatives were the stupidest party, Mill replied: "I did not mean the Conservatives are generally stupid; I meant that stupid persons are generally Conservative."

Mill's idea of liberalism was inseparable from his desire that the individual be able to determine his own fate and take responsibility for his decisions. Just how much respect Mill had for the feelings of individuals, and how much he wanted society to honor those feelings, is evident in the passage from Mill on capital punishment that Capaldi quotes near the end of his biography:

> Much has been said about the sanctity of human life, and the absurdity of supposing that we can teach respect for life by ourselves destroying it. But I am surprised at the employment of this argument. . . . It is not human life only, not human life as such, that ought to be sacred to us, but human feelings. . . . We show, on the contrary, most emphatically our regard to it [human life], by the adoption of a rule that he who violates that right in another forfeits it for himself.

Mill scholars and students of nineteenth-century thought and English Romanticism will find this biography engrossing. For the general reader, though, it is rather heavy going. Capaldi spends a little too much time setting to rights the misapprehensions of other scholars—never a good narrative move. And though I take his point about autonomy, the concept appears with such regularity that I longed for a more Johnsonian biographical investigation of how that concept played itself out in the philosopher's domestic privacies.

For all Capaldi's desire to elevate Harriet Taylor's importance, she does not quite emerge as the equal partner Mill took her for. Absent from the biographer's narrative and bibliography is any acknowledgment of Phyllis Rose's *Parallel Lives* or other recent works that have explored the Victorian marriage. Without that perspective, Capaldi does not quite escape the hermetic cell of intellectual biography.

Interviews

Telephone interviews are tough. I've done a great many of them, and somehow it never gets easier. But sometimes it is the only way to get information, or to get someone to respond to a letter. In-person interviews are not such a problem for me, though it is often hard to see someone more than once. Sometimes one interview is all I need, but sometimes several interviews are required to gain the interviewee's confidence. I also share with the interviewee a lot of what I have learned elsewhere, which helps to build confidence. See the chapter "On Interviewing and Evidence: Boston and Holmes," in Catherine Drinker Bowen's *Adventures of a Biographer* (1959).

Interviewing as a widely practiced biographical technique dates only from the nineteenth century, though Boswell and other eighteenth-century biographers did a certain amount of it. Samuel Johnson, however, was more typical of early biographers who saw no need to do interviewing, perhaps in part because historians were biased against oral testimony and found consulting documents a far neater task. It was a way, too, to avoid accusations of retailing gossip.

But oral history and biography constitute an academic discipline. University archives at Columbia University and the presidential libraries, for example, consider oral testimony an important part

of their collections. Techniques of interviewing, and ways to cor-
roborate oral testimony, have become the subject of many studies.
Biographers and historians have come to realize that while the written record may be more convenient to consult, it is not inherently
more reliable than verbal evidence.

FURTHER READING: See Robert Perks and Alistair Thomson, ed.,
The Oral History Reader (1998), and Shoshan Felman and Dori Laub,
*Testimony: Crises of Witnessing in Literature, Psychoanalysis and His-
tory* (1992).

James, Henry (1843–1916)

A major influence in modern discussions of biography, James wrote
not only *The Aspern Papers* and "The Real Right Thing"—two stories with biographers as protagonists—but two biographies as well.
Elsa Nettles, "Henry James and the Art of Biography" (*South Atlantic Bulletin*, November 1978, pp. 107–124), discusses James's book
reviews, which maintained that the biographer should present a balanced picture (strengths and weaknesses) with "real psychological
facts," situated in history, and in a style appropriate to the subject.
James's biography of Hawthorne expresses the assumption that "art
reflects the forces of heredity and circumstance which have shaped
the artist's mind and imagination." James's second biography (of
William Wetmore Story) suffered from an awareness that Story was
a "second-rate" artist, which the biographer tried to compensate for
by making him a "representative figure" of his age and dwelling
upon the "biographer's experience of recovering" the past. James did
not believe the biographer should pry into and publicize matters
writers deemed private. He wanted the truth, but presented with
"kindness, urbanity, and discretion."

SEE ALSO Biographers in Fiction; Edel, Leon.

Johnson, Samuel (1709–1784)

In *The Rambler*, No. 60, Johnson provides a classic defense of biography, demonstrating that through the use of the imagination the biographer is able to empathize with the "happiness or calamities" of others and thus excite in readers a similar experience. Endowing biography with a moral purpose, Johnson avers that it can "widely diffuse instruction to every diversity of condition." Better than history, biography inculcates lessons for private life. A "judicious and faithful narrative" can illuminate anyone's life since human beings share a common nature and experience basically the same feelings. "Domestick privacies" may tell as much about a person as do public achievements, and it is wiser to relate a subject's virtues and faults in due and candid proportion than merely to pay homage to the dead.

Johnson's theory of biography and his practice as a biographer have stimulated considerable comment and scholarship, much of it centering on his *Life of Savage* and his *Lives of the Poets*. Richard Holmes devoted an intriguing study, *Dr. Johnson and Mr. Savage* (1994), to exploring the relationship between biographer and subject. This highly speculative work probes the friendship of these two men, suggesting that Savage functioned as a kind of alter ego for Johnson.

Earlier studies of the *Life of Savage* praise Johnson's style, his comprehensiveness and compassion, even while correcting many of the biographer's errors. William Vesterman, in "Johnson and the *Life of Savage*" (*ELH* [*English Literary History*]), vol. 36, 1969, pp. 659–678), rehearses the views of critics who believe there is a "confusion of intention" in Johnson's biography, which shifts between condemnation and redemption of his subject. Vesterman locates this apparent confusion in Johnson's opposition to melodrama, the attribution of single motives for an individual's behavior, and the tendency to judge single motives as good or evil. Johnson's more open position is designed to prevent the betrayal of both himself and Savage—that is, to preserve a certain flexibility in the interpretation of motive, so that "he has made it impossible for there to be a last word on Savage."

The more expansive *Lives of the Poets* has been praised for Johnson's acute interpretation of personality and his awesome command of the history of literary criticism from Aristotle to his own age, and for the intellectual, moral, and social range of his commentary. Others laud his grasp of history and psychology.

Johnson's faults, however, are also canvassed, particularly his reluctance to do diligent research. Some of his "lives" lack structural coherence, certain critics claim. A representative example of scholarship discussing the strengths and weaknesses of Johnson's approach to biography may be found in *Domestick Privacies: Samuel Johnson and the Art of Biography* (1987), edited by David Wheeler.

Latin/Medieval Biography

The earliest written lives date back to the end of the seventh century and are the product of an oral tradition. These biographies celebrated the hero-warriors of God, conveyed moral lessons in story form, and showed the triumph of the righteous over evil forces. Until recently such biographies had been dismissed as untrustworthy, but in fact they reveal much about their own times, about monastic life, and eventually lead to more substantial and accurate works such as Bede's *Life of St. Cuthbert.*

In *Medieval Popular Culture: Problems of Belief and Perception* (1988), Aron Gurevich explores the nexus between hagiography and biography, the way saints lives were styled to appeal to a popular audience, the structure of medieval biographical narrative, the issue of plausibility, and how popular texts grew out of "parish practice." Readers of medieval hagiography were not concerned with causality, chronology, character development, analytical judgments—the hallmarks of modern biography and history—and instead favored concrete stories, exempla, and short "self-sufficient fragments."

Thomas J. Heffernan, in *Sacred Biography: Saints and Their Biographers in the Middle Ages* (1988), contends that saints' lives are more than "pious fiction." The product of a worldview very different from the modern age, medieval biographers, influenced by Greco-Roman models, explored radical new ideas of individuality and were not merely credulous and unthinking purveyors of miracles but conscious artists establishing a new language of the self and finding new ways of transforming the lives of medieval saints from oral tales to sacred texts.

A useful overview is provided in T. A. Dorey, ed., *Latin Biography* (1967), which includes chapters on Nepos, Plutarch, and Suetonius, "the three best-known Classical biographers," and on the period of Augustan history. Chapters on William of Poitiers, William of Malmesbury, and the lives of St. Francis demonstrate the development of Latin biography in the Middle Ages. Each chapter begins with a biographical sketch of the biographer, then proceeds to an analysis of his strengths and weaknesses in the context of scholarship in Latin biography. The chapters on Plutarch and Suetonius are especially valuable because of their contrasting methods as biographers, Plutarch emphasizing parallel lives and moral paradigms, Suetonius the vividness of personality and the intimacies of public figures. The first chapter provides a solid grounding in the tradition of Greek biography on which Roman and medieval biographers drew heavily.

Letters

Personal letters are, of course, one of the staples of biography. The search for correspondence is one of the first activities a biographer is likely to conduct when beginning a biography. Yet letters have their limitations. However many are available, they are not in themselves sufficient to construct a biographical narrative. Those letters that survive are partly a matter of accident, so certain letters may loom larger than they should if the subject's complete correspondence is not available.

Letters can also be quite misleading, especially when a biographical subject like Rebecca West uses them to vent complaints and seriously skew a view of her life outside her correspondence. Certainly her behavior toward her husband, Henry Andrews, as described in her letters does not square with what members of her family observed. A good deal of the affection and trust she showed him is absent from her correspondence.

And letters are obviously exercises in persuasion. How a subject writes to his spouse or parent or friend may vary greatly. So the recipient of the correspondence must also be considered.

Then there is the problem of publication—how letters are edited and presented for public consumption. These vexing issues are explored in the following two reviews of the letters of Martha Gellhorn and Jessica Mitford.

CRITIQUE: It is wonderful to have Caroline Moorehead's *Selected Letters of Martha Gellhorn* (2006). Gellhorn reported many of the last century's important wars: the Spanish Civil War, World War II, and Vietnam were brought to vivid life in her lucid and precise prose. Married to Ernest Hemingway (and the only one of his four wives who left him), she has always caught the attention of biographers—much to her dismay. Her letters reveal close friendships with Eleanor Roosevelt, Leonard Bernstein, H. G. Wells, and a host of other important literary and cultural figures.

One of Gellhorn's correspondents thought her letters constituted her greatest achievement. Certainly they are as striking as her journalism, more engaging than much of her fiction, and filled with the energy that led her to visit and write about almost half the countries of the world. She was always avid to be off somewhere, since nowhere ever quite fulfilled her idea of paradise—not Italy, Mexico, or Africa, to mention just the dozen or so homes she established in the course of her peregrinations. She was, as I implied in the title of my biography of her, a "beautiful exile" in search of a beautiful exile.

Martha Gellhorn lived in a nearly perpetual state of dissatisfaction, which sometimes made her a bore but often made her attractive precisely because she was so demanding. She could also be very, very funny about her naive search for the perfect world. *Travels with Myself and Another*, for example, is a comic masterpiece, one of the truly great travel books of our time.

But just how wonderful are her letters? And perhaps more to the point, how can we trust them? Gellhorn was writing about real people, events, and places. So unless her correspondence is regarded as fiction masquerading as fact, inevitably the nature of her perceptions must be explored and analyzed.

The trouble is that Caroline Moorehead is ill equipped to render this sort of service. As in her authorized biography of Gellhorn, Moorehead simply gives her subject her head. If Gellhorn denies she had an affair with H. G. Wells, Moorehead drops the subject. That Gellhorn wrote the sort of ingratiating letters to Wells that have prompted the suspicion of more than one Hemingway biographer; that Wells himself wrote quite directly about his affair with Gellhorn, means nothing whatever to Moorehead.

How much the editor of Gellhorn's letters ought to say about them is, of course, debatable. An editor who is constantly correcting or augmenting her subject's text might very well annoy some readers. But in this case both Gellhorn's own skewed accounts and the provenance of these letters are cause for concern.

What Moorehead's reticence and the letters themselves reveal is Gellhorn's fierce desire to define history solely on her terms. She adopted an attitude toward biography and history that essentially eviscerates both forms of writing. She believed exclusively in eyewitness history. If you weren't there with her at the Spanish Civil War, if you were not a friend of Dorothy Parker, then how could you possibly know anything? Thus Gellhorn writes as follows to the esteemed Parker biographer Marion Meade, who had sent a letter inquiring about Gellhorn's friendship with Parker:

Dear Miss Meade, Have a heart. I could talk to you about Dottie for hours, I knew her well . . . but I can't write a whole chapter for you. I haven't time to live let alone write letters.

Of course, Meade was not asking Gellhorn to write a chapter for her (I know, I checked with Meade), and besides, Gellhorn loved writing several letters a day. The real point of the letter was to put Meade in her place. Gellhorn was forever writing such letters to biographers.

In a letter to Alan Grover, one of Gellhorn's lovers, Gellhorn enunciated her lifelong distaste for biography: "I think it is barbarous, and the mark of microscopic minds, to confuse the man and his work; as long as the man, in his own life, is not the enemy of the commonwealth . . ." This letter, written in Cuba sometime in 1940 when Gellhorn was living with Hemingway, conveys the dread she felt in anticipating the public attention that would inevitably follow her marriage to one of the kings of American literature.

But Gellhorn was a part of history and had no trouble, when it suited her, promoting and writing about herself—as she did in *The Face of War* and *The View from the Ground*. She squirreled away her letters in the special collections department of Boston University's Mugar Memorial Library, presided over by the late Howard Gotlieb, who aggressively sought the papers of celebrities and literary figures. Gotlieb was quite willing to make his devil's bargain—in this case, promising Gellhorn that her papers would not be available to anyone until twenty-five years after her death (she died in 1998).

But if Gellhorn wanted no biography, why not destroy the papers? Why leave an estate free to hire an authorized biographer? Why allow Moorehead to edit the letters *now*? Why let her make a selection that no other scholar/biographer can check since the Gellhorn collection is still closed to other researchers? Moorehead mentions, for example, that she has chosen a few pages from a forty-plus-page letter that Gellhorn wrote to her lover David Gurewitsch. Perhaps those are the best pages of that letter, but what is the principle of selection? What are we really reading when only parts of letters appear?

Gotlieb justified his deals by saying that in order to preserve history he had to accept the terms he was offered. He also suggested that Gellhorn was trying to prevent the kind of "pop biography" that would appear before there could be any perspective on the events she participated in. But Gellhorn said she did not believe in perspective. She thought the perspective argument was fallacious since history and biography occur all the time. To be sure, there is perspective, but there is also the immediacy of biographies written on the spot, so to speak—as the historian John Lukacs notes in *The Hitler of History*. One of the best biographies of Hitler, Lukacs points out, was published in 1935.

So by all means, enjoy Gellhorn's letters, but *caveat emptor!* What to make of a writer who thought the Spanish Civil War had been the only just war fought during her lifetime? Or what about this passage on Alger Hiss, written on April 11, 1982:

> The man is 77 now, and with hurt eyes, still trying to restore his good name. And though he doesn't understand why Whittaker Chambers and Richard Nixon were out to kill him, I do; he was the very embodiment of everything they were not and could not be, the educated upper class American, an American gentleman; they hated him. It had nothing to do with Communism; it was like a private vendetta.

This passage can be easily turned on its head: Whittaker Chambers is dead now, and the old lefties cannot let go of vilifying him. I know why: he was fat and conservative and worked for *Time* magazine and had none of Hiss's elegance and education. How could someone as well spoken and with the right opinions possibly be a traitor?

Reducing history to such psychology and ideology is repugnant. There may be a grain of truth in it, but to make such explanations dominate, as Gellhorn does, makes her a very unreliable correspondent. Why didn't Moorehead at least include an introduction that explored the nature of Gellhorn's prejudices and blind spots? She mentions Gellhorn's Jewish background, yet makes no connection with Gellhorn's staunch support of Israel and how she related to Jews. Gellhorn made a Jew discovering the horror of Dachau the main character in her novel, *Point of No Return*, yet she never commented on how that character's sudden awakening to his Jewishness reflected her own obsession with protecting Israel.

Or did she? Since we have only a selection of letters and must wait nearly another two decades to see how Moorehead made her selections, we cannot know for certain. This half-baked collection of letters is certainly better than not having a loaf at all, but what will arise from a complete and uncompromising study of the letters remains to be seen.

"COMPILATIONS of correspondence are necessarily biographies of a kind—biographies of individual consciousness with less intrusive mediation and interpretation than one finds in a traditional biography," writes Peter Y. Sussman, editor of *Decca: The Letters of Jessica Mitford* (2006). But what constitutes "less intrusive mediation"? Jessica Mitford supplied an admirable answer, which Sussman quotes: "The whole point of letters is to reveal the writer & her various opinions & let the chips fall where they may. Censoring them for fear of offending the subjects is in my view absolutely wrong."

Why then does Sussman disregard Mitford's uncompromising conviction? Mitford belonged to a family of outspoken individualists, including her older sister, the novelist Nancy Mitford, who satirized her own family's peculiarities and their devotion to the fascist cause. Another sister, Diana Mosley, was unapologetic about her marriage to the British fascist Oswald Mosley, and Jessica herself publicly excoriated Diana and another sister, Unity, for their pro-Hitler activities. Jessica, for her part, became a Communist and later an outspoken critic of American institutions, and is perhaps best known for her watershed book, *The American Way of Death*, a hilarious but savage attack on the funeral-home industry.

What is more, unlike many of her fellow writers, Mitford applied her principles to herself and her friends, sparing (with one exception) no person or organization when she believed an important principle was involved. For example, when the biographer Joan Mellen asked for an interview with Mitford about her friend, the writer Kay Boyle, Mitford assented even when the capricious Boyle withdrew her support for Mellen's biography and enjoined Mitford to do the same. Mitford refused, preferring to anger her friend, and to honor an agreement, noting, as well, that she had a right to speak with anyone she liked. Friends should not impose gag orders on friends, she believed. Would that more writers obeyed that Samuel Johnson injunction: It is more important to reveal the truth than to worry about hurting people's feelings.

Yet Sussman wants to protect Mitford's correspondents, to mitigate their pain, and is even willing to hide the identities of Communist party members who have not, in his words, "outed" themselves. I cannot believe, based on the evidence of the very letters that Sussman has edited, that Jessica Mitford would find his concerns about the tender feelings and reputations of others worthy of respect.

Sussman's motives are all the more suspect since Mitford's own Communist party membership is one of the least attractive features of her biography. While the wayward Mitford was a problem for the party, since she was by nature and nurture such an independent soul, she nevertheless lent her talents to an undemocratic and conspiratorial organization that took its orders from a foreign power.

Why? Because for her the party stood for social justice, especially civil rights, a laudable concern that Mitford championed in countless ways in the San Francisco Bay area. She not only wrote about social issues, she put her day-to-day energies into the drive for equal rights.

At the same time Mitford, who prided herself on her investigative skills, turned a blind eye to the global and geopolitical actions of the party, headquartered in Moscow. I put it this way because of the astonishing letter Mitford wrote after visiting Hungary shortly before the 1956 uprising, which (Sussman notes) resulted in thirty thousand deaths in Budapest alone: "Why couldn't we see signs of this while we were there?" she wrote to her mother-in-law. Why indeed. Anyone who traveled, as I did, in Communist Europe through the end of the 1970s had to be aware of repressive and closed societies that produced sullen functionaries and a cowed populace that was nonetheless ready to unburden itself to visiting Americans if an appropriately secure location could be arranged.

Mitford (a member of the party until 1958) expressed some sympathy with the uprising, but look at how she frames her discussion:

> However, I gather from news releases that the rebels were quickly joined by fascists and that a "white terror" was being established. Because of this, I think in the long run the interests of the Hungarian people are best served by entry of Russian troops.

It takes your breath away. As Woody Allen said in *Annie Hall*: "Excuse me, I'm due back on planet earth."

While Mitford's criticisms of American social institutions often hit their mark, the Soviet Union until very late in the day got no more than wry wrist slaps. Her letters reveal a love of causes, and even the fawning Sussman has to admit that sometimes Mitford was doing little more than stirring the pot.

Mitford was a muckraker, and the downside of a continual raking of the muck is that the raker can get pretty soiled herself. I was dismayed to read, for example, these gloating passages:

> I was also successful in getting the book [a history of the Mitfords written from a pro-Diana bias] thoroughly trashed by reviewers in S.F. Chronicle, Boston Globe, & NYT Book Review, having pointed out to reviewers—all friends of mine—some of the stupider passages.

> More on OJ: Bob [Treuhaft, her husband] & I rather agreed with you . . . we were pleased with verdict but thought he's prob. guilty. . . . serves the cops right. A thought: sort of an Affirmative Action type of vote? Redressing centuries of injustice in our law courts?

Forget the brutality of the O. J. murder and find your solace in revolutionary justice. No wonder it took Mitford so long to leave the Communist party. Elsewhere she writes that she supported Stalin: "Mainly for pragmatic reason that his lot won. Trots lost. I think Trotsky wld have been more to our liking philosophically." Her inhumanity is striking.

For all the good Mitford did in exposing corruption, there was a corruption at her very core as well. She seemed to have little understanding or empathy for liberals like Hillary Rodham, who once was an intern in Bob Treuhaft's law firm but later turned to helping her husband reform the penal system in Arkansas.

Rebecca West, who in some ways had a temperament similar to Jessica Mitford's but drew very different political conclusions from her investigative reporting, might have said that Mitford lacked a sense of process, a grasp of the mechanisms by which genuine social change is accomplished. Mitford was curious about West and wrote to me, wishing to know more about my research for a biography of West. Too bad Mitford did not take to heart West's key insight: that no matter how slow and contradictory it might be, there is no substitute for the Rule of Law—a phrase West liked to capitalize. Resort to revolutionary justice results in no justice at all.

Libel

In the United States libel is rarely a significant concern for biographers. Since most biographies are about public figures, and U.S. law treats public figures as fair game, lawsuits for libel are relatively rare. The plaintiff must show that the biographer has deliberately written slander, and the latitude given to critics of public figures means that lawsuits except for punitive reasons are unlikely to be filed.

An exception was Lillian Hellman's lawsuit against Mary McCarthy. When McCarthy appeared on *The Dick Cavett Show* and said that every word Hellman wrote was a lie, including "and" and "the," Hellman sued her for libel. Most legal scholars believed that Hellman had brought a nuisance suit, forcing McCarthy to pay attorney fees even though in all likelihood she would, in the end, prevail. McCarthy's words were taken by most observers to be hyperbole, not a considered judgment for which McCarthy could be sued.

Hellman could afford to pursue her antagonist because Hellman's attorney, Ephraim London, was not charging her for his services, and Hellman, at any rate, was wealthy whereas McCarthy had only modest resources to draw upon. Hellman's sole purpose, in other words, was to punish her critic. To nearly everyone's surprise, the judge in the case dismissed McCarthy's move for a summary judgment. Such a ruling would have determined that Hellman had insufficient cause of action against McCarthy. Instead the judge determined that Hellman was not a public figure in terms of the law he was interpreting. This defied common sense, but the judge was never overruled because Hellman died, bringing an end to the case.

Susan Sontag's attorney, Martin Garbus, intimated there might be a cause of action against the biography my wife and I were writing of Susan Sontag. He vaguely referred to "third parties" who might be libeled. But the matter was never pursued, perhaps because our agent and our publisher refused to be cowed by efforts to suppress our book, efforts that included threatening letters from another law firm that Sontag employed.

In England libel is a much more serious problem for biographers. If a plaintiff brings an action for libel, the onus is on the biographer and publisher to prove they have not libeled the subject of the biography. In practice this means that the very threat of a libel action has been enough to stop certain biographies from being published in the United Kingdom. In my own case, my first biography of Martha Gellhorn could not be published there because she threatened a libel suit. No UK publisher wished to incur the legal costs of defending my biography, even though it had already been published in the United States. Recent court decisions in the UK will perhaps shift the burden away from the biographer and publisher, though it is too early to tell whether this is likely.

FURTHER READING: Three by Carl Rollyson: *A Higher Form of Cannibalism: Adventures in the Art and Politics of Biography* (2005);

"Susan Sontag: The Making of a Biography," in *Female Icons: Marilyn Monroe to Susan Sontag* (2005); and the forthcoming *Adventures of an Outlaw: A Biographer at Work*.

The Life and the Work

I've been amused by the reviews of Peter Conradi's Iris Murdoch biography. One reviewer said it was superfluous because you learn nothing about Murdoch's work. Another said the biography was quite useful because you learn a good deal about the work. I've noticed that editors seem to have less and less tolerance for any sustained discussion of a literary work. But this is not really new either.

It is possible to write a biography of a literary figure without doing extended discussions of the work. I learned a good deal from W. A. Swanberg's biography of Dreiser, even though Swanberg included no literary criticism.

SEE ALSO Modernism.

CRITIQUE: The history of the Theodore Dreiser biography provides a sketch of contemporary attitudes toward the life and the work:

Dreiser (1871–1945), one of the giants of American literature, has been blessed with the best of biographers. Dorothy Dudley's *Forgotten Frontiers: Dreiser and the Land of the Free* (1932) captures her subject live, so to speak, and "contains material available nowhere else," Jerome Loving acknowledges. Robert H. Elias got to know Dreiser in the late 1930s, and in 1948 published the first scholarly biography, *Theodore Dreiser: Apostle of Nature*.

These early pioneering efforts came to fruition in W. A. Swanberg's *Dreiser* (1965). The biographer of William Randolph Hearst, Swanberg was no literary critic. How then to deal with the literary aspects of Dreiser's life? In the author's note and acknowledgments, Swanberg announced:

> This book is intended solely as biography, not criticism. There have been many analyses of Dreiser's works, but no attempt to study the whole man. Not even during his busiest writing years was he exclusively a writer, being always a self-taught philosopher with strong views about society. He collided repeatedly with American culture, religion, and politics. For a quarter-century he waged a violent battle against the censorship of art, and his works, if not his words, had a large share in the victory. Indeed, Dreiser was a fighter incarnate, always battling something; his compulsion toward social criticism and mystic philosophy so overmastered him that he all but abandoned creative writing. If his prejudices and contradictions were awesome, the mature Dreiser represents in extreme enlargement the confusions of the era after 1929 when intellectuals everywhere sought a better society, and when thinkers more competent than he proved as mistaken as he. But Dreiser was, in the extreme sense, an original. There has been no one like him. He deserves study simply as one of the most incredible of human beings, a man whose enormous gifts warred endlessly with grievous flaws.

For many literary biographers, a subject's written work is, in the main, the life, and the point is to show how the work and the life are of a piece. Swanberg suggests that Dreiser's writing can be treated separately—indeed it is so treated in numerous works of literary criticism that do not deal with the "whole man." But how, a literary biographer might ask, can there be a "whole man" in a biography that does not interpret the subject's writing? To say that there were periods when Dreiser did not write does not seem a very convincing argument, since all authors, even the most prolific, have periods of inactivity. Other authors have been just as involved in the political and social issues of their age and yet have also created unique personalities for themselves that surely are located, in important ways, in their writing. Why should Dreiser be any different?

Has Swanberg simply ducked the issue of literary biography altogether?

Enter Jerome Loving with a literary biography that reaches Dreiserian heights as he recounts the fraught publication of *Sister Carrie* (1900) and carefully analyzes the language Dreiser employs to describe Hurstwood's harrowing descent from manager of a saloon to the derelict whose life disintegrates when Carrie abandons him. Loving's account of Dreiser's own breakdown after his publisher refused to stand by the novel has the same relentless drive as his subject's work. At one point Dreiser becomes a day laborer and is roused out of his depression only after his brother Paul lends him money, allowing him slowly to write himself back to recovery.

Just as impressive is Loving's account of *An American Tragedy* (1925), Dreiser's other masterpiece, the story of Clyde Griffths's murder of his pregnant sweetheart so that he can marry a high-society girl. Although often labeled determinist, Dreiser's work is suffused with a wonder about the human spirit and the circumstances that seem to conspire against it. What is striking about Clyde is his sense of aspiration—and Dreiser's dismay that it should become so twisted. To simply write of such characters in moralistic terms outraged Dreiser, a lapsed Catholic, who rejected his devout father's belief in the God of everlasting judgment.

Dreiser yearned to believe in the self-made man, yet everywhere he saw the American dream of individual distinction crushed by society and organized religion. The power of Dreiser's work is ultimately spiritual. He ended his life as a Quaker exhorting everyone to find his own way to God—or what Dreiser liked to call "the Creative force."

No matter the virtues of Loving's biography, he does not have the field to himself. Richard Lingeman's two-volume biography (1986, 1990) presents Dreiser as a great American character. Dreiser's battles against censorship, his attacks on the manners and morality of the time, his willingness to engage in political issues—not only his Communist party activities and staunch defense of the Soviet Union, but his visit to the striking miners in Harlan County, Kentucky—show

how he wanted to integrate literature and life. The vigor of Dreiser's mind and body had to find an outlet in public action. His words had to be tied to actions, Lingeman argues. Dreiser's mistress (later his second wife, Helen) called him a "great man." She had in mind, it seems, his capacity to move people, to make them suffer along with his characters and himself. Dreiser's appeal grew out of his ability to be both vulnerable and resolute. He was not a handsome man, but he had a hold over many women because there was something in him that needed mothering and nurturing even as he evinced a power that controlled the lives of his lovers. He empathized with both the "little" man and the tycoon, like Charles Yerkes, on whom he based Frank Cowperwood, the hero of his trilogy, *The Financier, The Titan,* and *The Stoic.* The relentlessness in Dreiser's fiction runs parallel to his passionate life. He amasses mountains of detail when describing his characters, providing a social fabric for their lives that meshes with his keen awareness of how his own character was caught up with the fate of his country. By packing his biography with a similarly dense set of particulars, Lingeman does homage to a writer who remains important in American fiction's effort to encompass and appraise American identity.

Loving's literary approach has its downside. Lest he prove a Swanberg, he feels duty-bound to discuss even minor Dreiser works in tedious detail. Yet Jason Epstein, writing in the *New York Review of Books* (June 3, 1965), praises Swanberg for not writing "a novelist's literary life, that often wearisome genre, with its dutiful summaries of plot and character and neat packets of themes and symbols tossed in to give the whole a savor of textbook serviceability. But by concentrating on biographical data, Swanberg has done much to elucidate the art of the man who wrote *Sister Carrie* and *An American Tragedy.*"

As I point out in *Essays in Biography*, it is as though Swanberg did not wish to remind the reader of what it means to examine a literary text, to submerse oneself in the writer's style. When Dreiser is divorced from his words, Swanberg is free to reconstitute and dramatize his subject's life without competition from the very text (*Sister Carrie*) on which the biographer actually relies:

> In *Carrie* for the first time of importance, Dreiser translated his own experience into the desperate, hopeless yearnings of his characters. *Ev'ry Month* [the magazine he edited] had held him in a tight little strait-jacket. His magazine articles were pot-boilers conforming to editors' wishes. Now the reluctant conformist was free to write as he pleased about life as he saw it. He let himself go far, far into unconformity, apparently not realizing the extent of his divagation, but surely there was unconscious rebellion against the restraints that had curbed him for four years. Although he had read Hardy with admiration and he was not forgetting Balzac, what came out of his pen was pure Dreiser tinctured with Spencer and evolution. He was simply telling a story much as he had seen it happen in life. . . . He wrote with a compassion for human suffering that was exclusive with him in America. He wrote with a tolerance for transgression that was as exclusive and as natural. His mother, if not immoral herself, had accepted immorality as a fact of life. Some of his sisters had been immoral in the eyes of the world. In his own passion for women he was amoral himself, believing that so-called immorality was not immoral at all but was necessary, wholesome and inspiring, and that the conventional morality was an enormous national fraud.

To cite passages in the novel itself to support what Swanberg says would have the effect of fragmenting his narrative, calling a halt to it in favor of addressing a text—which, no matter how smoothly done, cannot quite rectify the damage that is done to narrative values.

Such is the power of W. A. Swanberg, possessed of a novel-like energy that his rival Loving dare not acknowledge in his own formidable biography. Like Lingeman's account, Loving's book may continue to illuminate Swanberg's account, even as it does Dreiser's own writing. But only Swanberg stands alone.

Literary Biography

Literary biography begins with Samuel Johnson's *Lives of the Poets*, a series of essays written between 1777 and 1781. Johnson did little original research, but his method of treating lives as well as works elevated the notion of biography. At the same time Johnson did not fully integrate life and work but treated them, in most respects, as separate, if parallel realms.

Boswell surpassed Johnson as a researcher, but he more or less maintained the separation between life and work that Johnson promulgated. Even so, Boswell made the writer's life of intrinsic importance, providing a level of detail that did not interest Johnson.

The advent of Romanticism broke down the divide between the life and the work. Byron, in particular, used his own personality to inform the personas of Childe Harold, Manfred, Don Juan, and others. The poet became his own hero, so to speak. Biographers, however, were slow to capitalize on Byron's breakthrough. While they tended to the writer's personality more than previous biographers, nevertheless a full integration of the life and the work is not essayed until Lytton Strachey's *Eminent Victorians*. Although Strachey did not depict literary figures, he made axiomatic the connection between his subjects' lives and their accomplishments. Florence Nightingale, for example, became virtually a Freudian case study—her astounding accomplishments a matter of a kind of manic, even demonic, drive to succeed. Strachey seemed to spite an aggressive woman who exhausted the men in her employ. Whatever else Strachey's controversial work accomplished, he established the biographer's power to take charge of his subject, thus annihilating the Victorian obeisance to greatness in which the dutiful biographer did nothing to diminish his subject's superiority.

Modern literary scholarship contributed to literary biography a meticulous scouring of sources, establishing reliable records of writer's lives. But by and large academic biographies were not "literary" in Justin Kaplan's sense of the word. His work on Mark Twain, for example, was an attempt to elevate the genre of literary biography, making it "literary" in terms of its style and structure that would be worthy of comparison with the novel.

Without doubt the work of Leon Edel and Richard Ellmann reflected the fruition of literary biography, integrating life and art. Biography in the post–Ellmann/Edel world remains caught in their wake, with literary biographers compared to the standards Ellmann and Edel established. Among academic critics, in particular, attempts to link the life and work remain suspect in spite of Edel and Ellmann. Biographers tend to be viewed as violating the sacrosanct literary text.

In "Literary Biography in Our Time" (*Sewanee Review*, Summer 1984, pp. 495–505), George Garrett points out the limitations of the genre, especially the fact that "all literary biographies are to some extent controlled, indeed censored," because of the way authors and their estates determine the flow of information. Even in cases where biographers are not authorized, their ability to interview sources and quote material depends upon their subject's "tacit cooperation." Few biographies attain the status of art, the "magic of a sensuous affective surface," and "whether the conventional form of the biography can do justice to a literary artist of our times remains in doubt. It will remain so until a more adequate and inclusive form develops—if it does."

In the Winter 2001 issue of the *Virginia Quarterly Review*, Garrett updated his view of literary biography, explaining how my work had attempted to surmount the difficulties he enumerated in his *Sewanee Review* article: "Rollyson deliberately and successfully aims to create a thorough and accurate literary biography without dealing with the complicated arrangements and permissions uniformly required by living authors or the estates of the dead, using instead the available public materials that can be found and effectively used by anyone willing and able to do the hard work."

In *Historical Fictions* (1990), Hugh Kenner attacks literary biography, criticizing the distinguished contemporary biographers Richard Ellmann and Deirdre Bair for sloppy handling of facts, fomenting a view of their subjects which is largely fiction, and for dignifying gossip in the guise of footnotes and other documentation. He prefers Boswell, who did not assume an air of omniscience and who allowed the voices of his sources to speak directly to the reader.

Georges May, in "'His Life, His Works': Some Observations on Literary Biography" (*Diogenes*, Fall 1987, pp. 28–48), insists that in spite of recent attacks on literary biography, it seems more popular than ever and has enjoyed a longevity (with origins in fourth-century B.C. Greece) unmatched by any other literary genre. He analyzes Sainte-Beuve's method of linking the life and the work, noting that it has been vulgarized by his followers. Even if Sainte-Beuve's contention that understanding of the life improves understanding of the work is rejected, his method contributes to a demystification of the author's image. Calling literary biography a "natural" genre in that one writer attempts to establish an intimate relationship with another, May notes that readers of literary biographies crave something of the same: the effort to put themselves closer to the mysteries of creation.

Peter Nagourney, in "The Basic Assumptions of Literary Biography" (*Biography*, Spring 1978, pp. 86–104), provides a well-documented and skeptical discussion of literary biography's claim to reveal the essence of a subject's life. Nagourney suggests that literary biography's chief elements—"the premise of a unified life," "the use of anecdotal evidence," "the assumption of development and growth"—are characteristic of the genre and not necessarily of the lives biographers portray. Literary biographies, like their subjects, use words and should be viewed as art, not science, inventions of the biographer's and reader's need to shape a coherent, meaningful life.

CRITIQUE: Two books, about Erich Maria Remarque and Richard Yates, raise questions about the requirements that are often applied to literary biography.

How literary does a literary biography have to be? The biographer Justin Kaplan believes the literary biographer should aspire to write in a style that turns biography into an aesthetic object. This achievement is what reviewers seem to be lauding when they claim that certain biographies read like novels. But how to attain that art and at the same time do justice to the literary subject's work? Literary criticism is the nemesis of narrative, the cross on which so many literary biographies come to grief. Analysis anesthetizes the story; interpretation distances the reader from the flow of events; plot summaries become roadblocks on the biographer's route to the evocation of a life.

Hilton Tims, a British journalist, novelist, and critic, surmounts these difficulties in *Erich Maria Remarque: The Last Romantic* (2003) by selecting telling details, deftly providing one-paragraph synopses of novels, quoting distinctive passages, and then placing the work in the context of the writer's life and career. This is all accomplished in a few pages, resulting in a streamlined, sensible, and often elegant book—a state-of-the-art specimen of literary biography.

Tims's subject, Remarque, is best known for his anti-war novel, *All Quiet on the Western Front* (1929), a sensitive and passionate revelation of the horror of war as it impinges on Paul Baumer, a teenage recruit in the German army. An international best-seller, the novel became controversial in Germany because, unlike so many of his countrymen, Remarque did not attempt to justify his nation's participation in the war or to mitigate its sense of humiliating defeat. It is altogether fitting, then, that the biographer begins his book by describing the night of May 10, 1933, when the Nazis staged a public burning of Remarque's most famous book— arguably the most renowned anti-war novel of the twentieth century. It has never gone out of print. The fine film adaptation of the novel made the young Lew Ayres not only a star but also a lifelong pacifist. (The actor, Tims reminds us, jeopardized his career by refusing to fight in World War II, even though he came under fire as a paramedic.) This is a story worth knowing since Remarque would also be branded a pacifist for the rest of his life because of his unflinching, documentary-like depiction of the horrors of war. He was obliged to flee Germany when the Nazis took power, and Germany never forgave him for writing novels about the Holocaust from the safety (so his countrymen believed) of exile. It did not matter to them that the Nazis beheaded his own sister for sharing her brother's "defeatist" views.

But the novelist was no pacifist, Tims explains. Not only did Remarque see action in World War I, he was also wounded—and, rather like Ernest Hemingway, later dramatized and expanded on his own brush with death. Remarque supported the fight against fascism in World War II. But to Communists, to Nazis, to almost any fervent political ideologue or nationalist, the novelist remained an example of the defeatist mentality that made him feel like an exile all his life—no matter where he resided, be it New York, Hollywood, or his beloved Casa Remarque in Switzerland.

The biographer calls his subject "the last Romantic" because Remarque remained the sensitive outcast, unable to commit himself fully to any culture outside of Germany and unable to feel he could ever return to live in his native land. Love—the pursuit of beautiful, famous, and bossy women like Marlene Dietrich, Greta Garbo, and Paulette Goddard—became his method of inventing his own world. These strong women found the unpretentious but courtly Remarque irresistible, even though he was not a high-powered lover (indeed his diaries note instances of impotence). But he indulged drama queens and had the right passive-aggressive qualities to keep the game of love going. Here is Tims's adroit handling of Remarque's relationship with the complicated Dietrich:

> Marlene's dalliance with Joe Carstairs [a lesbian] became a torment. Almost certainly there was an element of manipulation behind it, her fickle moods testing him [Remarque], provoking his jealousy, creating situations she could resolve with some generous or affectionate gesture or a brief resumption of intimacy. And Remarque at his lowest emotional ebb was a pitifully easy target for her capriciousness.
>
> His diary entries are a jagged graph of his feelings . . . The musical chairs of comings and goings, finding Marlene's door locked against him and knowing Joe is behind it with her . . . the intensi-

ties seething below the surface of all these relationships would take on a quality of farce were it not for the anguish Remarque was genuinely suffering.

The biographer never assumes too much—note his "almost certainly." He employs his novelist's sense of immediacy by shifting to the present tense: "Joe is behind it with her."

This excellent biography includes only one disappointment. Where is the summing up? It is one thing not to burden the narrative with literary criticism; it is another to leave the reader wondering how good a writer the biographer believes his subject to be. Tims quotes reviews but only occasionally ventures an opinion himself. His book ends with an epilogue—a good place to learn which of Remarque's novels still matter—but the biographer remains mute on the subject, which seems strange behavior for a novelist and critic.

WHO FIRST suggested the preposterous notion that writers' lives do not make for good biography? Supposedly nothing important happens in a writer's life except for the writing. Most writers are not men or women of action. E. L. Doctorow once told me in an interview that his biography would make dull reading. That's like saying that the life of the imagination has no story to tell. Or was it just the writer's way of warding off a prospective biographer? Writers—even autobiographical novelists like Richard Yates—have a horror of the naked narrative and are shocked when one of their fellows forsakes fiction for the starker precincts of memoir, as William Stryon did with *Darkness Visible*, an account of his suicidal depression. Even though Yates put himself, his family, and writer-friends like Stryon into his novels, he was appalled when Stryon denuded himself in nonfiction.

Biography strips bare—that's why novelists like Joyce Carol Oates detest what she calls "pathography," a term she coined when reviewing a biography of Jean Stafford that faithfully reported the prolonged mental and physical debilitation that made writing virtually impossible in Stafford's later years. The biography was true to the arc of Stafford's life but not to the importance of her writing. When a later biography focused on Stafford's writing and downplayed her foibles, critics applauded.

Such hostility to biography, especially among the literati and the academic community, requires rectification. "It is frequently objected to relations of particular lives that they are not distinguished by any striking or wonderful vicissitudes," Samuel Johnson wrote. This desire for dramatic doings is prompted, he argued, by "false measures of excellence and dignity." Biographers should eradicate such prejudices by passing "slightly over those performances and incidents, which produced vulgar greatness, to lead the thoughts into domestick privacies, and display the minute details of daily life, where exterior appendages are cast aside, and men excel each other only by prudence and by virtue." Johnson was not speaking only for himself; he relied on no less of an authority than Montaigne, who confessed: "I have a singular curiosity to pry into the souls and the natural and true opinions of the authors with whom I converse." He would much rather learn about what Brutus said in his tent the night before a battle than about the speech the hero delivered the next day for public consumption.

Fortunately Blake Bailey does not spare us Richard Yates's agonies in *A Tragic Honesty: The Life and Work of Richard Yates* (2003)— his lifelong alcoholism, psychotic episodes, failed marriages, and doubts about the value of his writing—any more than Yates spared his characters their indignities. April and Frank Wheeler, the principal figures in his greatest novel, *Revolutionary Road* (1961), begin their marriage in a 1950s Connecticut suburb—terrain familiar to readers of John Updike and John Cheever, to whom Yates has often been compared—with a sense of superiority, a dream of greatness that they manifestly will not be able to fulfill. It is an old story, the gap between aspiration and achievement, but Yates redeems the cliché by the vividness of his observations and his unrelenting, unsentimental revelation that this couple is not much different from their mediocre neighbors. This Gatsbyesque fable of thwarted dreams became Yates's signature tale, told again and again in exquisitely wrought stories and novels that critics praised for their art and condemned for their pessimism. As a result he failed to capture the larger audience that gravitated toward Cheever and Updike. Yates might have been in the running for awards, but he was always the kind of writer who just missed the prize. Let us hope Bailey will be the one finally to thrust Yates into the literary canon. He has written not merely a splendid biography of Yates—one that makes a compelling case for his subject's greatness and explains why he has been neglected—but one of the most moving and engrossing literary biographies of our times. Bailey seductively interweaves the facts and fiction of Yates's life into a fine mesh of life and literature, which, the biographer candidly notes, cannot always be disentangled. First drafts of Yates's work used real names, and even the final drafts made only superficial changes, so that, for example, his mother's nickname, Dookie, becomes Pookie. Mark Twain once said that history did not repeat itself, it rhymed. That is how Yates used fiction—as a kind of rhyme for his life.

There is wonderful comedy in Yates's self-destructiveness, just as there is in the lives of his self-destructive characters. Bailey knows how to present it:

> He wanted to be a proper country husband, a productive member of his household and community. He wanted to show he could "pull his weight," "stay on the ball," and "cope" as well or better than the most banal bore in Redding, but his efforts had a way of ending badly. One morning while his wife was fixing breakfast he went outside to burn some trash. A few minutes later he let loose an aria of obscenities, but the jaded Sheila [his first wife] simply assumed he'd stubbed his toe and went on with her business. Finally, she glanced outside: there was a brushfire in the backyard, on the edges of which Yates gamboled ineffectually. The volunteer fire department arrived in time to save their house, and a penitent Yates agreed to become a member, faithfully attending meetings every Saturday night.

Literary life is often portrayed as a competitive free-for-all; it may be that, but it can also be a heroic world in which writers like

R. V. Cassill, Grace Schulman, and George Garrett treat Yates with
an uplifting generosity and respect. Biography may strip its subjects
bare, but in this case it also brilliantly restores the life and work of
a great artist.

Living Figures

I wouldn't draw the line, as Michael Holroyd does, between the living and the dead. I do think he is right that people have a right to
"sentimentalities and silences," but I also believe a biographer has
a right to write about those sentimentalities and silences even while
the figure is living. One could easily turn Holroyd's argument
against him. It's rather sneaky to wait until the subject is dead to
expose "sentimentalities and silences." I use the word sneaky because that is exactly what Agnes de Mille said to me about her biography of Martha Graham. She wrote it while Graham was alive
and then waited more than thirty years to publish it as soon as Graham died.

De Mille called herself "sneaky," but she could live with it and
be amused by it. And I'm not criticizing de Mille. What I am criticizing is Holroyd's assumption of right and wrong. There is de
Mille's right to write and Graham's right to protect whatever she
wants to protect. Those rights clash. This is an impasse that biography simply cannot get over unless one draws artificial lines as Holroyd does. It may make the biographer feel better to think he has
such principles, but Holroyd is really no more principled than the
biographer of a living figure. He just chooses to shy away from a difficult problem.

In a "prelude" to *The Life of Henry Moore* (1987), Roger Berthoud
describes the process of researching his biography of the sculptor
during Moore's last days—the countless interviews, Moore's efforts
to be helpful and yet to remain aloof from the biographical query:
"But I've told you that before, haven't I, Roger." Berthoud remarks

on the "strange sensation" of writing a life of a living subject while knowing that subject is "unlikely to be in a fit state to read the end product, and might well not survive to see its publication, as indeed he did not." Consequently the biographer develops a "double relationship" with the subject, sociable and friendly, yet "clinical and critical."

In *Leon Edel and Literary Art*, edited by Lyall Powers (1988), Joseph Blotner writes about his friendship with William Faulkner. In "On Having Known One's Subject," Blotner describes the last seven years of his subject's life. This provided the biographer with enormous advantages, since he had a "visual memory" of his subject, of how he comported himself and spoke on different occasions. With the sanction of Faulkner's family, Blotner could approach sources in full confidence and gain their trust. Yet he admits that authorized biographers are sometimes shunned because it is assumed they are writing to please the subject's family. Friendship with Faulkner's family did prevent Blotner from asking certain intimate questions that a later biographer thought to ask. His unusually thoughtful essay describes how the biographer becomes implicated in his subject and struggles—not always successfully—to attain a proper sense of proportion and discrimination.

Lockhart, John Gibson (1794–1854)

Lockhart, an important editor of *Quarterly Review*, is best known as Sir Walter Scott's authorized biographer. His seven-volume life was an attempt to write a work that was commensurate with Scott's renown as the greatest writer of his age. Like Boswell, Lockhart had befriended his subject. Indeed, Scott was Lockhart's father-in-law. But Lockhart's work has been criticized as more of a compilation than a well-shaped book. Nevertheless Lockhart advanced the cause of biography by including so much intimate detail and, like Boswell, delving into the dynamics of the creative mind. Yet, like other authorized biographers, Lockhart tended to protect his subject and take him at his word.

FURTHER READING: Marion Lochhead, *John Gibson Lockhart* (1954); Francis R. Hart, *Lockhart as Romantic Biographer* (1971).

Malcolm, Janet: *The Silent Woman* (1994)

This provocative inquiry into the controversial life of the American poet Sylvia Plath and her husband, the English poet Ted Hughes, also probes the nature of biography and attacks contemporary biographers.

Janet Malcolm's sympathies lie with the subjects of biography, and with their families who must withstand the prying of biographers. She investigates Sylvia Plath's life in order to understand why it has occasioned so many biographies that tend to idealize her and demonize her husband, Ted Hughes, a brilliant English poet and a ruggedly handsome man whom Malcolm believes biographers have maligned.

Malcolm calls biographers professional burglars, voyeurs, and busybodies, rifling through the most intimate places in their subjects' lives. This crude delving into gossip is masked by the elaborate apparatus of notes and other documentation which make biography appear to be a legitimate enterprise. Malcolm attributes the great popularity of biography to a collusion between biographers and readers, both slavering to read other peoples' mail and to discover the secrets of other peoples' lives.

Biographies raise the same sort of ethical concerns Malcolm has identified in her book on journalism, *The Journalist and the Murderer*. The biographer, like the journalist, is driven by reportorial desire, the urge to get a story no matter how it may affect its subjects, their friends, and their families. Like the journalist, the biographer uses the interview to con people into spilling the beans, as she puts it.

To her credit, Malcolm does not absent herself from criticism. Once she decides to do a book on the Sylvia Plath phenomenon, she realizes she classes herself with other biographers rooting around for information. She too has to deal with the Hughes estate, chiefly Ted's sister Olwyn, who has been the bane of every Plath biographer. But the difference in Malcolm's case is that she is not writing a full-dress biography of Sylvia Plath, she is studying the whole literature of biography that has grown up around this intriguing poet.

Plath died a suicide in 1963 by gassing herself in an oven. She had attempted suicide once before as a teenager, and, as one of Malcolm's informants tells her, the poet was always a borderline personality, someone on the edge of doing herself in. Plath wrote poetry about suicide and attracted the attention of other poets—such as Anne Sexton, who also committed suicide.

Malcolm suggests that certain key events and texts ensured Plath's canonization as poet and feminist martyr. First, she wrote her best poetry, collected in her book *Ariel,* in the last year of her life. Until then she worked in the shadow of her husband, who later became the Poet Laureate of England and whose collections of poetry won major awards while Plath struggled to place her poems in magazines and publish them in book form. Her last poetry is vivid and sometimes extremely painful. Its highly personal tone and its use of historical metaphors—such as her allusions to the Holocaust—have attracted both intense praise and condemnation. Virtually no critic, however, denies that her final poems demonstrate genius.

Naturally, biographers would want to know why such a brilliant woman killed herself. But in 1963, the year of her death, there was no woman's movement, and Plath's work was not yet well known. What turned the corner in Plath biography, so to speak, was a brilliant memoir by A. Alvarez, a British poet and critic, writing for a British paper, *The Independent.* As its poetry editor, Alvarez had published some of Plath's poems and was one of the first to recognize their startling power and originality. He had attempted suicide himself, and he had known Plath in her last years in London. So his prose had a special authority, which reached a general audience when he included his memoir of Plath in his acclaimed book *Suicide*, frequently reprinted in paperback.

Alvarez revealed for the first time some key details of Plath's biography—her growing mastery as a poet, her estrangement from her husband Ted Hughes, and her acute suffering during her last days in a bitterly cold England, trying to take care of her two children and getting up at five in the morning to write her poetry. Alvarez, a friend of Hughes's as well, was discreet and did not mention many of the details of the Hugheses' married life. But as Malcolm shrewdly points out, the very omission of material on Hughes in Alvarez's memoir raised suspicions. What was Ted Hughes's role in Sylvia Plath's death? Ted Hughes himself was quick to see the damage Alvarez had done, but he couched his objections to Alvarez in the form of concern for Sylvia's young children and the pain that Alvarez's speculations would cause them when they were old enough to read them. Alvarez replied that he had treated Plath's life with considerable tact, reserve, and sensitivity. Malcolm does not disagree, but she persuasively demonstrates that once Alvarez articulated a vision of Plath's life and death, he opened the door wide to every sort of biographical speculation—exactly what Ted Hughes feared, and exactly what has come to pass.

Much of *The Silent Woman* concerns the efforts of Ted and Olwyn Hughes to keep the lid on Sylvia's life, to discourage and even censor unlicensed biographical interpretation. Malcolm sympathizes with them, feeling they have a right to protect their privacy, especially when it is violated by biographers looking to make a buck, or get an academic promotion, or punish Ted Hughes for his supposedly vile treatment of Sylvia Plath. For Hughes has become the villain of the story. Tales of his violence and womanizing darken the Plath biographical myth. His own poetry is violent, and it is easy to see him as a modern-day Heathcliff. He even hails from Yorkshire—Brontë country, the world of Emily Brontë's *Wuthering Heights*.

Although Ted Hughes opposed the Plath biographers because he said he wanted to protect the privacy of himself and his family, several biographers have suggested he was merely attempting to stifle and even destroy the evidence that placed him in a bad light. Hughes has contributed to this image of himself by destroying one of Plath's journals and by claiming another had been lost. His sister Olwyn, even in Malcolm's sympathetic portrayal of her and her position as literary executor, has harried biographers—even Plath's own authorized biographer, Anne Stevenson, whose biography was lambasted by many critics as a put-up job from the Plath estate.

How can Malcolm be so sympathetic to Ted and Olwyn Hughes, especially when Malcolm honestly admits their many faults and mistakes in the treatment of Plath biographers? Because Malcolm sees biography as an epistemologically problematic genre. She doubts that the biographer can know the truth about much of anything. She raises all sorts of problems with the so-called data biographers collect. Interviews, for example, are done after the subject's death or, at the very least, after the events that the biographer seeks to study. Memories fade and contradict each other. Witnesses to the events have their own agendas. There is no infallible way to tell the truth. Similarly, letters are unreliable. They seem to fix experience, but they are only expressions of the moment and cannot be taken for the subject's final or complete attitudes.

Malcolm seeks to strengthen her point by noting that biographers often overstate and dramatize. Her particular target is Paul Alexander, who reconstructs scenes from Plath's life with an immediacy and detail that cannot be verified. Even if some of his details can be traced to letters, interviews, journals, and memoirs, those details are the product of individuals with their own biases. Alexander misleads readers, Malcolm argues, by presenting a story as if it could be objectively told, when the whole mass of it is actually a collection of subjective accounts.

Of course, Malcolm is right about Alexander's sources, but her conclusions are curiously naive. If she knows that Alexander's book is skewed, she must have an idea of how to unskew it. In fact that is exactly what she attempts by analyzing Alexander's narrative. She is unfair to Alexander by making him a special case. Every biography, indeed every work of history, is open to another reading, another interpretation. The answer to a flawed biography—and every biography is flawed—is another biography, also flawed, but which corrects some of the errors in the previous biography. This is why Plath has had five biographers and will have more.

Malcolm apparently believes there is such a thing as truth, and it is whole. But the other way to look at truth is to regard it as a slow, often interrupted, accumulation of knowledge which is never whole at any point but which is constantly growing and constantly subject to revision. The great sin against knowledge and against biography that the Hugheses have committed is their effort to short-circuit this process because they feel wounded by it. Certainly they are injured by crude biographical speculation. But the Hugheses have led high-visibility lives; they have attracted precisely the kind of speculation they now want to squelch.

Malcolm concedes this point when she explains that Ted Hughes authorized the publication of Plath's autobiographical novel, *The Bell Jar*, in order to buy a piece of property. This is hardly the action of a man interested only in preserving his privacy. He does not mind profiting from Plath's literary estate, yet he insists he is on high moral ground and that only the biographers are money grubbers.

Malcolm suggests that Hughes's pecuniary motives were laced also with literary ones; that is, he had authorized the publication not only of *The Bell Jar* but of Plath's journals (with significant excisions) because of their literary quality. Even when these works showed him to disadvantage, or at least raised questions about his behavior, he was willing to release them to the public because, Malcolm argues, he could not bear to suppress literature. Malcolm may be right, but her argument is no more than ingenious speculation, because Hughes never made a clear statement about his motivations. Indeed, he never granted an interview, never cooperated even with Anne Stevenson, the authorized biographer, except to respond to a few of her questions conveyed through his sister Olwyn.

If Malcolm is shrewd in pointing out the faults and ethical dilemmas of unauthorized biographers, she is curiously blind to the shortcomings of authorized biography. Her sympathies go out to

Anne Stevenson, but Malcolm never fully acknowledges that the authorized biographer is just as likely to present a skewed version of the subject's life as the unauthorized biographer, because the authorized biographer is fatally compromised by giving up his or her independence. Malcolm even criticizes authorized biographers such as Bernard Crick, who insisted on a written guarantee that George Orwell's widow would not interfere in any way with his collection and interpretation of the data. Malcolm finds Crick's position arrogant and unfeeling, and implies that a more cooperative attitude with the subject's widow and literary executors would yield a more intimate and humane biography. It might. But the biographer knows there are tremendous pressures to see things the subject's way, or the way of the subject's family. Malcolm would be on stronger ground if she were to admit that neither biographers nor their subjects can occupy the high moral ground, and that the very process of writing biographies, whether they are authorized or not, is fraught with epistemological and ethical problems. She comes close to this position several times, but she keeps backing away from it, lured by her obviously romantic attachment to Ted Hughes, her Heathcliff, who has been done dirty by a legion of biographers.

A more academic study of biography and literary criticism, which also uses Plath as a focus, is Jacqueline Rose's *The Haunting of Sylvia Plath* (1992). The literature on Plath shows how difficult it is to separate literary and biographical interpretation, especially since Plath used the "living as figures or images" in her work, and those figures have copyright control over what they write and thus over what biographers and critics are allowed to reprint. To such living figures, literary analysis can have a personal significance unintended by the critic. Since Plath's representation of living figures is by its very nature incomplete, the efforts of critics and biographers to come to closure about her life and work cannot succeed. Rose demonstrates that the biographer or critic must maintain an open-ended and tentative approach to both Plath's biography and art.

SEE ALSO Authorized Biography; Unauthorized Biography.

The Marketplace

Since the eighteenth century, biography has been a staple of the publishing industry, and though fashions in publishing have changed,
and biography itself has gone through various developments as a literary genre, it is remarkable how constant the market for biographies
has been for nearly three hundred years. One reason for this extraordinary stability—at least in the English and American markets—is
the premium that has been put on individual experience. Anglo-
Americans have elevated individuality to a sacrosanct doctrine and
have worried whenever they espied signs that it was under attack.
John Stuart Mill fretted in the mid-nineteenth century that the English were losing some of their vaunted eccentricity, and William
Faulkner lamented in his midcentury novel *Requiem for a Nun* (1951)
that his region was being swallowed up in the uniformity of modern-
day mass society. Faulkner, at least, detected countervailing forces:
the further people are removed from their origins and sense of identity, the stronger is their desire to recover them. His insight has surely
been borne out in the success of books and television programs that
are, in essence, group biographies—best epitomized by Alex Haley's
Roots and Ken Burns's *The Civil War.*

At the beginning of the book market for biographies, eighteenth-
century booksellers had to be convinced that biographies would sell
as well as novels and histories, the mass and elite entertainments, respectively, of their day. Biography then, as today, could be made appealing if it concentrated on the famous and infamous, on heroes
and scoundrels. As now, it was then the mode to write up the lives of
criminals, adventurers, explorers, the shipwrecked, and the disaster-
prone. Robinson Crusoe, for example, had his real-life counterpart
in Alexander Selkirk.

But biography could also draw upon a distinguished ancient author, Plutarch, and claim a moral purpose in narrating individual
lives. Let it be remembered that Samuel Johnson, now such an august figure in the annals of biography, began as a hack, busily writing up the lives of the renowned and notorious while arguing on be-

half of biography as a literary form. On one occasion he conflated literary and commercial interests by writing an eloquent biography of a rogue, Richard Savage, who also happened to be a noteworthy minor poet whom Johnson had befriended.

It was the market that dictated what came to be known as Johnson's *Lives of the Poets*; a group of London booksellers persuaded him to write the acclaimed prefaces to poetry anthologies. Johnson drew on a lifetime of learning, conducted relatively little research, and wrote rapidly—like the glorious hack he was.

Biography, then, went hand in hand with the expanding capitalism of the eighteenth-century Anglo-American market. Then, as today, a poet or novelist—Robert Southey, for example—would turn to biography, writing a life of Admiral Nelson the way Norman Mailer has done with Marilyn Monroe and his book on Picasso. Curiously, Mailer has been accused of faults that could be equally detected in Johnson—slipshod research and tendentious conclusions. Yet in both cases, what made their biographies popular—notwithstanding their defects—was not merely the sensationalism of their material but the liberties they took with the evidence, allowing them to propose creative insights into their subjects that are beyond the reach of more plodding and ostensibly more serious biographers, who are also less marketable.

Does the market, then, drive biography? To a large extent it does, though not quite in the simplistic way that the term "market-driven" implies. It is not the case that only the biographies publishers want get published. Or, to be more precise, it is writers who make publishers want to publish certain biographies. Begin with what the trade publisher* needs: a biography that will sell. This almost surely means, one would suppose, a life of a well-known figure. True enough, but as soon as a biographer proposes a subject instantly recognizable to the public, the publisher is likely to say: "No,

---

*I say "trade publisher," meaning one that is concerned with turning a profit in the open marketplace, though increasingly university presses have turned to biography as a way of attracting a broader audience and significant profits.

so and so has already been 'done.'" Professional biographers refute that objection by writing book proposals* that demonstrate how much new material is to be had, or how different their treatment of the subject will be from previous biographies. The publisher's attitude, in this instance, has been a boon to biography, for it has made the contemporary biographer search sources diligently and innovatively and come to grips with style and structure.

Style and structure were precisely what nineteenth-century biographies often lacked, when it was enough to write an idealized, bowdlerized, life-and-letters treatment of a subject that a Victorian public accepted, indeed craved, in a century that celebrated progress and prosperity. Without the kind of aggressive market mentality that is manifested by twentieth-century publishers, biography as a genre, with a few significant exceptions, languished in the nineteenth century, which turned it into a reliable but staid form of literature.

Freud destroyed forever these Victorian panegyrics of the great by speculating boldly on the repressed sexuality of Leonardo and other great artists and leaders. He did not thereby destroy biography. On the contrary, individuality now became not a happy given—something one was born with and developed—but what one struggled to achieve and then maintain. The heroic battle became internalized, and the hero could be not only the soldier but the literary figure—the subject not merely of a biographical essay on the life and work, as in Johnson's day, but of the most penetrating,

---

*The advent of the book proposal, fostered by the super agent, Scott Meredith, certainly aided biographers, in that the same proposal could be submitted to several publishers at once. Not only did this increase interest in biographies, it aided biographers by providing them with immediate feedback on their subjects—not merely on whether the subjects would sell but on how publishers, who are, after all, the author's first readers, reacted to the subject. How intrinsically interesting was the subject? How would a general audience be likely to react to the biography? And since proposals traditionally contain a section on "the competition," the biographer was also forced to take a hard look at what had already been done on his or her subject—not necessarily the first thing a biographer would otherwise do.

microscopic reading of personality that seemed, even if it promised more than it delivered, scientific in its rigor.

The reading public has responded well to this new biography, pioneered by Lytton Strachey in the 1920s, which, like Freud, refused to take its subject at face value. Biographies that attempt an intimate view of the subject are often accused of purveying gossip and of uncovering secrets for the sheer delight, as it were, of creating scandal. Of course there is truth in this criticism, but it misses the point. Contemporary biography is not merely hauling down its subjects to the level of its readers, it is making accessible precisely the process of self-formation that can only be glimpsed in minute particulars, in the gradual accumulation of experience that represents the modern self.

Publishers have abetted biographers more than the critics and the academy* because they have been so open to multiple treatments of the same subjects. Although a publisher may be skeptical at first, a well-researched and well-written proposal on a familiar subject will often be bought, even as reviewers groan that they must read yet another biography of Napoleon or Lincoln or Marilyn Monroe. Certainly there can be a glut of biographies on a particular subject, but in the main several biographies on the same subject teach that the same life may be read in many different ways, depending on the nature of the available evidence (which changes as new discoveries are made and restrictions are lifted from research collections) and of the

---

*It is remarkable how little interest scholars have shown in biography, either as a literary form or as an important element of popular culture. In recent years this has been somewhat rectified with studies of the history of biography and with scholarly biographers writing books and essays on the theory and practice of biography. Nevertheless, compared with the incredible volume of work on the novel, for example, biography has clearly been slighted. It can be argued, of course, that as a genre biography has not produced the range of first-rate work found in the novel, but from a historical point of view, given the undeniable importance of biography in shaping literary opinion and in establishing a canon of great writers, the academy has been remiss both in neglecting the merits of biography per se and in failing to recognize how, practically speaking, biography has contributed to the development of literature itself.

biographer. And it is not certain that there would be as wide a field for biographers were it not for the demands of the market seeking novelty and new ways of telling old stories.

It is also true that a biography of an obscure figure, or of a slighted subject who deserves major treatment, may excite a publisher because of the quality of the biographer's writing—though publishers do seem increasingly conservative and unwilling to take risks on unknowns. Happily, university presses are beginning to publish more biographies, sometimes filling the gap opened up by trade publishers who see no profit, or not enough profit, in certain kinds of biography. Brian Boyd's biography of Vladimir Nabokov is a case in point. His contract with Simon and Schuster was canceled as soon as the publisher learned that Boyd insisted on dividing his work into two volumes. In most cases, multi-volume biographies are not a good financial investment for the largest trade houses, since after the first volume is published sales drop significantly—even for such acclaimed work as Michael Holroyd's volumes on Shaw. Boyd was fortunate not only to have Princeton University Press publish his biography in two volumes but to make it a lead title, which enjoyed large sales by university-press standards.

Similarly, university presses have sometimes acquired titles from trade houses for paperback publication. The University of Tennessee Press, for example, has published in paperback Ann Waldron's fine biography of Caroline Gordon, and the University of Massachusetts Press published in paperback Ann Hulbert's acclaimed biography of Jean Stafford. Such titles appeal to a broad literary audience while also satisfying the scholarly mission of university presses.

That university presses have not published more biography in the past is largely due to fashions in the academy. For years the "New Criticism" taught that there was virtually no value in studying an author's life, that the work of art must be discussed only in its own terms, and that it was illegitimate to bootleg biography, so to speak, into legitimate literary criticism. More recently the deconstructionists have attacked the very notion of an author and have been, for the most part, hostile to biography.

It is difficult to predict the future of biography in publishing. Based on current trends, biographers of certain subjects without mass appeal will have to turn to university or small presses, but these alternatives to trade publishing have sometimes been able to produce best-sellers and have their own impact on the market for biography. A small press may understand how to target a biography for a specific audience, relying on independent bookstores that have often been instrumental in promoting nontrade titles. But smaller publishers also need the chains: there are so few independents remaining that their influence on sales is vastly diminished. On balance, publishers' continued willingness to consider biography from virtually every kind of writer—from the journalist to the academic to the novelist and so on—bodes well for the genre. It has been said, sometimes with scorn, that anyone can write a biography—perhaps because in the lowly estimation of some, all that's required is to collect and arrange the facts. For the health of biography in the marketplace, however, the idea that one can not only read but perhaps also write a good biography has always served as the best tonic for the form, a tonic publishers have always been willing to patent and to distribute to the widest possible audience.

Modernism

Montaigne mentions how writers' lives (including his own) are a part of the writing. He just assumes this, as do Johnson and Boswell. But modernists say it's the work, the work, the work, and they coin terms like "pathography" to denigrate the biographer's interest in the life. Modernism makes a separation between art and life, elevating art into a kind of religion, and thus the biographer becomes a Judas who betrays the writer and the written word by exposing his subject's life.

Reviewing a biography of Proust in *The New Yorker* (April 3, 2000), John Updike seconded Proust's attack on the critic Sainte-Beuve for not viewing "literature as a thing apart, or at least detachable from the rest of the man and his nature." Updike favored a distinction between what he called the "creative self and the social self." In effect, said Updike, biography adds not only a new dread to the writer's life, it also subverts the autonomy of literature.

Johnson insists biographers must deal with the whole life—not just what relates to the writing. Indeed, he says the life may be more important than the writing. It often is, as with Richard Savage, one of Johnson's subjects. To me, biography is the whole story. Not just what made *Alice's Adventures* a wonderful work of literature. And no, I don't believe that art is sacred. It comes out of the glory and mess of life, and to call it sacred even "to a certain extent" is to rip away its roots. I don't claim you have to read biography in order to understand art, but if you are going to read biography, you have to have a much broader conception of what the genre is. That's what Johnson understood, and that's what has been lost in the contemporary discussion of biography.

In his biography *Samuel Johnson* (1977), Walter Jackson Bate rejects the radical split between literary biography and literary criticism begun in the 1930s and 1940s. No other form of biography separates the man from his work: "only with writers was it assumed that there should be a division of labor," with the biographer enjoined to "stay clear of critical discussion of the writer's works" and the critic to "tiptoe around biography and history. . . . If we are to find our way into the inner life of a great writer, we must heal this split between 'biography' and 'criticism,' and remember that a very large part of the 'inner life' of a writer—what deeply preoccupied him, and made him a great writer—was his concern and effort, his hope and fear, in what he wrote."

Movie-Star Biography

Until the 1980s, biographies of movie stars were the province of journalists. Often based on magazine profiles and interviews, the books were often called "clip jobs," meaning they were superficial and aimed at simply appealing to an audience of fans and other curious readers. In some cases, where the reporting was diligent and based on a solid grounding in the movie industry, these biographies were quite valuable. Writers like Maurice Zolotow and Fred Lawrence Guiles exemplify the more serious side of popular-culture biography.

Academic writers tended to focus on film directors. Influenced by the auteur theory of film developed by French writers and directors such as Francois Truffaut, American scholars equated film directors with authors. This theory made it much easier to treat films as texts akin to the literary study that academics had been trained to pursue.

Not until the early 1980s did attention shift from directors to actors. My own *Marilyn Monroe: A Life of the Actress* (1986) was the first such scholarly biography, viewing Monroe not merely as some kind of tool of Hollywood or extension of directorial styles but as an artist who contributed significantly to the shaping of her roles and of Marilyn Monroe movies that had a consistent identity regardless of who the screenwriter or director was.

Since the late 1980s it has become commonplace for scholarly presses such as Oxford University Press and the University Press of Kentucky to publish biographies of movie stars. At the same time writers like Barbara Leaming and Donald Spoto have combined accessible popular styles with a rigorous use of documentation and archival research.

One of the first books to acknowledge the full range of movie-star biography, and to assess the different styles and techniques of movie-star biographers, is Sarah Churchwell's *The Many Lives of Marilyn Monroe* (2005). Where Churchwell shines is in her anatomy of the biographer's rhetoric. Too often biographers engage in a kind of circular logic and paraleipsis (a new word for me), which means indulging in a story which the biographer then dismisses. Norman Mailer and Anthony Summers are convincingly arraigned on these charges.

The Many Lives of Marilyn Monroe is a wonderful introduction to the field. Churchwell has deftly sorted out the merits of the

major contenders—Mailer, Gloria Steinem, Summers, Spoto, Leaming, and myself—though she does not seem to realize just how much
we owe to Zolotow (who knew Monroe and saw her in action on
movie sets) and Guiles (who interviewed crucial witnesses no longer
available by the time other biographers arrived on the scene).

But Churchwell's scope extends beyond biography to include the
entire image-shaping apparatus that made Marilyn Monroe—the ad-
vertisements, photographs, magazine stories, memoirs, documentaries, docudramas, the art of Andy Warhol and others. To disagree
with some of her conclusions and to wish she had done some leg-
work is not to dismiss what is an impressive, even encyclopedic effort
to provide some order to the chaotic world of—if you will pardon
the academic expression—Marilyn Monroe and movie-star studies.

Musical Biography

Fully developed biographies of composers and other musical artists
are largely due to the advent of Romanticism. The history of musical biography has no equivalent to Vasari, who celebrated the lives
of Renaissance artists and brought to biography a keen interest in
both the artist's personality and the development of art.

The first biographies of Bach and Mozart, for example, do not
appear until the early 1800s. Such composers were regarded as heroes and prophets. Not until after Lytton Strachey's work did biographers probe the musical artist's psychology and intimate life.

Scholarly lives of composers as well as serious biographies of
popular performers—such as Peter Guralnick's two-volume biography of Elvis Presley (1994, 1999) and Gary Giddens's *Bing Crosby: A
Pocketful of Dreams, The Early Years, 1903–1940* (2001)—do not
emerge until the late twentieth century, at the same time debunking
or anti-romantic biographies appear, such as Albert Goldman's *The
Lives of John Lennon* (1988) and Kitty Kelley's *His Way: The Unauthorized Biography of Frank Sinatra* (1986).

CRITIQUE: Edmund Morris's biography of Beethoven demonstrates the contemporary biographer's effort to write for both a popular and a scholarly audience. Morris, better known as the biographer of Theodore Roosevelt and Ronald Reagan, is also a classically trained musician with a lifelong devotion to Beethoven; he writes about his "immortal beloved" with brio and wit. This book amply fulfills the promise of the "Eminent Lives" series in which it appears: short biographies to appeal to the general reader, the student, and the scholar, "To preserve a becoming brevity which excludes everything that is redundant and nothing that is significant."

Morris's subtitle—*The Universal Composer*—says it all: Beethoven is the Shakespeare of music. The composer appeals to listeners on all levels, and Morris aims to do the same, which is difficult when confronting the technical aspects of music. "The greatness of Beethoven's music cannot be fully expressed without some analysis and some reference to technical matters. Wherever possible, this has been done in plain language."

In the main, Morris succeeds in the tricky balancing act of engaging the full range of musical readers:

> The huge sonorities of the organ, particularly in the pedal register, and its capacity to prolong tones ad infinitum, combined with yet more lessons in viola and horn to produce the characteristic "sound" of Beethoven the composer: spacious, projective, multi-layered, muscular.

Packing this much into a paragraph is a good way to evoke Beethoven's resonance.

There are moments in human experience, Morris suggests, when only Beethoven will do. The biographer describes how, for example, in the aftermath of a tremendous storm that brought six feet of snow to New England in February 1978, some invisible person in Harvard Yard "threw open a second-floor window, mounted a pair of speakers on the sill, and blasted the finale of Beethoven's Fifth Symphony into the crisp air."

But there are moments, I confess, when Morris—never Beethoven—is boring, when the music lover/biographer is both too technical and too impressionistic at the same time: "The soft A-major haze introducing the second sonata turned out to be a mirage that burned off a hard landscape in D minor." A "Glossary of Musical Terms" helps but cannot really diminish the sedative effect of such sentences.

What interests me as a biographer is how Morris handles speculation: "In court, he performed piano pieces and acted as répétiteur for the elector's opera singers. (Those stage folk, we may presume, taught him a thing or two about sex.)" Boswell called biography a "presumptuous task" and then, like Morris, went on to presume. Beethoven, Morris assures us, has to fit in with adolescence as we know it: "He would have been a rare teenager if he did not delight in mounting the palace organ loft in all his finery, and letting go with the loudest possible blast from the big pipes."

How to police presumption? Describing how Beethoven wrote on the outside of an envelope that he intended to leave Vienna for Westphalia and the patronage of Jerome Bonaparte (a ploy, actually, to get the Viennese to cough up more money), Morris adds: "A biographer should resist the speculation that his envelope was allowed to lie upside down on a silver tray in the hall, preparatory to being posted, but the fact is Countess Erdödy at once embarked on a frantic campaign to keep Beethoven in Vienna." There should be a literary term for this, for invention followed by fact.

Lured into the precincts of psychobiography, Morris finds the work of Editha and Richard Sterba, two Viennese psychoanalysts, helpful in describing Beethoven's fixation on his nephew. The composer treated him as a son, wresting custody of the boy from his mother, whom he attacked in court as an unfit parent during a seven-year legal assault. Morris agrees that while Beethoven "redeemed himself with perfect works of art," he was "deeply disturbed, even psychotic." Then the biographer comments on the Sterbas: "Their arguments are persuasive, although it is in the nature of psychobiography to infer what cannot be proved."

This kind of biographer's slither is rare in Morris's straightforward narrative. He is quite aware of the perils of presumption: "When disease, and money maneuvers, and family politics, and eccentricity mix as much as they do in Beethoven's personal dealings from 1813 through 1820, speculation as to what was going on in his mind is even more risky than it normally is in biography."

What is apparent is that Beethoven had an "overengined mind and body"—he could not have produced such great art without it. But Morris's book is no throwback to biographies of earlier days that linked genius and madness. The creative mind remains undaunted no matter what the emotional upset. As Morris observes:

> Ordinary psyches often react to bad news with a momentary thrill, seeing the world, for once, in jagged clarity, as if lightning has just struck. But then darkness and dysfunction rush in. A mind such as Beethoven's remains illumined, or sees in the darkness shapes it never saw before, which inspire rather than terrify.

This is the courage of creativity. Such passages go a long way toward describing how a man who was often so wretched and overwrought could produce such sublime art. What more can one ask of biography?

BUT WHAT does a musical biographer owe the general reader? And who is this GR anyway? In Robert Gutman's sumptuously produced *Mozart: A Cultural Biography* (1999), he refers to the "nonspecialist" and the "layman" who may wish to "pass over" his "excursions into cultural, musical, and traditional history . . . without loss of biographical continuity." In other words, the GR craves the life story and must be seduced into other concerns that will yield, Gutman promises, "wider perceptions."

The GR's wishes came to mind while reading Oxford University Press's description of Julian Ruston's *Mozart* (2006), the newest addition to the Master Musicians series: "An engaging biography for general readers that will also be an informative resource for scholars." Rushton, however, puts it quite differently: "My objective has been to supply an introduction and guide to Mozart's output, usable for reference, with the appendices (calendar, worklist, and personalia) usual in the Master Musicians series."

GRs will find Rushton's biography a bore, I believe, precisely because it is not an engaging narrative and certainly no introduction, judging by language that refers to Mozart's "output" (as if he were a musical machine) and passages that begin: "The opening four bars present the simplest elaboration of tonic harmony. The chromatic touch in bars 5–6 enhances the modulation to the dominant." And it only gets more technical. The book was too much for me, a GR when it comes to music, since my credentials include a year of piano lessons when I was twelve, six months on the trombone a few years later, and a rudimentary ability to read music (learned in high school and mostly now forgotten).

Gutman cajoles the GR, whereas Rushton would prefer not to be biographical at all, concluding: "nobody would take the slightest interest in Mozart's or his wife's illnesses, his debts, his relationship with his father—still less would anyone have invented love-affairs for him, and theories of his being poisoned—if his music did not compel attention to the man behind it."

This oft-expressed denigration of biography is absurd. We all invent very rich and imaginative lives for ourselves and others, regardless of what we achieve. Liza Doolittle was certain that "they" (never mind the vague pronoun) had "done in" one of her relatives. What elaborate scenarios we invent for our neighbors and nearest of kin—whether they can compose a note or not!

Although Gutman instructs us to attend to the music, notice how thoroughly the humanity of his subject has seduced the biographer:

> The decades I have passed studying Mozart have rich recompense in both acquaintance with and loving admiration for this affectionate and generous man, an austere moralist of vital force, incisiveness, and strength of purpose who, though—like all—bearing the blame of faults and lapses, yet played his role in the human comedy

with honor, engaging with grace the frustrations of his complicated existence: his goodness of heart, unaffected charm, winning ways, and self-humor run like gorgeous threads through its web.

This is what the GR is looking for: the measure of the man who made the music. Yet Mozart biography has a long history of discounting the man, making him into the myth of the eternal child, as Maynard Solomon writes in his acclaimed *Mozart: A Life* (1995). The composer possessed an antic, childlike quality, to be sure, Solomon acknowledges. But there is also a tradition of infantilizing him, of wishing him to remain the child prodigy his father Leopold cultivated and sought to control even as he matured.

Romanticism played the hand of Mozart's father, Leopold, who believed that the "child is father of the man," and that musical talent (to paraphrase Hegel) could be expressed by empty heads. The philosopher had Mozart in mind, Solomon suggests, when Hegel wrote that "very great achievement in musical composition and performance [is] combined with considerable indigence of mind and character." Enter Tom Hulce and his daffy and diverting impersonation of Mozart in the movie *Amadeus*.

So where, dear GR, to find a book less demanding than Gutman's and Solomon's weighty works but nonetheless stimulating and in the three-hundred-page range? Not Stanley Sadie's *Mozart: The Early Years: 1756–1781* (2005), in which no major work and "very few minor ones are passed over without discussion in terms of both context and of the music itself." Sadie, who did not live to complete the second volume, depsychologizes Mozart, calling him a "professional of his time, [who] never wrote a piece of music simply because he felt like it or because of some 'inner need' but virtually always because it was in some sense a requirement." Me, I'd like to know more about the "virtually" and whether the quotation marks around "inner need" mean there is no such thing.

Sadie notes that it is "easy to criticize Leopold Mozart for his readiness to 'exploit' the talent of his children." Indeed, Solomon uses that very word, and the somewhat more circumspect Gutman nevertheless refers to the father's "raw opportunism." Such interpretations, Sadie argues, are "misguided. The notion that it could in some way be damaging to the children [not only to Mozart but to his talented sister Nannerl] to be exhibited as they were [all over the courts of Europe] is a wholly modern one, representing attitudes to upbringing and child psychology that would have been incomprehensible to a man of the eighteenth century."

But this defense of Leopold can only be maintained by ignoring Solomon's powerful picture of the father's lifelong efforts to infantilize his son, to deprive him of any emotional gratification outside his family, and to convince Wolfgang that without his father he could not function as man or musician.

And here the GR, still seeking that page-turner of reasonable length, might alight on Jane Glover's *Mozart's Women: The Man, the Music, and the Loves in His Life* (2006). Although the enticing title might arouse suspicion—is this just a potboiling, bodice-ripping biography?—it is in fact a shrewdly told story by a longtime conductor of eighteenth-century music, including twenty-five years at Glyndebourne and with London's Mozart Players.

Leopold receives no mercy from Glover. He is "tyrannical and paranoid," a man of "staggering insensitivity" to women's feelings. Cultural explanations of Leopold's character do not wash with Glover. Leopold was a brute who kept his wife, Maria Anna, at home while he toured with Wolfgang and Nannerl. Leopold's letters to Maria Anna are hectoring while Wolfgang's letters to both his mother and later to his sister (when she stopped touring) are generous and entertaining.

Mozart biographers make much of Mozart's closeness to his father, emphasizing that Leopold was responding to, not coercing, his son's genius. But it is the women, Glover maintains—especially his mother and sister, his wife, Constanze, and her three sisters—who made Mozart a man, providing him with emotional support and, in Constanze's case, a business manager.

In a chapter devoted to the composer's operas, Glover demonstrates how Mozart's affinity with women resulted in a "penetrating understanding" of his female characters. A later chapter shows that it was the women in his life, chiefly Nannerl and Constanze, who worked hardest to preserve the documents and testimony that subsequently made Mozart biographies possible. Glover's biography is not based on new material; her interpretations are not original. Instead she fulfills Gutman's idea of a biography that realigns "materials into fresh and balanced configurations." Her nemesis, Leopold Mozart, never fulfilled his desire to write a biography of his own son, but nevertheless has overshadowed Mozart biographers well into the twentieth century. Now he has been bested—to his eternal horror—by a woman! The cunning Glover ends her biography with a "Postlude," an excerpt from a letter Mozart wrote to Gottfried von Jacquin on November 4, 1787. The words explicate the chain of affection and influence that helped make Mozart into the man she so admires:

> My great-grandfather used to say to his wife, my great-grandmother, who in turn told her daughter, my grandmother, who reported it to her daughter, my mother, who used to remind her daughter, my own sister, that to talk well and eloquently was a very great art, but that an equally great one was to know the right moment to stop. So I shall follow the advice of my sister, thanks to our mother, grandmother, and great-grandmother, and put a stop not only to my moral digression, but to my whole letter.

The same can be said of Glover's matriarchal biography: She knows how to end a most diverting and perceptive narrative.

New Biography

Virginia Woolf coined the term "new biography" in a review of Harold Nicolson's *Some People* (1927). Inspired by Lytton Strachey's *Eminent Victorians*, Nicolson not only wrote with verve about his biographical subjects—some of them his friends or acquaintances— but verged on the novelist's depiction of character, inventing details, changing the names of famous people, and employing an irony that made the biographer's voice paramount. Woolf favored Nicolson's approach because it caught the lineaments of personality rather than just reporting facts and events. Biography had become a stodgy genre, in her view.

Biographers such as Emil Ludwig and André Maurois began writing the "new biography" in this Woolfian vein, presenting their subjects in dramatic relief, figures emerging boldly out of their periods, dominating their times by force of personality. By doing so, these biographers detached character from history, in so far as they were willing to go beyond the documented record. Eventually, however, Nicolson and Maurois retreated from some of their larger claims, recoiling from some of their experiments, concerned that biography would lose its moorings in fact and history.

FURTHER READING: See Ruth Hoberman's *Modernizing Lives: Experiments in English Biography, 1918–1939* (1987); James L. Clifford, ed., *Biography as an Art: Selected Criticism 1560–1960* (1962); and Peter France and William St. Clair, eds., *Mapping Lives: The Uses of Biography* (2002).

New Critics

The "new critics"—usually identified as John Crowe Ransom, Robert Penn Warren, and Cleanth Brooks—began in the 1930s to challenge historical and biographical criticism, a way of studying literature prevalent in American higher education. The new critics believed that only the work of literature itself was the critic's province. The author's biography, cultural background, and anything else extrinsic to the work of art should not be considered. Instead the author's language and style and the form of the work ought to be of paramount consideration. Even the author's own intentions should be discounted.

The merit of this approach was that it sharpened an awareness of art as an autonomous work. The critic did not have to be concerned with any criteria other than mastery of the text. Studies of metaphor and structure in the spirit of the new critics provided enormously insightful interpretations.

In practice, however, few new critics could actually separate knowledge of an author's biography and culture from the work of art. Cleanth Brooks, for example, drew on his own Southern background and understanding of Southern culture in interpreting William Faulkner's work.

Nevertheless the new critics have continued to exert influence over academic responses to biography and biographical criticism—so much so that biography per se remains a neglected aspect of literary study in spite of an explosion of literary biographies since Richard Ellmann's and Leon Edel's pioneering work in the 1950s. English majors rarely receive any grounding in literary biography, and literary biography is not itself a subject of study in the college curriculum.

FURTHER READING: For a discussion of the academic response to biography, see the introduction to Carl Rollyson, *Biography: An Annotated Bibliography* (1991).

Nineteenth-Century British Biography

One of the standard studies is A. O. J. Cockshut's *Truth to Life: The Art of Biography in the Nineteenth Century* (1974), which explores the general themes of nineteenth-century biography (especially the tension between considering the "moral welfare of the reading public" and the "personal dignity of individuals") while demonstrating a coherence of thought among biographers in dealing with "the mid-Victorian ethos of decency." Arguing for the influence of the English evangelical tradition—even on liberals and agnostics—Cockshut contends that conscience more than reason, feeling rather than thought, was the paramount value for Victorian biographers. This survey is soundly balanced by highly perceptive chapters on individual biographers: Arthur Stanley (Thomas Arnold), Samuel Smiles (*The Lives of the Engineers*), George Otto Trevelyan (Thomas Macaulay), James Froude (Thomas Carlyle), John Morley (William Gladstone), and Wilfred Ward (Cardinal Newman).

In *Victorian Biography: A Collection of Essays from the Period* (1986), the editor Ira Bruce Nadel notes the paucity of critical literature on nineteenth-century biography. His volume begins with Carlyle, who began the nineteenth-century discussion of biography that expanded into considerations of "sincerity, ethics, an suppression." Nineteenth-century critics were concerned about the biographer's motives, sense of responsibility, and art. Should a biography merely collect the facts, regardless of length, or be more selective and interpretative?—Nadel notes a tendency toward shorter, more incisive work later in the century. The volume includes essays by Thomas Carlyle, Edmund Gosse, and Sydney Lee.

Joseph W. Reed, Jr., *English Biography in the Early Nineteenth Century, 1831–1838* (1966), argues that nonliterary standards—respect for privacy and the dignity of the subject—led to the devaluation of biography as art in the early nineteenth century. Moore not only acceded to the destruction of Byron's autobiography, he suppressed important aspects of the poet's relationship with family, friends, and lovers and skewed the design of his biography by trying to interpret every aspect of the poet's life in terms of a theory of genius. In biographies of Nelson and Scott, Southey and Lockhart avoided these pitfalls, Southey elegantly selecting only those details that provided an integrated, unified vision of Nelson, and Lockhart (eschewing Boswell's reliance on dramatic scenes and conversations) evoking the characters and backgrounds of Scott's life with the assurance worthy of a great novelist.

Obituaries

Obituaries became a staple of newspapers in the nineteenth century. Local newspapers carried accounts of notable citizens but also brief notices placed by families of the bereaved. Obituaries may serve as news, informing the public of death of a prominent or famous person of achievement. They honor the death but may also be the occasion for expressing community values. Or an obituary notice may recount the scandalous life of criminals and other controversial figures.

As biography, as documented and verifiable records, however, obituaries must be treated with caution. They are often culled from secondary sources—that is, from books and other periodicals. These kinds of sources often repeat errors because they are not the product of original research or of access to primary sources (letters, diaries, public records, and so on). For example, every obituary of Jill Craigie, one of my biographical subjects, stated that she had been born in 1914 whereas my checking of her birth certificate and passports established 1911 as the correct date. Some of the obituaries got her place of birth wrong as well.

More substantial errors also appear in obituaries—often errors of omission. A controversy erupted, for example, over the *New York Times* obituary of Susan Sontag. Several editorialists pointed out that the *Times* had not mentioned the obvious fact that she was a lesbian. A *Times* editor said this fact could not be corroborated. Everyone in New York City knew the truth, however, and Sontag herself in interviews given after publication of the biography I wrote with my wife, admitted to affairs with women. This curious omission by the *Times* received national attention, especially since no other newspaper dealt candidly with Sontag's sexuality, except for the *New York Sun*, which printed my obituary.

Thus obituaries may present the public myth that the biographical subject has perpetuated rather than the actuality that can be obtained only through diligent research.

Oral Biography

Oral biography and history are probably as old as the human interest in the past. Herodotus is said to have interviewed sources, col-
lecting and preserving information that would otherwise disappear.
But as an academic discipline and a genre in itself, oral biography is
the product of the 1930s, when slave narratives were first recorded
and deposited in the Library of Congress. Then, in 1948, the historian Allan Nevins established the first oral history collection, at Columbia University.

But the methodology of oral history and biography has been a
subject for academic study only since the mid-twentieth century,
when anthropologists, sociologists, psychologists, and other professionals in the humanities and social sciences turned increasingly to
interviewing live subjects as a way of recapturing past events. Techniques of interrogation, the structure of the interview, the staging,
so to speak, of the interaction between interviewer and interviewee
have become important areas of research in themselves. How to
evaluate the role of memory, what constitutes "evidence" in an interview, how to evaluate eyewitnesses, how to assess the interviewer's
point of view—even the gender of the interviewer—are now con-
tentious issues to be explored. How to deal with ideology, folklore
(legend), individual and group dynamics are all concerns for the
scholar of oral biography and history.

In recent years oral biographies—"tape-recorder books"—have
become popular. Wallace Stevens, Norman Mailer, and Truman
Capote, for example, have been subjects for wide-ranging testi-
monies elicited from family members, fellow writers, friends, and
acquaintances. In "The Oral Biography" (*Biography*, Summer 1991,
pp. 256–266), David King Dunaway, a biographer of Pete Seeger
and Aldous Huxley, argues from his own experience and from a survey of recent oral biographies and their methodologies, noting
problems of reliability, interviewing techniques, the nature of memory, verbal performance, and the oral biographer's influence on his
subject. Dunaway points out that literary historians, folklorists, an-

thropologists, and other professional oral historians share common concerns in developing "collaborative, interactive narration," vivid detail, and "life-like phrases" while "producing comprehensive, dependable records."

In "Tough Talk: A Conversation with Peter Manso" (*Provincetown Annual,* Summer 1987, pp. 22–25, 124–128), the biographer explains his friendship and falling-out with Norman Mailer and his method of putting together his oral biography: "The premise . . . is that no one's single version of an event can be taken as accurate." Manso admits that his closeness to Mailer influenced the materials he selected and rejected, and probably contributed to Mailer's desire (in Manso's view) to control the image of himself presented in the biography.

Perhaps the most popular oral biographer/historian of our time has been Studs Terkel, whose work covers virtually the entire range of twentieth-century American history. His best work is *Hard Times: An Oral History of the Great Depression* (1977). For scholarly studies, see Michael Frisch's *A Shared Authority: Essays on the Craft and Meaning of Oral and Public History* (1990), and *Women's Words: The Feminist Practice of Oral History* (1991), edited by Sherna Berger Gluck and Daphne Patai.

Pathography

Joyce Carol Oates coined this term in the *New York Times Book Review* (August 28, 1988), apropos of David Roberts's biography of writer Jean Stafford. Pathography is "hagiography's diminished and often prurient twin." This subgenre focuses on "dysfunction and disaster, illnesses and pratfalls, failed marriages and failed careers, alcoholism and breakdowns and outrageous conduct." Its scenes are sensational, wallowing in squalor and foolishness; its dominant images are physical and deflating; its shrill theme is "failed promise" if not outright "tragedy."

According to Oates, subjects are mercilessly exposed, and the mystery is taken out of writing. In sum, writers are humiliated in this form of biography, and their achievement is obscured by sensationalistic scenes—in Stafford's case involving her alcoholism.

Like so many others of her generation, Oates falls into the modernist pitfall of elevating the work over the life (a proper notion for literary criticism but not for biography). A writer's life is his or her books, Oates insists. She seems unaware that this sentiment, in terms of biography as a genre, is of rather recent vintage.

In fact Roberts gets the proportions of Stafford's life just right. To do otherwise might satisfy readers interested in only literary achievement but certainly not those interested in biography per se, or biography as a genre.

SEE ALSO Modernism.

Plutarch (c. 46 A.D.–120 A.D.)

Plutarch is the greatest biographer of antiquity, who taught his successors how to combine depth of psychological and moral insight with a strong narrative that evokes the greatness and excitement of his subjects' lives.

Most of Plutarch's writing was not accomplished until late middle age. He was born in a Roman province to an old and wealthy Greek family. He received a comprehensive education in Athens, where he studied rhetoric, physics, mathematics, medicine, the natural sciences, philosophy, and Greek and Latin writing. His worldview was strongly influenced by Plato (c. 427–347 B.C.), and he took considerable interest in theology, serving as the head priest at Delphi in the last twenty years of his life. By the time he was twenty he had rounded out his education by traveling throughout Greece, Asia Minor, and Egypt.

Before his writing career began, Plutarch worked in Chaeronea as a teacher and was its official representative to the Roman governor. Later he undertook diplomatic trips to Rome, where he befriended several important public servants. The prestige of Greek learning stood very high in the Roman Empire, and Plutarch eventually was invited to lecture in various parts of Italy on moral and philosophical subjects. Sometime in his late thirties he began to organize his notes into essays. Evidence suggests that by the time he was forty, Plutarch enjoyed a highly receptive audience for his lectures.

Although Plutarch could easily have made a career of his Roman lecture tours, he returned to his home in Chaeronea at about the age of fifty. There he served in a number of administrative posts with the evident intention of reviving Greek culture and religion. His principal great work, *Parallel Lives*, was written in these years when his sense of civic responsibility and leadership had matured, and when he was able to draw on his considerable experience of political power.

In *Parallel Lives*, Plutarch chose to write about actual historical figures. The lives were parallel in the sense that he paired his subjects, so that Alexander and Julius Caesar, Demosthenes and Cicero, could be written about in terms of each other. It was important to have a basis of comparison, to show how equally famous men had arrived at their achievements in similar and different circumstances, with personalities that could be contrasted and balanced against each other. For Plutarch's aim was not merely to describe lives but to judge them, to weigh their ethical value and to measure their political effectiveness. Clearly he believed that human beings learned by example. So he would present exemplary lives, complete with his subjects' strengths and weaknesses, in order to provide a comprehensive view of the costs and benefits of human accomplishment.

Plutarch has often been attacked for being a poor historian. What this means is that sometimes he gets his facts wrong. On occasion he is so interested in making a moral point, in teaching a lesson, that he ruins the particularity and complexity of an individual life. He has also been guilty of relying on suspect sources, of taking reports at face value because they fit his preconceived notion of his subject.

While these faults must be acknowledged and accommodated, they should not be allowed to obscure the enormous value of Plutarch's biographies. In the first place, he realized he was not writing histories but lives, and that some of his sources were questionable. Unlike the historian, he was not primarily interested in the events of the past. On the contrary, it was the personalities of his subjects that had enduring value for him. To Plutarch, there was a kind of knowledge of human beings that could not be found in the close study of events or in the narration of historical epochs. As he puts it, "a slight thing like a phrase or a jest often makes a greater revelation of character than battles where thousands fall, or the greatest armaments, or sieges of cities." Plutarch found his evidence in seemingly trifling anecdotes about great personages. He was convinced that an intense scrutiny of the individual's private as well as public behavior would yield truths about human beings not commonly found in histories.

Plutarch thought of himself as an artist. He was building portraits of his subjects: "Just as painters get the likenesses in their portraits from the face and the expression of the eyes, wherein the character shows itself, but make very little account of the other parts of the body, so I must be permitted to devote myself rather to the signs of the soul in men, and by means of these to portray the life of each, leaving to others the description of their great contests."

As the founder of biography, Plutarch was pursuing psychological insight. Individuals were the expressions of a society, the eyes and face of the community, so to speak. He would leave to historians the description of society, "the other parts of the body."

What makes Plutarch convincing to this day is that he is loaded with perception. No biographer has surpassed him in summing up the essence of a life—perhaps because no modern biographer has believed so intensely as Plutarch did in "the soul in men." Each line in Plutarch's best biographical essays carries the weight and significance of a whole life. It is his ability to make his readers believe that he is imagining, say, Caesar's life from the inside, from Caesar's point of view, that makes Plutarch such an attractive source that Shakespeare and many other great authors have freely borrowed from him.

It has often been said that no biographer can truly penetrate his or her subject's mind. But Plutarch perfected a way of reading external events, of shaping them into a convincing pattern, until—like a great painting—his prose seems to emit the personality of his subject. Here, for example, is his account of Caesar's ambition:

> Caesar's successes . . . did not divert his natural spirit of enterprise and ambition to the enjoyment of what he had laboriously achieved, but served as fuel and incentive for future achievements, and begat in him plans for greater deeds and a passion for fresh glory, as though he had used up what he already had. What he felt was therefore nothing else than emulation of himself, as if he had been another man, and a sort of rivalry between what he had done and what he purposed to do.

These two long sentences, with their complex clauses, are imitative of Caesar's life itself, for they demonstrate how ambition drove him on—not satisfying him but actually stimulating more exploits. Here was a great man who had set such a high example for himself that his life had turned into a competition with itself. Plutarch manages the uncanny feat of having Caesar looking at himself and thereby gives his readers the sensation of momentarily occupying Caesar's mind.

Plutarch was by no means interested only in men of great political and military accomplishment. His pairing of Demosthenes and Cicero, for example, is his way of paying respect to mental agility and the power of the word. Both men prepared for their public careers as orators through long, careful training, but their personalities were quite different. Cicero was given to extraordinary boasting about himself whereas Demosthenes rarely spoke in his own favor. If Cicero was sometimes undone by his penchant for the joke, there was nevertheless a pleasantness in him almost entirely lacking in Demosthenes.

That two such different men should have parallel careers is surely part of Plutarch's point. There is no single pathway in life to success or failure, and personal faults, far from being extraneous, may determine the fate of a career. Shakespeare realized as much when he based much of his *Coriolanus* upon Plutarch's interpretation of the Roman leader's choleric character and his devotion to his mother.

Most of *Parallel Lives* seems to have been written in the last twenty years of Plutarch's life—precisely at that point when he was most seriously occupied as a religious official, statesman, and diplomat. His studies of philosophy and religion surely gave him the confidence to assess the lives he would have his readers learn from.

As suggested in the second edition of the *Oxford Classical Dictionary*, Plutarch was most concerned with the education of his heroes, whose stories proceeded from their family background, education, entrance into the larger world, climax of achievement, and fame and fortune (good and bad). He exerted a profound influence on the Roman world of his time, on the Middle Ages, and on a group of important writers—chiefly Montaigne (1533–1592), Shakespeare (1564–1616), Dryden (1631–1700), and Rousseau (1712–1778). If his impact is less obvious in modern times, it is probably because there is less confidence in the moral patterns that Plutarch boldly delineated. What biographer today can speak, as Plutarch did, to the whole educated world, knowing that he had behind him the prestige and the grandeur of Greek literature and religion?

FURTHER READING: C. J. Gianakaris, *Plutarch* (1970); D. A. Russell, *Plutarch* (1973); Alan Wardman, *Plutarch's Lives* (1974); Scardigli, Barbara, ed., *Essays on Plutarch's Lives* (1995).

Political Biography

Candid political biographies do not emerge in Britain or the United States until the twentieth century. Victorian political biography amassed considerable documentation and remains valuable as fact-gathering. But political biographers then tended to extol their subjects and suppress unflattering, intimate details. In America, political biographers saw their task as contributing to nation-building tasks, so that preserving the iconic power and probity of subjects remained their paramount interest.

The advent of Freud and Strachey, however, destroyed the surface polish of political biography. Suddenly the biographical subject's peculiarities, quirks, and unconscious behavior became fair game. Freud's collaboration with William Bullitt on a biography of Woodrow Wilson is one sign that political figures no longer were taken at their word—not just about politics but about their lives in general.

It is still the case, however, that certain kinds of political biographies operate with blinders. Britain has what might be called the policy biography, written by a group of British historians who take a major political figure and transform his life into a kind of policy debate. One can read, for example, half a dozen biographies of Neil Kinnock and learn very little about his marriage, his children, and the internal dynamics of his intimate world.

When I made it clear that I would include in Jill Craigie's biography a chapter on her husband Michael Foot's affair with a young Pakistani woman, Michael's friends put considerable pressure on me to suppress the story, even though it was a central event in his life (the woman threatened blackmail) and a major disruption in his marriage. They worried that this former leader of the Labour party would suffer not only embarrassment but that many in the party who thought of him as a sort of saint of the left would be disillusioned. Brian Brivati, author of a biography of Labour leader Hugh Gaitskill, confronted the wrath of Gaitskillites who deplored his candid description of Gaitskill's Conservative mistress.

Perhaps the finest political biographer of the age—if the criteria includes an effort to measure all aspects of the man and his politics—is Robert Caro, who is as penetrating about LBJ's love life as he is about his subject's drive for power. Similarly Blanche Wiesen Cook's two-volume biography of Eleanor Roosevelt provides a far more probing portrait of Eleanor (especially her relationships with women) than did Joseph Lash's hagiographic volumes.

A really outstanding study of the development of political biography has yet to be written. The best one can do is consult collections of essays by biographers such as Ben Pimlott, *Frustrate Their Knavish Tricks: Writings on Biography, History, and Politics* (1995).

FURTHER READING: Eric Homperger and John Charmley, ed., *The Troubled Face of Biography* (1988).

CRITIQUE: Another kind of political biography, of course, is the politician's account of his own life. Here personal and public life often appear in rather evasive and uneasy tandem—as I suggest in this review of Governor James McGreevey's autobiography.

Autobiography is often an exercise in absolution—and never more so than when it is titled *The Confession* (2006). James Mc-Greevey, former altar boy and New Jersey governor, invokes church fathers (St. Thomas Aquinas, for example), in his quest to come clean. But the genre he has chosen is not the appropriate form of apologia, since by its very nature it is also an exercise in exculpation. Even more so when the subject has a collaborator, in this case David France, who possesses, in McGreevey's words, "the gift of language."

To put it another way, McGreevey is still a politician, and his book has to be regarded as a political act. Why should France, who gets only one sentence in the acknowledgments, be regarded as other than a kind of speechwriter and damage control expert?

The back of McGreevey's book jacket features his proclamation: "History books will all say I resigned in disgrace. That misses the point entirely. Resigning was the single most important thing I have ever done. I'd rejected a political solution to my troubles and took the more painful route: penance and atonement, the way to grace." But resigning was a political solution. When McGreevey announced he was leaving office because he was gay, I joined my South Jersey neighbors in wondering what was really behind the governor's resignation. That he was gay was no surprise to many of us, since tales about his cavorting in Cape May were common.

What bothered his constituents (Democrats and Republicans)— at least the ones I talked with—was his duplicity. Evidence of corruption in his administration was mounting, and the gay tie-in mattered only in so far as he had appointed Golan Cipel, his lover, to a position in homeland security that, in McGreevey's own words, reflected a "spectacular lapse of judgment."

You can say that again. Cipel's appointment, remember, was an outrage not merely because the governor was in love with him (Cipel claims he was sexually harassed but never had consensual sex with McGreevey) but because Cipel had no qualifications for the sensitive role he occupied. This was no minor office but one that involved overseeing the safety of New Jersey citizens.

Writing an autobiography, especially one that avoids detailed exploration (naming names) of "pay to play" (the phrase now used for awarding government positions and contracts to major campaign contributors), obfuscates what had to be the more complicated and compromising circumstances under which McGreevey resigned. His personal story is riveting (kudos to France), but McGreevey's former constituents and historians deserve much more.

Perhaps legal reasons restrain McGreevey, as well as a desire not to embarrass his political mentors and allies. Just so. That is why autobiography—at least at this stage—is problematic. Even on the personal level, though, McGreevey cannot convey the full story of his gay sensibility. He disguises the names of former lovers going all the way back to early adolescence, and mounts a fierce defense of his parents, rejecting the clichés about familial and environmental factors that shape a gay sensibility. McGreevey is squarely in the biological camp, believing that nature, not nurture, produces homosexuals. Consequently he never forthrightly analyzes the nexus between his Roman Catholic upbringing and his sexual orientation.

When referring to his closeted life, McGreevey notes that all politicians are in the closet, hiding from public view the deals they make to get elected and to stay in power. Like McGreevey, all politicians, in other words, are duplicitous.

McGreevey does not seem to realize that there are many aspects of his troubling life that amount to more than he can say—even with the best of intentions. What is needed here, of course, is biography, not autobiography. What is required is an independent biographer with access to McGreevey but also an unflinching dedication to flushing out the sources that McGreevey would just as well hide. In other words, what is essential is a writer whose first loyalty is to the truth and not to concerns about hurting others. It is understandable that McGreevey wants to protect friends and former lovers, but that is exactly why he should not be the one in control of the story.

I can only hope there is already a biographer on the case, investigating not only McGreevey's life but also the New Jersey political machine that makes McGreeveys possible. Now that would be an edifying tale!

SOME BIOGRAPHIES of political figures effectively eviscerate politics and instead concentrate, to the detriment of the biography, on personality, not policies. A case in point is Disraeli, whose colorful character makes it easy to focus on the man and not his career.

You must meet two requirements to enjoy *Disraeli: The Victorian Dandy Who Became Prime Minister* (2006). First have a profound ignorance of British politics and no desire to rectify the problem. Second, venture no curiosity whatsoever about Benjamin Disraeli's place in British literature and be content with potted summaries and reports of what the critics said about his novels.

Christopher Hibbert breezes through Disraeli's political career, not stopping to explain what was at stake in the Reform Bill of 1867, the rivalry between Gladstone and Disraeli, or how it was that this "sham-Jew" (as Thomas Carlyle indelicately called Disraeli) attained the pinnacle of power, serving twice as prime minister and being hailed as one of Britain's greatest political leaders.

To be sure, Hibbert lauds Disraeli's powers as an orator and cites his indefatigable electioneering, his savoir faire in both the social and political spheres. And an apt summary comes at the end of this biography that alludes to its subject's compassionate conservatism, which attracted the middle and working classes to the Conservative party's program. But for the most part the biographer seems content to quote extracts from Dizzy's letters demonstrating what a wit and flatterer he was—"laying it on with a trowel," Dis (another of his nicknames) said, especially when it came to advising Queen Victoria.

As a personality, Disraeli is superbly drawn. Here is Hibbert at his best:

> When he went out in the evening he was careful not to dress as the articled clerk he was determined not long to be [Disraeli reluctantly assented to his father's plea that he study the law], setting himself apart from his colleagues by a style of dress—a black velvet suit with ruffles and black stockings with red clocks—as well as a manner which was considered flamboyant, even in those early years of the reign of King George IV. 'You have too much genius for Frederick's Place [where Disraeli clerked],' a lady pleased him by suggesting one day. 'It will never do.'
>
> His manner, so another lady remarked, was entirely fitted to his 'rather conspicuous attire' and his theatrical gestures as he 'delivered himself of high-flown compliments and sharp asides.' He performed his duties in Frederick's Place adequately; but, like Charles Dickens, who started work in a small firm of solicitors a few years later, he yearned for other things. The books he read in his father's library, the distinguished men he met at work, and the conversations he had heard at [the publisher] Murray's dinner table stirred his imagination and ambition. He felt himself worthy of a more dramatic future than that promised by the testaments and conveyances and ledgers of Frederick's Place, Old Jewry.

Disraeli never lost his sense of drama. In the House of Commons he would introduce his salient points with a modest cough while waving an immaculate white handkerchief under his nose. When attacked during parliamentary debate he remained immobile, seeming to repose like the Sphinx itself.

Assailed at a time when liberals, conservatives, and radicals alike indulged in anti-Semitic slurs, Disraeli did not even try to stem the prejudicial tide. Although his father had him baptized in the Church of England, Disraeli was proud of his Jewishness and did not trouble to assimilate as a conventional public man. On the contrary, he was Byronic and opportunistic, a favorite of the ladies but also an increasingly forceful figure in Conservative party circles because he worked hard for other candidates and pulled his weight.

A careerist, Disraeli attacked the Conservative prime minister, Sir Robert Peel, after Peel declined to admit Disraeli into his Cabinet. Not content to register his own dissent, Disraeli became the leader of several rebellious Conservatives who called themselves "Young England."

It was this latter move that fueled Disraeli's ascent, making him the champion of a cause: the renewal of the British aristocracy, on the one hand, and the promotion of enhanced respect for the common people, on the other, a combination that would lead to a new national spirit. While this program was somewhat fanciful, it nevertheless provided a kind of emotional patriotic platform that catapulted Disraeli beyond the bigotry of party regulars.

Hibbert shows no interest in exploring how Disraeli attached the engines of a political party to his personality, or the extent to which Disraeli's fiction furthered his success. What influence did Disraeli's novels actually have? Were they any good? These are elementary questions that any reader of a Disraeli biography wants answered. One novel, *Sybil, or the Two Nations* (1845), which is part of a trilogy, drove home Disraeli's understanding of the plight of the poor and the complacency of the upper classes. The other two parts, *Coningsby* (1844) and *Tancred* (1847), "may be regarded as the first truly political novels in English," Margaret Drabble writes in *The Oxford Companion to English Literature.*

Why Hibbert does not address Disraeli's novels as important turning points in his life, let alone in British literary history, is puzzling. Critics disagree about how seriously to take Disraeli's novels, but Hibbert does not even try to adjudicate between them. Indeed, when he says that, like Dickens, Disraeli rarely created believable female characters, his judgment must be challenged. Disraeli felt more comfortable in the company of women—as Hibbert himself reports—and he took them seriously, evincing, Drabble observes, "a skill in the characterization of clever women."

Disraeli the novelist and Disraeli the politician were of a piece, as his statement in 1848 (seventy years before women were granted the vote) shows:

> In a country governed by a woman, where you allow women to form part of the other estate of the realm—peeresses in their own right, for example—where you allow a woman not only to hold land, but to be a lady of the manor and hold legal courts, where a woman by law may be a churchwarden—I do not see, when she has so much to do with State and Church, on what reason . . . she has not a right to vote.

Why Hibbert, who quotes the above passage, steadfastly refuses to link the writer and the politician is mystifying. Evidently the biographer and his publisher believe plenty of readers will be satisfied with his lively style and his focus on Disraeli as suave diner-out, a fancy-pants young man playing the exotic Jew, a gustatory traveler to foreign parts, an uxorious husband, and a wily pol. So he was— but he was so much more.

A GOOD EXAMPLE of a biography that manages to maintain a sharp political focus without forsaking a full development of the subject's personality is Richard White, Jr.'s study of Huey Long. Fortunate is the biographer who has Huey Long as a subject. The colorful King-fish (a nickname Long appropriated from the popular radio show *Amos 'n' Andy*) has always been good copy because his whole life was politics, thus there is no strain involved in distinguishing the private from the public man. Politics consumed him; as he told his wife, Rose, it was not possible for him to lead a normal life. His son, Russell, remembered his father taking him to the movies only to slip out shortly after the film began in order to attend yet another political meeting.

Often called a demagogue—in American terms, a rabble-rouser—Long had a gift for the homespun analogy and thought of himself as a man of the people. T. Harry Williams, Long's 1970 Pulitzer Prize–winning biographer, quotes his unapologetic subject as pointing out that his depression-era political program amounted to demagogy "because in the old Greek parlance that meant the language that was acceptable to the majority."

In *Kingfish: The Reign of Huey P. Long* (2006), Richard White provides many examples of the down-to-earth Kingfish. Responding to those who deplored his destroying of the old mansion that had been good enough for previous Louisiana governors and replacing it with a towering Art Deco edifice, Long memorably said: "I can see where the criticism is sound. It reminds me of the old man who keeps a boarding house. When one guest complains that the towel is dirty, he says, 'People have been wiping on that towel for a month without complaining. I don't see what's the matter with you.'"

No Long biographer is certain about Long's sex life. Little is known about his marriage or if he had affairs. Williams interviewed nearly three hundred family members, friends, associates, and enemies and never could determine whether, for example, Long had an affair with his pretty secretary, Alice Lee Grosjean, whom he later made secretary of state. She was efficient and utterly loyal, but was she also his mistress? To this day no one seems to know.

But one thing is certain: if Huey had had his way, everyone in Louisiana—and in the country—would have been Longized. His opponents referred to his corruption of the state legislature by calling it the Longislature. A brilliant attorney, despite never having completed law school—or much other formal schooling, for that matter—Long drafted laws by the hundreds. At the height of his power he compelled lawmakers to pass his bills without even reading them. He even abolished the state bar organization, recreating it à la Long. He undermined the judiciary, packing courts with his own cronies, and placed, it seemed, every member of his large family on the state payroll—except (he liked to joke) those in the penitentiary. Elected to the U.S. Senate in 1930, he installed a puppet governor and continued to run Louisiana, all the while blasting Franklin Roosevelt for not instituting Long's radical Share the Wealth program, which would make "every man a king"—the catchphrase of Long's autobiography and the call to action that at one point inspired more than eight million people to join Share the Wealth clubs.

Long had a Napoleonic restlessness and was often accused of running a dictatorship. But, like Bonaparte, Long also had a code— a populist program aimed at annihilating the old guard and the corporations that supported it. Long supplied the state's children with free textbooks. He built thousands of miles of roads, and he modernized Louisiana.

Undeniably Long was unscrupulous in achieving his often laudable ends, as Robert Penn Warren eloquently dramatized in his Pulitzer Prize–winning novel, *All the King's Men* (1946). Headed for a great fall (he would die by an assassin's bullet in 1935), Long provided the model for Warren's Willy Stark, a more self-aware and tragic character who dies lamenting that it could have been different, that he need not have so confused means and ends. The closest Huey Long came to adopting that point of view was expressing regret that no means other than his ruthlessness seemed available to achieve equity for the majority.

White has produced a taut and riveting narrative that is true to his subtitle. He is concerned with a reign of power, not with the whole man or with the myth that is greater than the man. For White, Long's finest period was his first two years as governor (1928–1930), when he made good on many of his promises to the people. After that he degenerated into a demagogue, pure and simple, one who talked reform but actually did little to change the structure of politics or government. Perhaps the worst crime in White's indictment is Long's exploitation of the state's natural resources—chiefly oil—which through government leases lined the pockets of a few multi-millionaires, thus depriving the state of the means to better the lot of its citizens.

Call White's book, then, a political biography of the highest order, but not, certainly, a full-scale biography. White calls Williams's
1969 biography "a landmark in oral history" that "stands alone in
size and detail," though it is also "at times needlessly apologetic regarding Long's ruthless methods."

Strike "needlessly" and replace "apologetic" with "empathetic."
Perhaps because Williams spoke with so many of Long's contemporaries, perhaps because the historian taught at Louisiana State University (which Long built into a first-class institution), and perhaps
because he seemed swayed by the myth of the man Warren portrayed, Williams presented a more appealing biographical subject.

Whereas White zeroes in on Long's subversion of state laws,
Williams focuses on the conservative opposition, which used those
laws to concentrate power in their hands. After only a year in the
governor's office, Long was impeached, only to be saved by the state
senate. White emphasizes that Long's opposition had a good case,
and while Williams does not deny the point, he shows that the opposition did not hold the ethical high ground and that, in fact, one
of its leaders, Lieutenant Governor Paul Cyr, who would have re-
placed Long, was detested by many of the impeachers.

Thus the two biographers do not disagree on the facts so much
as on where the emphasis should lie. They also divide company
when it comes to the rhetoric of biography. White is all business,
deftly laying out Long's devious politics. Williams, in contrast,
might almost be Plutarch, enveloping his central figure in a rich historical context (devoting ten pages or so, for example, to what it
meant to be a Southern demagogue and why Long, who did not
play the race card but did actually implement reform, was no typical demagogue):

> It is sometimes said, by reputable historians who like to think that
> the course of history is foreordained, that Huey Long was an in-
> evitable product of conditions in Louisiana. . . . Sooner or later a
> reform leader would have appeared. But that leader could have
> been a very mild reformer who would have satisfied popular desire

for change with relatively little change, or he could have been a charlatan who would have propitiated the people with mere rhetoric. He did not have to be a Huey Long. But it was Huey Long who appeared, a man of great power, with the capacity within him to bring about large and even revolutionary change, and to do much good—or evil.

Elsewhere, Williams calls Long "an artist in the use of power," lauding his political imagination, as did W. J. Cash and other profound commentators on Southern politics. The symbiosis here between Warren's novel and Williams's biography is intense. Whereas White wraps up Huey's final hours, spent dying from a gunshot wound, in a few paragraphs, Williams brings us to the deathbed:

> At times he passed into unconsciousness and then revived and talked wildly, as though he saw visions beyond the hospital walls. He saw the people out there, the poor people of America, a mass of faces, staring at him, needing him, wanting to give him power so that he could help them . . . the one-gallus farmers of the hill lands of the South . . . the white and black sharecroppers in the broad cotton fields . . . the gaunt and debt-ridden farmers of the Great Plains . . . the unemployed factory workers tramping the streets of the Northeast . . . the small businessmen all over the country pushed to the wall by big business . . . the pathetic elderly couples in countless towns and villages whose life savings had disappeared with the collapse of the banks . . . the fresh-faced boys and girls eager to gain an education . . . they looked at him and trusted him . . . and they would give him power.

At other times, Williams reported, Long spoke quite rationally and soberly. Most eyewitnesses to his passing remember Huey, a man of titanic energy, saying, "God, don't let me die. I have so much to do."

This Long is glimpsed occasionally in White's parsimonious prose, such as when Huey inspects the new LSU grounds and halts the cement mixers, telling the construction crews to wait a year and lay down cement paths where the students actually walk; when he shows up at a bank threatened with failure brandishing a $265,000 check, telling depositors not to attempt a withdrawal because he will take the state's money out first, leaving them with nothing (the bank was saved); and when he tells that story about the dirty towel in the boardinghouse.

For Huey Long, politics was the great leveler, whether we know it or not. White's many virtues notwithstanding, that Long is available only in the work of T. Harry Williams.

ANOTHER recent development in political biography is the focus on political wives, who present a problem for biography. Insofar as Dolley Madison was a perfect helpmeet—and she did set the standard for later first ladies—she is not a subject in her own right. What did Dolley think of the War of 1812? Was there a shade of difference between her view of slavery and her husband's? There is no way to tell because she subsumed herself in President Madison's political program.

In *A Perfect Union: Dolley Madison and the Creation of the American Nation* (2006), Catherine Allgor deals with aspects of the person inside the larger historical and political context. Dolley was particularly fond of one of her sisters and worked hard to corral family members within her political compound, so to speak. She was gracious to everyone and included her husband's political enemies in her parties in an effort to soften the harsh rivalry between Federalists and Republicans.

Dolley (everyone seemed to call her Dolley at a time when even husbands and wives referred to each other by last name) cultivated what we now know as the aspiration to be "well liked." She dressed elegantly and fashionably but also wore American fabrics and made sure she did not appear too queenlike at the court she constructed during her husband's presidency.

James Madison, a rather fragile physical figure in comparison to Jefferson, Burr, and other robust contemporaries, needed an outgoing mate to attract a social following in the raw environs of Washington City, as it was then called. Congressmen like John Randolph brought their hunting dogs to public meetings and thought nothing of settling debates by coming to blows. By promoting a lively social scene, Dolley tempered these excesses, since even Randolph would not strike another man in a woman's presence.

Allgor provides this background to Dolley's triumphs with scholarly aplomb. Dolley shines among a stunning cast, especially in comparison with the shifty, rather thuggish Jefferson, who enjoyed humiliating British envoys when Madison was his secretary of state, and with the wily Henry Clay (the "Great Compromiser"), who exclaimed, "Everybody loves Mrs. Madison"—to which she rejoined, "That's because Mrs. Madison loves everybody."

Of course, not everyone did love Dolley, nor Dolley everyone. Malicious critics accused her of having an affair with Jefferson, though Allgor's account offers no evidence of that. She once told a close friend, "It is one of my sources of happiness, never to desire a knowledge of other peoples' business." If true, of course, that sentiment would have made her a pitiful political wife. But to the contrary, she served as her husband's spy. Her parties were intelligence-gathering activities.

Here again is where Dolley herself fades into the big picture:

> Dolley's role in the [her husband's presidential] victory proved paramount. Though psychological effect is hard to quantify, no election can be won without it. Always a person who put on a good public face, she submerged her true feelings, presenting a serene and gracious persona to the outside world. The work of political campaigning—the weekly parties, the daily visits, and the constant entertaining—paid off.

Acrimony abounded in the Republican ranks, but Dolley knew how to assuage it. What she thought of her husband's rivals, however, and how she learned to temper her own opinions, are unanswerable questions. Historians do not even know, Allgor points out, if Dolley kept her grievances to herself or dispatched them in her correspondence, since a considerable number of her letters were destroyed at her behest.

On one matter, though, Dolley is starkly shown. She had a cousin, Edward Coles, who served as Madison's secretary. He was, in Allgor's words, a "charming, intelligent, deeply thoughtful man," and a bachelor devoted to the Madisons. Dolley said he was a "great fidget & is hard to marry." But as Allgor points out, Coles had much to fidget about: he did marry, years later, when he had resolved the dilemma of his life. The immorality of slavery troubled Edward Coles, and he often argued with James Madison about it. Edward would go on to move his slaves to Illinois, free them with land of their own, and settle there himself for a time, his life a reproach to slaveholders and to his Albemarle County neighbor and friend, Thomas Jefferson.

Did Edward also quarrel with Dolley about slavery? And what did she say? Allgor evidently does not know. But it is not hard to surmise Dolley's response to her uneasy cousin, for she had next to no ability to imagine slaves as human beings. Allgor makes plain Dolley's deficiency: "On occasion, [she] acknowledged emotions in enslaved people but only for the purpose of manipulation, to ensure good and dependable service." This is an extraordinary mind-set, not to be excused by the customary notion that Dolley was simply a product of her age. While furnishing the White House, for example, she employed free blacks as well as her own slaves. She could not, evidently, see that to engage the services of free men of color made a mockery of her own pretense of ownership over the lives of others. And yet, Allgor points out, the Madisons, "in direct contrast to their neighbors, also freed slaves on occasion."

What to make of these "occasions"? Allgor rightly concludes:

> Celebrated as she was for her good heart and her warm personality, Dolley seems to have been quite cold on this particular subject. This affect, along with Dolley's refusal or inability to understand why her slaves might steal or otherwise resist, might well have stemmed from the need to distance herself from the reality of the situation and to deny her participation in it.

Indeed, without that distancing device, who knows, the polished and poised first lady might have begun to fidget. It is in fugitive moments such as the above passage on slavery where Dolley comes alive. Fortunately Allgor, an astute historian and biographer, makes the most of them.

THE VAST literature of political biography is a good way to assess the different options open to the political biographer. Consider Winston Churchill, who is central to our understanding of twentieth-century historical and biographical writing. This claim would have sounded preposterous a generation ago when—as historian John Lukacs noted in *Churchill: Visionary, Statesman, Historian* (2002)—there was a lull in Churchill studies. Even now, in some quarters, my contention may seem extravagant; it isn't.

Robin H. Neillands, in a sparkling new biography for beginners of Churchill—*Churchill: Statesman of the Century*—reports that more than five hundred books on the subject have been published since Churchill's death in 1965. The state funeral—a very rare honor that put Churchill in Admiral Nelson's and the Duke of Wellington's company—partly accounts for his apotheosis. Broadcast in the television age, the ceremony and its awesome sense of the past coming to a close in pageantry expressing the continuity of British history is powerfully evoked in the closing chapter of Lukacs's book.

The Churchill revival is also a stunning rebirth of a vision of history that professional historians spent a century censuring. Thomas Carlyle's great-man theory of history was regarded as protofascist when it was not being derided as a simplistic, romantic conception. It is the events that make the man, not the man who makes the events, the chastising anti-Carlyleans averred, and they dominated historical writing for the better part of the twentieth century. For such thinkers, biography distorted the historical process by making politics and much else a matter of personality.

This devaluation of individuality is precisely what Martin Gilbert confronted at Oxford in 1960, several years before he embarked on the official biography of Churchill—eventually eight volumes, with fifteen more of accompanying documents. As Gilbert wrote in his indispensable biographer's memoir, "In Search of Churchill: A Historian's Journey" (1994), he began his graduate work on the

> post-1917 struggle for power in the Ukraine, then on British rule in India. I have since learned that Churchill had rather a lot to say on both, and had taken a lead in policies and controversies regarding both. Yet neither of my supervisors, both of them deeply versed in their subjects, directed me towards any of his writings either autobiographical or historical.

Gilbert's knowledge of Churchill was, in his own word, "abysmal." Indeed, there is still little place for Churchill's biography or his own historical writings in the academy; but outside of it, there is a mania for Churchill. Why?

To be sure, he had his day in the spring of 1940, when Britain stood alone against Hitler, though even an admirer like Lukacs admits in *Five Days in London, May 1940* that Churchill could not win the war but only keep his country from losing it. Debunking historians like John Charmley in *Churchill: The End of Glory* (1992) argue that Churchill would have done better by Britain if he had made a separate peace with Hitler, thereby preserving as much of the British Empire as possible and avoiding a humiliating postwar reliance on an ascendant America.

Charmley's views are as much anti-American as they are anti-Churchill, but in an ironic way Charmley's animus reveals the heart of Churchill's continuing appeal. The essential sources here are Gilbert's book, *Churchill and America*, and John Ramsden's *Man of the Century: Winston Churchill and His Legend Since 1945*, because both historians regard the United States as the key player in elevating Churchill to world historical status.

Roosevelt and Stalin were the victors of World War II, and Churchill was the junior partner, representing an empire on its way out. Yet Churchill was the one who recognized the United States' potential as a world leader. This is the foundation of his unassailable place in this nation and what made him a world power even as his own land declined. Gilbert might as well have called his book "The American Churchill" or "Churchill: The American," since from Churchill's earliest days he embraced this country's potential as a world leader and what he liked to call the partnership of the English-speaking peoples.

Churchill's pro-Americanism was no mere sentimental tic—a product of the fact that his mother, Jennie Jerome, was born in Brooklyn—or a ruse to edge Roosevelt into the war on Britain's side. As Gilbert documents in an appendix, Churchill made sixteen trips to the United States, the first in 1895 and the last in 1961. He loved American energy and what we call "makeovers." In Britain, Gilbert reports, Churchill's changes of party (Conservative to Liberal to Conservative again) provoked a political opponent to call him "half alien—and wholly reprehensible." Gilbert cites a World War I colleague commenting: "There's a lot of Yankee in Winston. He knows how to hustle and how to make others hustle too."

Yet in 1940, at the age of sixty-five, Churchill was regarded as not merely a failure but a reckless adventurer; he seemed to many a dicey replacement for the steady, if not very imaginative, Neville Chamberlain. Churchill's dismal record is retailed in Robert Rhodes James's impressive *Churchill: A Study in Failure, 1900–1939* (1970). He had never really recovered from his part in the World War I disaster in the Dardanelles. As early as 1913, Rebecca West referred to Churchill as "that pathetic figure whose lack of political success is an eternal warning to opportunists that there are some souls for which the devil does not care to pay a price."

In *In the Footsteps of Churchill: A Study in Character*, Richard Holmes identifies a narrowness in the British character, especially among intellectuals, which made the expansive, "American" Churchill—especially during the 1930s—the odd man out, with his tiresome opposition to appeasement and his emphasis on rearmament. Holmes, a British historian who takes a very American tack by calling Churchill "Winston," demonstrates that his subject was indeed struggling against a mind-set. As Churchill himself put it in a speech to the Royal Society of St. George (April 24, 1933, quoted by Holmes):

> The worst difficulties from which we suffer do not come from without. They come from . . . a peculiar type of brainy people always found in our country, who, if they add something to its culture, take much from its strength. Our difficulties come from the mood of unwarrantable self-abasement into which we have been cast by a powerful section of our own intellectuals.

With his American bravado, Churchill was energized. And it was precisely the "can-do" spirit in Winston Churchill—and in Winston Churchill alone—that enabled him to save his country. In his several books on Churchill, John Lukacs shows what a near thing it was for Churchill in those tense Cabinet meetings in May 1940. Arriving at an understanding with Hitler did not seem an unreasonable proposition to British leaders who did not have Churchill's conviction that sooner or later America would enter the war, and that it was worth fighting on even if it meant, in guerrilla fashion, taking the action to the very fields and streets of Britain. Churchill was not a man, he was *the* man, thanks to the force of his will and his words.

Many recent books make this point. Geoffrey Best's *Churchill: A Study in Greatness* (2003) is the best one-volume Churchill biography. "I have been pleased," he writes, "to adopt other writers' judgments where they have said things better than I could have done or have at any rate said them first. I am grateful to have found so many sturdy shoulders to stand upon. . . . Regarding the many aspects of Churchill's life which have become matters of persisting controversy, however, I have enjoyed making my own mind up." With such an attitude, it is not hard to understand why Best's work is unsurpassed in its synthesis and insight.

But there are many worthy competitors to explain Churchill's greatness. Paul Addison's elegantly compact *Churchill: The Unexpected Hero* (2005) concludes with this provocative assessment: "Churchill is no longer the hero he used to be, but in the end the recognition of his frailties and flaws has worked in his favor. It has brought him up to date by making him into the kind of hero our disenchanted culture can accept and admire: a hero with feet of clay." John Keegan's Penguin life, *Winston Churchill* (2002), contains a wonderful brief analysis of Churchill's world-stirring language. And Roy Jenkins's *Churchill: A Biography* (2001), which draws on the biographer's own experience as a Cabinet officer, concludes with this judgment:

> I now put Churchill, with all his idiosyncrasies, his indulgences, his occasional childishness, but also his genius, his tenacity and his persistent ability, right or wrong, successful or unsuccessful, to be larger than life, as the greatest human being ever to occupy 10 Downing Street.

Here is a case where history and biography have become one. We need to know everything about the man in order to understand why he made so much history.

John Keegan stands out among the biographers for his effort to understand the whole man. It is rare to find a Churchill biography that makes much of his sexuality or finds it relevant in assessing his achievement:

> Churchill, as he himself recognized with uncharacteristic insight, had a weak sexual drive. He was innocent in his judgment of others' sexuality and apparently personally innocent of sexual experience until his marriage, at the age of thirty-four, to Clementine Hozier, herself serenely pure minded. Churchill was a moral oddity: a man who was world-wise without being a man of the world. It may have been his indifference to the lures of the flesh that heightened his susceptibility to the seduction of words and to the spell of history as romance.

So far as is known, Churchill never committed adultery. Keegan might have added, though, that the serene and pure-minded Clemmie had one short-lived, discreet affair in the 1930s.

John Ramsden, on the other hand, in *Man of the Century*, suggests that Churchill's true significance can only be caught by quoting

Churchill himself. The words are the man, and the words shaped history. Here is Ramsden quoting from Churchill's memoirs describing the end of 1940, after having served eight months in office:

> We were alive. We had beaten the German air force. There had been no invasion of the Island. The Army at home was now very powerful. London had stood triumphant throughout her ordeals. . . . With a gasp of astonishment and relief the smaller neutrals and the subjugated states saw that stars still shone in the sky. Hope, and within it passion, burned anew in the hearts of hundreds of millions of men. The good cause would triumph. Right would not be trampled down. The flag of freedom, which in this fateful hour was the Union Jack, would fly in all the winds that blew.

Churchill writes as a man with the world on his mind, and his words remind me of Walt Whitman's assertion, "I contain multitudes." Historians have often pointed out the mythifying that suffuses Churchill's prose, and Ramsden himself calls Churchill the original spin doctor. Yet he concludes:

> It is difficult not to be carried away by such powerful words, especially for the British. But perhaps we should not try to resist, if we are fully to understand the impact that Churchill had on so many people, both at the time and since. The man, the message, and the way in which he so effectively expressed it were and are indissolubly one.

It seems to me that Lincoln is Churchill's only equal as political icon; they shared the indispensable ability to write great prose. Churchill won the Nobel Prize for Literature in 1953. And deservedly so. Such is the prestige of the novel that we often forget that some of the modern world's greatest literature is biography and history. No one should think Churchill won it because his books were influential best-sellers or because he was a great man. He was one of the great writers of the century, as John Lukacs demonstrates in his *Churchill: Visionary. Statesman. Historian.* In a brilliant chapter on "Churchill's Historianship," one of our finest historians demolishes the "gifted amateur" denigration of Churchill's work.

Churchill the historian had faults: a tendency to write self-exculpatory prose, an excessive desire to vindicate his father, Randolph Churchill, and the Duke of Marlborough. But his early books were military classics, his autobiography is a masterpiece, and two great memoir-histories are tour-de-force reconstructions of the past. Churchill's power as warrior, statesman, and writer was his historical imagination.

To those who dismiss Churchill as a mere stylist, Lukacs asks, "If you have a right (and fine) sense of the past, can your history be entirely wrong?" Lukacs concedes that "there exist bad histories that are written tellingly or even well," but he adds, "there can be no good history that is not told or written well. After all, whatever the research, there is no historical fact the meaning of which exists separately from its statement, from its very phrasing." In those words I recognize the author of *Historical Consciousness* (1985), still one of Lukacs's best books and one that can be invoked to show what made Winston Churchill great: in his person he embodied historical consciousness, and in his writings he recreated that consciousness, over and over again. This is the very thing that binds together a single identity and with it informs the whole world.

Popular History and Biography

In "Popular History and Biography" (*Handbook of American Popular Culture,* edited by M. Thomas Inge [1988]), John Scott Wilson describes the enormous influence of Parson Weems's biography of Washington (there were seventy editions by the beginning of the twentieth century) and of other popular works concentrating on mythic aspects of the country's heroes. In the nineteenth century, historians and biographers such as George Bancroft and John Fiske managed to write books that were both scholarly and popular, albeit not at the level of the most profound historians, Parkman and Prescott. The rise of scientific history, influenced by German historians and universities, divided popular and scholarly history, the latter consigned to journals in which primary evidence was investigated, while the former appeared in popular magazines. Paine's life of Twain and Sandburg's life of Lincoln represent the continuing appeal of popular narrative biography.

The distinction between popular and scholarly biography is likely to persist. David McCullough's biography of Harry Truman, for example, is a best-seller highly praised for its narrative drive but also criticized in academic circles for a certain lack of rigor in evaluating Truman's policies. From a scholarly perspective, McCullough is regarded as burnishing certain national myths about leadership. His accuracy has not been faulted but rather his penchant for orchestrating a story that fits a certain tradition of what might be called patriotic biography. Other writers in this vein include Doris Kearns Goodwin, Joseph Ellis, and Stephen Ambrose.

The latter two biographers, however, are academics who have bridged the gap between the popular and the scholarly. Their works are distinguished by a strong narrative drive but also by rigorous archival work. Even so, biography itself is viewed as lacking in certain scholarly qualities.

In "The Complexities and Rewards of Biography Should Be Better Appreciated on Campuses" (*Chronicle of Higher Education*, January 10, 1990, pp. B1–B2), Elizabeth Young-Breuhl notes that in spite of its increasing popularity biography has not found "an academic niche." Compared to autobiography, which literary critics favor because of its suitability to current theories about the unstable self, biography seems old-fashioned, a perception biographers understand but find difficult to counter, since any significant confrontation with epistemology is likely to destroy the story value of biography. Yet contemporary biography is a complex story usually ignored by reviewers who merely sum up the life without assessing how it has been told. Rarely do reviewers contemplate a biographer's choices, or whether the kind of narrative selected is suitable to the subject. Perhaps as outstanding biographies accumulate, reviewers will begin to notice that the recreation of a life does not appear from "nowhere, fully formed."

Since Young-Breuhl wrote, reviewers continue to ignore—because they do not know how to do otherwise—the form and method of biographies. On the other hand, the academic study of biography has burgeoned.

Some years ago I coined a term, Bio-Pop, to describe the legitimacy of popular-culture biography. This term, I suppose, is meant to lend a sort of sanction to a genre that has not been accorded much respect. Here is my full definition of the term:

> A species of biography concentrating on popular personalities held in low esteem—chiefly by academics who think they write far more sophisticated lives of literary, political, and other cultural figures of permanent importance. Bio-pop positively emphasizes biography as a crude literary form and openly entertains the notion that the continuity of lives in biographies has been vastly overrated, and that—indeed—human lives are more fragmentary than has usually been acknowledged. The bridge between its two truncated terms proclaims the forever unfinished but dynamic state of the lives it writes.

There is still a great deal of academic snobbery and condescension toward popular-culture studies. In the early 1980s an editor of a new scholarly journal that accepted an article I wrote on Eugene O'Neill asked me if he could omit from his "Notes on Contributors" a reference to my forthcoming biography on Marilyn Monroe, "so as not to offend more conservative scholars." I can imagine many reasons for the editor's timidity, but instead of speculating on his motivations I would rather concentrate on a statement by Leon Edel that has provoked this prolegomenon on the legitimacy of popular-culture biography:

> We need not concern ourselves with "camp" biographies or daubs, the ephemeral figures of movie stars, dope addicts, Boston stranglers; they belong to certain kinds of life histories by journalists in our time. They belong in a waxworks. They are documentary and often vividly mythic; they are more related to the photographic,

the visual moment, the changing world of entertainment or crime, the great and flourishing field of interminable gossip disseminated by the media. This is quite distinct, as we know, from serious artistic biographical and pictorial quests to capture the depths and mysteries of singular greatness.

I especially like that interjection of utter confidence that Edel employs to include his audience in the rightness of his observation— "As we know." But there is much to learn from precisely the kinds of biographies he dismisses. We learn that, in a certain sense, the human personality is ephemeral—even waxen in its malleability and perishability—and it is precisely through documentaries and through photographs from which documentaries are made that we have come to see that "the depths and mysteries of singular greatness" are part of a powerful biographical myth.

Edel is deeply disturbed over the massive clutter of contemporary archives. How is the biographer expected to sort out the "essences" of his subject's character in the "mountains of trivia" he must scale? Edel's solution is to adopt the investigative tools of the psychologist and the detective, of Sigmund Freud and Sherlock Holmes, both of whom have indeed become partners in much of contemporary fiction and biography. It is hard to conceive of doing without these two masterful problem posers and solvers, yet my own research for a popular-culture biography has prompted me to restrain if not to shun the use of their models of the human mind. Unlike Edel, I am not sure the biographer should strive for "the clean mastery of the portrait painter unconcerned with archives." I cannot deny that Edel may be right in suggesting there is a "figure under the carpet," a hidden, inner myth that makes an individual's life cohesive; but that myth depends largely on the biographer's selection of details that fit the myth and on a narrative that itself mimics the myth. Once the mimesis is established between a life and the narrative of that life, the biographer's understanding of his or her subject profoundly impresses us. This is so because—as in good fiction—inevitability is established between the individual's actions and the words used to describe those actions. This is why Edel lauds Virginia Woolf's biography of Roger Fry; it is artistic: it sets a scene, paints a portrait, and vividly renders a man in motion. If one carefully examines Woolf's narrative, however, it is clear that she is not so much offering evidence of a life as she is transmuting it into a compelling fiction by the use of figurative language. The "essences" of character that Edel prizes are inseparable from the seemingly inevitable words in Woolf's vocabulary of Fry's life.

I argue against Woolf and Edel only to the extent that their view of biography is the most prominent one we have. Even when the academic biographer is inclined toward the documentary rather than the artistic side of a life narrative, he or she is likely to regard the subject as one person with "depths and mysteries of singular greatness," and not—which may be the case—as an ambiguous assortment of bits and pieces tenuously held in place by an assertive but embattled multiple personality. It is fashionable to acknowledge the role of deconstruction in our lives, and perhaps it is also true. No doubt Edel distrusts the "interminable gossip disseminated by the media" because it fragments our sense of self, focuses on the immediate and the popular but not on the permanent constituents of culture. Might it not also be true, however, that this "interminable gossip" has always been with us, and that the media have simply forced us to confront how our grand sense of ourselves has always been ground down and dissolved by tittle-tattle, by what in an earlier age used to be called "table talk"? How many different photographs do we have of Norman Mailer? Hundreds? Suppose we had only five painted portraits of him, like the five Joshua Reynolds did of Dr. Johnson? Would Mailer's greatness seem more singular? Would Dr. Johnson's uniqueness suffer from the various replications of his likeness in photographs?

In any case, it is certain that at least some contemporary biographers have been especially taken not with Edel's vision of biography as a portrait of essences but with a picture of biography as a tentative tracing of a personality that is essentially photographic. Thus in his life of Virginia Woolf, Quentin Bell describes biography as "an outline that is consistent and convincing, but which, like all outlines, is but tenuously connected with the actual form of the sitter in all lights, poses, moods and disguises." There is embedded here an analogy with the cinema and with acting that rivals Edel's parallel between portrait painting and biography. Film, as Walter Benjamin pointed out long ago, has made us acutely aware of the minute shifts in personality from second to second—indeed within fractions of seconds, as if the human personality were composed of intricate atomic particles. In fact, in *Golden Codgers*, Richard Ellmann has adopted such a model of the mind in his forecast of the next generation of biographies.

Here is precisely where popular-culture biographies can teach us something about ourselves, about our plural identities. Studying an atomic blonde like Marilyn Monroe gets us away from an antiquated—albeit perennially attractive—notion of "singular greatness." Her various name changes, her plastic surgery, and her elastic autobiographies make her stand out in some respects, I admit, but—as Mailer says—she is the "magnified mirror of ourselves." From her we learn what is essential about the composition of our diverse identities rather than about the "essences" of character, which may not exist at all, though, like most of us, she tried to find the final determinants of what she hoped could fuse into a unified personality.

Mailer's main sources of information for Monroe's life are two journalistic biographies, *Norma Jean* by Fred Lawrence Guiles and *Marilyn Monroe* by Maurice Zolotow. Guiles is the most thorough guide to her life, even though his book lacks detailed documentation. Zolotow is more prone than Guiles to use hearsay, but Zolotow hones the events of her life into a stimulating interpretation of a multiple personality trying to piece herself together through a single-minded dedication to acting. Mailer, in a way, goes Zolotow one better by integrating the psychology of Monroe's life into *his* style, and vice versa, of course. That is, it's hard to tell where Monroe begins and Mailer leaves off, for there is reason for supposing that in both their lives the splitting of personality into various roles for various occasions goes hand-in-hand with the search for a definitive self. This novelistic freeing of fact in favor of recreating the rhythm of a life that is perhaps in tune with the biographer's own probably pleases Edel.

Mailer's book is something of a breakthrough work in the field of popular-culture biography, and Edel gives it a measure of grudging respect:

> And Norman Mailer, whatever his motivations, revealed a proper sense of biography when as a novelist he sought to capture a figure as elusive and as delicate as Marilyn Monroe. Even if we judge his work a failure, we must praise his undertaking.

I guess Mailer has merit because he is a novelist and not one of those "journalists in our time" from whom Edel wishes to remove himself as far as possible. I suspect he admires Mailer for his close to surgical penetration of Monroe's psychology; the biographer is excavating his subject's roots. But Mailer never quite arrives at the heart of the matter, and we remain suspended between various scenarios of Monroe's life and death. Is this why Edel's approval is qualified? For me, it's to Mailer's credit that he never comes to closure, even though biographies have taught us to expect considerable neatness in perspective.

Yet Mailer does not go far enough in un-concluding Monroe's life—at least this is what I have come to feel in writing my own biographical narrative. Except for *The Misfits*, he is not nearly curious enough about her movies, about the way films provided her with multiple frames around which her behavior was delimited. What is often missing from his book, and what I have tried to supply in my own, is some sense of the rhythms of moviemaking, of the interruptions and extensions of selves that the imprinting of images on celluloid enforces. Monroe's flickering life was almost literally a series of short takes strung together to exhibit the illusion of wholeness. Mailer covers but does not sufficiently probe her use of "the Method," which by its very name must have implied to her a oneness, a knowledge of self that could be used to inform the parts, the bits, the personas she had to play.

Opposed to the Method is montage, that quick cutting and juxtaposition of scenes to form a gestalt that is not the direct result of the actor's efforts. The best the actor can hope for is that his or her projection has been all of a piece, so that later editing can build on rather than shatter a performance. Biographies of popular-culture figures, I would argue, have much to teach us about biographical form, about how biographers must employ both method and montage. The patchwork of the individual's performances can never quite coalesce into the biographer's or the subject's search for singularity, yet we cannot seem to live without Edel's fondness for essences. Let us not fool our many selves, however, by insisting upon a coherent biography that is far more fastidious than any life, great or small, could hope to be.

FURTHER READING: See Quentin Bell, quoted in Dennis W. Petrie, *Ultimately Fiction: Design in Modern American Biography* (1977); Walter Benjamin, "The Work of Art in the Age of Mechanical Reproduction," in *Illuminations* (1969); James Clifford, "Hanging Up Looking Glasses at Odd Corners: Ethnobiographical Prospects," in *Studies in Biography* (1978), pp. 41–56; Leon Edel, "The Figure Under the Carpet," in *Telling Lives* (1979); Richard Ellmann, "Literary Biography," in *Golden Codgers: Biographical Speculations* (1973); Robert Gittings, *The Nature of Biography* (1978); Fred Lawrence Guiles, *Norma Jean: The Life of Marilyn Monroe* (1970); Peter Nagourney, "The Basic Assumptions of Literary Biography," *Biography* I (1978): 86–104; Alan Shelston, *Biography* (1977).

SEE ALSO History and Biography.

Privacy

Two words in Samuel Johnson's definitive essay on biography (*The Rambler*, No. 60) haunt me: "vulgar greatness." Johnson is attacking the idea that biography ought not to stray very far from the public arena. He argues in favor of portraying "domestick privacies" and of displaying the "minute details of daily life."

As has been observed with increasing frequency these days when discussing public figures, including politicians, the line between public and private has eroded. Received wisdom would have it that this development somehow reflects a culture obsessed with the prurient biographical details of its famous figures.

I would argue to the contrary that Samuel Johnson's vision of biography might finally have its day. After Boswell, Johnson's disciple, one would be hard put to find another biographer as revealing, as dogged about domestic privacies, or as extravagantly bullish about biography as a form of knowledge. On the contrary, biographers seemed to suppress as much as they revealed. Thus Thomas Jefferson's biographers were silent on the subject of Sally Hemmings or dismissed her family's detailed oral histories of the affair. The daily struggle of President Roosevelt just to move around was never documented in photographs or film.

By the time George Wallace was shot and proceeded to campaign in a wheelchair, this kind of suppression no longer prevailed. And we are just beginning to return to a faith in the intrinsic value of biography for its own sake that Johnson exudes in his life of Richard Savage, a poet and criminal whose life Johnson transformed into a fascinating study of human individuality.

In the presidential elections of 2000 and 2004, when either candidate continued talking after they thought the microphones had been turned off, and we heard something else besides George Bush's singsong and John Kerry's drone, we were electrified. It is therapeutic, it is biographical, to overhear George Bush employ a profanity to describe a reporter and John Kerry mutter about crooks and liars.

Such incidents remind me of Tony Bennett's refusal to allow *60 Minutes* to watch his warm-up before a performance. Bennett does not want us to see the hard work, the behind-the-scenes business of being a singer anymore than politicians want us to see them off duty.

But without some alternative to the public persona, all we have is "vulgar greatness." Those words turn the current cant upside down, reversing the notion that it is vulgar to pry into private life. All that should matter—say the moralists and aesthetes—is whether we are persuaded by the politician's policies, the literary figure's work—in short, the public figure's public record.

I do not think, however, that in truth anyone really believes in such a narrow-minded concern with the public realm. Anyone who does can be easily fooled. We need some way to measure the public personality, because whether we like it or not, we dwell daily side-by-side with George Bush and John Kerry.

I am reminded of a chilling *Alfred Hitchcock Presents* television program I saw as a child. A young woman attends the theater and falls in love with a dashing ventriloquist whose performance she watches raptly. Star-struck, she gains entrance to his dressing room, and overcome with emotion she rushes to him. At her touch, her idol collapses, for he is the "dummy," a tool of the false dummy, the ugly dwarf who then jumps up and screams at the terrified woman.

What has always made that story so evocative for me is that it occurred backstage. The tale provides an especially compelling metaphor for me, since I had begun a brief career in the theater. Early on I was introduced to the idea of public life as a drama, a role, a fiction that hid the behind-the-scenes reality.

Domestic privacies and daily details help place the public personality in perspective. And we do not need to worry much about invasion of privacy where public figures are concerned. Our nation's eighteenth-century founders, Samuel Johnson's contemporaries, wisely wrote a constitution that gave the press considerable latitude, for they knew that those with political power have more than enough resources to thwart their biographers.

Other democracies, like Great Britain, that do not have a First Amendment, suffer every day because libel laws place the burden on biographers to prove they have not damaged their subjects. Biographies like mine have been suppressed in Britain with a frequency that would astound Americans who complain that the press here has too much freedom.

But without that freedom, as Samuel Johnson understood, there is only "vulgar greatness."

SEE ALSO Libel.

Psychobiography

The use of psychology in biography has always aroused suspicion. Psychobiography has been called a pseudoscience and just another way of fictionalizing biographical figures. Psychological approaches cannot explain the whole man, critics argue, and psychobiography cannot sufficiently distinguish one subject from others with similar psychological makeups. Psychology also panders to the contemporary need to debunk public figures and reduce them to manageable size. Even the best psychobiographies are conjectural, employing tentative language such as "it is not at all improbable" or "it would seem."

Psychobiographies have also been used to make fallacious links between creativity and neurosis, or they have been used in judgmental fashion—as in Nancy Clinch's *The Kennedy Neurosis*. Much of the anxiety, phobias, and sexual inhibitions that psychobiographers discover in their subjects are characteristics found in millions of people. The subject's behavior gets labeled "anal" or "oral," but what does that really explain about an individual's behavior?

The term critics most often use for psychobiography is "reductive." Psychobiographers do not attend closely enough to historical, sociological, and other factors that determine an individual's behavior. In *Shrinking History: On Freud and the Failure of Psychohistory* (1980), David E. Stannard rejects psychohistory (there is "little, if any psychohistory [that] is good history"), and he questions the validity of psychoanalysis itself, arguing that it has not been shown to have much empirical validity, and that its practitioners have been loath to submit it to the kind of verification that any important system of thought, let alone therapy, must confront. Calling his book a "primer" accessible to the general reader, Stannard aims to open a discussion that has "for too long been rendered impossible by the protective smokescreen of functionless private jargon and cant and dogmatic Alice-in-Wonderland logic that has marked the psychoanalytic and psychohistorical enterprises."

How can psychobiographers treat their subjects as patients? is another familiar criticism. One reason why psychobiography has been so controversial is that it is still largely a Freudian enterprise. The biographer's use of psychology per se is not the problem. Modern biographers focus on the development of personality as opposed to Boswell's eighteenth-century assumption that the biographer deals with the mature character already formed. As soon as the modern biographer begins to question his subject's motivations, he enters the realm of psychology. Not to inquire into the subject's psychology, then, is to restrict the biographer to an aloof, outside view of his subject.

Sigmund Freud produced the first psychobiography in 1910: *Leonardo da Vinci and a Memory of His Childhood* is highly speculative and based solely on secondary sources. Freud is aware of his more extravagant speculations, noting that he may be accused of writing a "psycho-analytic novel." Nevertheless his attempt to identify those features of Leonardo's early years (especially in infancy) that have the most impact on his style is suggestive. His effort to ascribe virtually all of Leonardo's mature art to its origins in the sexual fantasies of childhood makes his work seem reductive and deterministic to most contemporary practitioners of psychobiography.

Lytton Strachey turned psychobiography into the form of elegant suggestive essays in his landmark *Emminent Victorians* (1918). Strachey uses psychology to undermine Victorian earnestness and devotion to high principle. Thus Florence Nightingale seems, for all her high achievement, an obsessive, tormented spirit. Dr. Arnold's strenuous efforts to reform the British schools is made to seem like the actions of a man with profound religious doubts that he has repressed in his energetic dedication to progress. Other Victorian heroes, like Cardinal Manning and General Gordon, are shown to have enormous egos and towering ambitions reflected in certain psychological tics. But this undermining of Victorianism is done by and large through narrative understatement. Only in his letters did Strachey explicitly confess, "Is it prejudice, do you think, that makes us hate the Victorians, or is it the truth of the case? They seem to me to be a set of mouthing bungling hypocrites; but perhaps really there is a baroque charm about them which will be discovered by our great-great-grandchildren as we have discovered the charm of Donne, who seemed intolerable to the 18th century. Only I don't believe it. . . . I should like to live for another 200 years (to be moderate)."

Strachey's American counterpart was Gamaliel Bradford. In *Bare Souls* (1924), Bradford describes his "psychographies" of Voltaire, Thomas Gray, Horace Walpole, William Cowper, Charles Lamb, John Keats, Gustave Flaubert, and Edward Fitzgerald. In "A Clue to the Labyrinth of Souls," Bradford discusses the difficulty of interpreting the inner selves of his subjects, how he looks for telling details in "minor, insignificant actions," sifts through the reports of others, analyzes his subject's writing (published works, diaries, and letters) in order to dissect and penetrate the core of self. Some kinds of evidence are better than others: Bradford favors diaries and letters that may be more spontaneous than retrospective works such as autobiographies and memoirs. The "naturalist of souls" must learn to distinguish between the subject's poses and determine which evidence is most self-revealing.

Strachey died in 1930; no writer since has been able to capture the flair and panache of his biographies. Instead writers such as Marie Bonaparte used Freudianism in rather mechanical ways to reveal the neuroses of literary and political figures. Freud himself contributed to a dubious entry in the genre of psychobiography by co-writing with the diplomat William C. Bullitt, the posthumously published *Thomas Woodrow Wilson: A Psychological Study* (1967).

A new era seemed to dawn, though, with *Woodrow Wilson and Colonel House: A Personality Study* (1956) by Alexander L. and Juliette L. George, which is often cited as one of the best psychobiographies. The Georges concede (in a preface to the 1964 Dover edition) that while no biographer can psychoanalyze a subject, psychoanalysis has empirical justification, and it is a theory of personality that can be employed to understand the "functioning and development of human personality." Personality traits do not determine events; the context of political action limits and defines how such traits are expressed. But, "It is by relating Wilson's overt behavior, which sometimes seems naive or unreasonable, to some of his emotional needs, which were given their particular hue by his upbringing as a child, that the inner logic of his actions becomes clear," they conclude in their introduction.

In *Thomas Jefferson: An Intimate History* (1964), the biographer Fawn Brodie argues that "a man's inner life affects every aspect of his intellectual life and also his decision-making." Nuances and metaphors are as important as facts and events. Quoting Freud, Brodie claims that Jefferson's previous biographers have been reluctant to inquire directly into his emotional and sexual life, into the impact of his parents, his marriage, and his relationships with other women, because of their desire to canonize and sanctify their subject. Taking his private experience into account makes Jefferson's "ambivalences less baffling" while leaving his genius "undiminished."

In *After Great Pain: The Inner Life of Emily Dickinson* (1971), John Cody, a practicing psychiatrist, uses an analogy with paleontology to suggest that psychoanalytic inferences can bridge the gap in biographical facts by functioning as the equivalent of plaster bones used to reconstruct fossil skeletons. Whether his approach enhances an understanding of Dickinson's art depends on how art is conceived (as self-contained or as a social and psychological phenomenon). He concedes that the psychoanalytic biographer cannot understand a subject in the way that a practicing psychoanalyst can understand a patient, yet the former often has a rich life record unavailable to the latter, and Dickinson had a prescient sense of psychology, making it possible to recover something akin to her "free associations" by studying her letters and the symbols in her poetry.

Bruce Mazlish's *James and John Stuart Mill: Father and Son in the Nineteenth Century* (1975) has a high place in the canon of psychobiographical texts. Mazlish employs the Oedipus complex as a way of dealing with the father-son conflict and with generational change, which Mazlish states (in his introduction) became "pivotal" as a way of effecting social change in the nineteenth century. Mazlish also aims to "reexamine Freudian concepts in the light of our general historical materials" as a way of testing their universality.

In *Clifford Odets: American Playwright. The Years from 1906 to 1940* (1982), Margaret Brenman-Gibson, a psychoanalyst/biographer, acknowledges that it is "not only conceptually but humanly pernicious" to have a "wide chasm between the vocabularies often used to describe a patient's case history and those used to tell the story of a neighbor's or a creative leader's life." Her biography is an effort to bridge the divide between psychoanalysis and biography that Leon Edel has discussed, and that Brenman-Gibson recognizes in the early jargon-ridden psychobiographies. Her model is Erik Erikson. For clinical researchers she has devised a special symbol in the text referring to a footnote in which she gives detailed explanations for professionals.

Undoubtedly Erik Erikson has contributed most importantly to psychobiography in theory and practice. In *Children and Society* (second edition, 1963), Erikson engages in extended studies of Hitler and Gorky, which are preliminary efforts at an integration of psychoanalysis and history that Erikson would later develop in *Young Man Luther*. Concentrating on the childhood and youth of these two figures, he attempts to modify Freudianism so as to take more account of the interaction between the self and society, and to fashion a historically based psychology that is faithful to historical method, to the historian's handling of evidence and understanding of change. As Erikson concludes in his foreword to the first edition: "Psychoanalysis studies psychological evolution through the analysis of the individual. At the same time it throws light on the fact that the history of humanity is a gigantic metabolism of individual life cycles."

In *Dimensions of a New Identity* (1974), a study of Thomas Jefferson and his legacy, Erikson elaborates on the origins of psychohistory, which derives from the psychoanalytical investigation of what has gone wrong in an individual's development. A life history, on the other hand, "describes how a person managed to keep together and to maintain a significant function in the lives of others." The psychohistorian must "understand in himself such unconscious motivation as he analyzes in others," just as "historians

. . . have always expressed some awareness of their own place in history." For history is "also a record of how historical concepts influence as well as reflect both the writing and the making of history." It is the particular role of psychology, says Erikson, to sharpen that awareness.

His *Identity: Youth and Crisis* (1968) includes chapters on Bernard Shaw, Freud, and William James which seek to integrate a psychobiographical view of self and society. In the case of William James, for example, Erikson discovers a "protracted identity crisis as well as the emergence of a 'self-made' identity in the new and expansive American civilization." What Erikson calls "identity" is a process located *"in the core of the individual* and yet also *in the core of his communal culture,* a process which establishes, in fact, the identity of those two identities."

Gandhi's Truth: On the Origins of Militant Nonviolence (1969) begins by exploring how Erikson became involved in a biography of Gandhi, demonstrating his belief that the biographer must show how his personality interacts with his subject's. After examining the conditions in which Gandhi wrote his autobiography in order to determine its usefulness to the biographer, Erikson provides a narrative of Gandhi's early years before concentrating on "the event"— how it was that Gandhi and his followers "converged in Ahmedabad in 1918" to develop the "philosophy of nonviolence" as a *"political instrument."*

"On the Nature of Psycho-Historical Evidence: In Search of Gandhi" (*Daedalus* 97 [Summer 1968]: 695–730) traces the roots of psychohistory to Freud, pointing up the flaws in his method, particularly in the biography of Woodrow Wilson, where Freud allowed his co-author, William C. Bullitt, too much autonomy in presenting the historical evidence for their interpretation. Erikson explains how the psychoanalyst makes a "family affair" out of history, though he entertains the question as to how much an individual can "deal with the cast of his adult life on its own terms." Certainly Gandhi drew upon his family experience, making of the event at Ahmedabad "something of a family affair" while establishing it as the crucial event for the definition of his doctrine of nonviolence and of his position as the nation's leader.

Young Man Luther: A Study in Psychoanalysis and History (1958) regards psychoanalysis as a "historical tool" and as a "system of ideas" that interprets history. Emphasizing that he will abide by the rule of historical evidence, Erikson aims to avoid a major failing of psychoanalysis: "reducing every human situation to an analogy with an earlier one," and finding the origins of everything in infancy. Taking a developmental view, he declares that human beings grow "stage by stage into a social world." At the same time historians have too often ignored the "disguises, rationalizations, and idealizations" of historical figures, and psychoanalysis can therefore help the biographer keep his distance from the subject.

Historians have not been greatly impressed with Erikson's approach to biography and to the past. They concede certain valid insights, but they are wary of his investigation of the unconscious. Motivations attributed to the unconscious are not based on any sort of empirical evidence and are therefore suspect. Erikson also tends to ignore evidence that contradicts his views. And the probing of Luther's psychology, for example, for signs of anality is fruitless since Luther's feelings are rather representative of his time.

Quite aside from what psychobiography may have to contribute to an understanding of the subject is the ethical question. In *The Nation* (March 23, 1992, pp. 385–387), Paul Alexander, a biographer of Sylvia Plath, describes his own experience with her psychiatrist and discusses the ethical issues concerning the release of psychiatric evidence. He rehearses the controversy over Diana Middlebrook's biography of the poet Anne Sexton (which used recordings of her psychiatric sessions). Alexander argues for a case-by-case evaluation of the use of psychiatric evidence, carefully noting that both he and Middlebrook took into account their subjects' attitudes toward revealing such information as well as the psychiatrists' reasons for relinquishing confidentiality.

Religious Biography

In the medieval period, religious biography was hagiography, an account of a saint's life as an inspiration to the faithful and instruction to the wayward. These biographies did not question the veracity of miracles or the principles of religion. Biographers like the Venerable Bede were concerned to document saints' lives, so that Bede went to considerable trouble to interview those who knew his subject, St. Cuthbert. Nevertheless Bede and Cuthbert shared the same worldview, and it would have been unthinkable to challenge the metaphysical premises of the saint's life.

In a secular world the religious biographer, depending on his biographical subject, may need to address hostility to religion itself. Or the religious biographer—one who remains an adherent to specific religion—must decide how to couch his narrative for an audience that will include unbelievers or disbelievers. And for the biographer who is not religious, or not a member of the religion his subject espouses, the challenge is how to portray a particular religious experience with respect, if not acceptance.

SEE ALSO Latin/Medieval Biography.

FURTHER READING: See Carl Rollyson, *Biography Before Boswell* (2005), which includes Bede's *Life of St. Cuthbert* and places hagiography and religious biography within the context of the development of biography.

CRITIQUE: Biographies of Father McGivney, Pope John Paul II, Calvin, Brigham Young, and St. Thérèse of Lisieux reflect different kinds of religious biography:

"But even when the servant of Christ was dead and buried, the miracles which he worked whilst alive did not cease." So wrote St. Cuthbert's eighth-century biographer Bede, intent on showing how his subject had become a saint. Biographers then had forsaken Plutarch's focus on the peculiarities of personality and the vagaries of the self. Plutarch's biographies contain an inherent psychology, Bede's include an intrinsic piety. These two biographers exemplify the genre's extremes: the desire to lay bare the minute particulars of the self, which Samuel Johnson so prized, and the wish to exalt the qualities that make the self a model for others.

In Plutarch the subject is uniquely himself within the rich context of his culture. Coriolanus is a noble Roman but also a mama's boy, brought up in an era, Plutarch emphasizes, that valued martial valor above all else. His life comes to grief because he cannot reconcile the rigid discipline of the soldier with the pliability of a politician. In a vulnerable moment he surrenders his plan to invade Rome, succumbing to his mother's plea while crying out, "What hast thou done to me, my mother! . . . Thou art victorious, and thy victory means good fortune to my country, but death to me; for I shall withdraw vanquished, though by thee alone."

In Bede's case the biographer becomes a postulator, that "combination of researcher and advocate who shepherds the cause [the process of canonization] through its many steps," as Douglas Brinkley and Julie Fenster write in *Parish Priest: Father Michael McGivney and American Catholicism* (2006). Father McGivney's actual postulator is Father Gabriel O'Donnell, and if he is successful— documenting two miracles "attributed to the intercession of Father McGivney"—the "canonization is complete." Father McGivney would become the first American-born parish priest to be made a saint.

Unlike Bede, who provides evidence of St. Cuthbert's miracles in nearly every chapter ("How He Changed the Winds by Prayer, and Brought the Scattered Ships Safe to Land"), Father McGivney's biographers do not establish their subject's miraculous powers in the medieval sense. If there is a flaw in Father McGivney's saintly life, however, they have not found it.

Samuel Johnson, a devout man as well as an impassioned biographer, would have rejoiced in *Parish Priest*. Father McGivney (1852–1890) achieved a sort of "vulgar greatness"—to use Johnson's term—when he founded the Knights of Columbus, now nearly two million strong and expanding into countries like Poland, where it provides aid and comfort to individuals and their families.

Father McGivney grew up in an era still rife with hostility to Catholicism (his work was attacked, for example, by the *New York Times*), and his native state of Connecticut had just emerged from an era in which Catholics were not allowed to purchase land. Accused of giving their allegiance to Rome, papists were regarded as a kind of fifth column subverting the American commonwealth. In a stroke of genius, Father McGivney decided to call his nearly all-Irish-immigrant founding membership the Sons of Columbus, before agreeing to a member's suggestion that "Knights" would be an even more popular term. In public relations argot, Father McGivney mainstreamed Catholicism.

Yet, as Brinkley and Fenster insist, he was just a parish priest. His good work is mirrored by thousands of parish priests, whose mission and methods—unlike those of other professions—have not changed for centuries. The lives of any of those priests, Johnson would say, would be a biography worth reading.

After establishing the Knights of Columbus (against the wishes of certain members of the church hierarchy, who condemned secret organizations, such as the Masons, as well as the apathy of Catholic businessmen absorbed with their worldly pursuits), Father McGivney relinquished control over the burgeoning organization and returned to obscurity, remaining, as his biographers call him, "the most unassuming of Catholic clerics."

Not hagiographers in the medieval sense, Brinkley and Fenster write with one eye on modern skeptics when they describe Father McGivney's retirement from his Knights of Columbus work: "Whether or not he had been under any pressure within the diocese to surrender direct influence over the order, he was comfortable in being, once again, nothing more or less than a parish priest."

Absent from this biography is the supposed psychodrama of being a priest. If Father McGivney suffered inner turmoil or temptation, his biographers are not privy to it. They acknowledge the damage done to the American priesthood because of recent sex scandals but affirm: "Like many others, we each counted at least a few priests among the most impressive people we had ever known."

The photographs and portraits of Father McGivney included in this biography represent a rather dour man, especially in the firm set of his mouth, which his biographers see as revealing a man of "indomitable will." That will had a harsh side, which Father McGivney occasionally exercised on his recalcitrant parishioners. But his biographers are also quick to cite evidence of his humor—and are positively giddy with delight that he liked to watch and to play baseball.

Modern biographers seek what the distinguished biographer Leon Edel called the "figure under the carpet," the secrets Freud saw lurking in every biographical subject. Gazing at Father McGivney's portraits, his biographers observe that his "grim expression . . . was typical of him, at least in repose. Or maybe, like most people, he had an image he wanted to project whenever his picture was taken and, like most, he tried a bit too hard to project it."

Such a fascinating sentence recalls the investigations of the sociologist Erving Goffman and others into the self as persona or actor, a concept inconceivable in the world of the Bedeian biographer. There is no gap between Cuthbert the man and Cuthbert the saint. Neither St. Cuthbert nor his biographer had image issues. Yet Bede, for all his credulity about miracles, still acknowledges a surprisingly modern skepticism.

Like Brinkley and Fenster, Bede believed in his subject's goodness but felt he had to prove it. Explaining the provenance of one of St. Cuthbert's miracles, the biographer emphasizes that he received his account from "one of the most worthy brothers of our monastery . . . [who] heard it from one of those who were present, a man of the most rustic simplicity, and altogether incapable of telling an untruth."

Like the interrogating Bede, Father McGivney's biographers scour the testimony of their subject's parishioners, analyze his few surviving letters, and collate contemporary newspaper accounts. Ultimately, though, their faith in the exemplary man makes their narrative possible, and that makes biography itself a form of model-building and pattern-making.

As the philosopher Nelson Goodman has suggested, such narratives are half perceived and half created, a matter of evidence and projection. To use the title of one of Goodman's books, biography is one way of world-making, a genre that has perhaps not changed as much over the millennia as we might suppose.

HAGIOGRAPHY is often a term of abuse, as though a biographer has idealized or sentimentalized the subject, or emphasized the heroic over the humble, the saint over the sinner. To be hagiographic is to be atavistic, harking back to the pre-modern, pre-secular world where the fraught dynamics of human psychology were suppressed in favor of extolling the exemplary figure. And yet here is Peggy Noonan, a believing Catholic, describing an audience with Pope John Paul II:

> His cassock was too short—six inches off the floor. We could see his white cotton sports socks. We could see his worn brown shoes! He wears old brown loafers, like a working man, and not the traditional dainty slippers of a pope.

Biographies excite a craving for such details about the late and the great. John Paul II, Noonan implies, remained always the same man who had worked in a chemical factory in Nazi-occupied Poland while studying clandestinely for the priesthood.

John Paul the Great: Remembering a Spiritual Father (2006) seems to me nothing less than a rehabilitation of hagiography. Noonan is unabashed in calling the pope a saint and in speaking the language of faith. She believes that God is a person and that John Paul is in heaven. "These thoughts seem sentimental, but I do not mean them so," she insists. "I have become a person who believes these things."

This confession—and Noonan's book is as much autobiography as biography—reminds me of St. Augustine's *Confessions*. His gift to biography was to make the saint's life both a study in sanctity and an acknowledgment of sin. If John Paul the Great, as Ms. Noonan styles him, is her spiritual father, it is because, like Augustine, his holiness is of this world—a matter not of dainty slippers but of work shoes.

Noonan notes that the pope was a poet, a playwright, and an athlete, a man very much at home in his body and comfortable, for example, with the idea of human sexuality. If he maintained the Catholic church's traditional teachings about birth control and abortion (it is curious that she does not explore his attachment to the celibacy of the priesthood), it was not out of some kind of puritan rejection of sensuality. On the contrary, it was because sexuality was such a powerful driving force in the human psyche that he felt it ought to be channeled into the love of the body and soul that graces a marriage.

Noonan sees the very strengths of her spiritual father as allied to his failings. Because his own calling to the priesthood came at a time when it was a crime, he could not grasp the catastrophe that has overtaken the American Catholic church. In Poland, priests were the very bulwark of society, and as a parish priest, John Paul II participated in the intimate lives of his spiritual community. That American priests could so abuse their privilege and authority as to molest the children in their charge was hard for him to believe. It was, he thought, an overblown press controversy.

Noonan is unsparing in revealing the pope's blind side, even as she delineates his saintly life, his robust workingman's sensibility, and his courageous public dying, making himself a symbol of the virtue of suffering and taking his life to its full term because life is sacred in every sense.

I was reminded of Noonan's working-class pope in his old brown loafers when she calls on Bernard Law and the other fathers of the church to relinquish their mansions and limousines. The biographer holds the American cardinal directly responsible for the church's sexual scandal, and in one of her book's most dramatic moments confronts Cardinal Law about his luxurious lifestyle. He tells her, "Well, the cardinal only lives in a modest room, and there have to be conference rooms, and how would it look if I'd refused to live there, what would it say about my predecessor, how would it look?" Noonan's reply (I think made only to herself) was, "How would it look? It would look good. But more to the point, they should not be worrying about how things look; they should be worrying about how things are."

Noonan believes that the church hierarchy in this country still does not understand how devastating the sexual scandal has been, and that only a new generation of priests and nuns can rectify the damage. This hope is not quite fleshed out in the biography and is countered by a troubling awareness: "We are suffering, in the West, through an imbalanced period of cultural history, a time that seems to mark both an obsessive interest in and an anxious, even combative attitude toward the human body."

When Noonan writes that "we seem not so comfortable in our own skin," she is responding to the rift between body and soul that poets like John Paul II and William Butler Yeats sought to heal. Noonan is no Crazy Jane, but I could not help but think of Yeats's great poem, "Crazy Jane Talks with the Bishop," and Jane's retort to the holy man who scorns her "bodily lowliness": "nothing can be sole or whole / That has not been rent."

Hagiography seeks to heal the split. If Noonan cannot quite bring off that miracle, the sensitive nature of her quest is such that she has written a work of a high order.

CLASSIFY *A Heart Promptly Offered: The Revolutionary Leadership of John Calvin* (2006) as a didactic biography, since David W. Hall is intent on proving a point: our common understanding of John Calvin is wrong. Hall believes his subject has been maligned as an authoritarian with a bleak view of humanity and an intolerance that separate him from all that is modern and humane.

To the contrary, Hall argues, both the man and his doctrines are the bedrock of our democratic society. No Calvin, no America— this is what the American historian George Bancroft and a host of other authorities have suggested, as Hall points out. Why, then, such a huge discrepancy between the real Calvin and his caricature?

To answer that question, turn to "The Legacy and Decline of Calvinism," in Part 3. Hall argues that Calvinism was overtaken by Enlightenment values, unable to compete in a Rousseauistic world that touted the innate goodness of man and the perfectibility of human nature. In America the Puritans, the heirs of Calvinism, came to seem a very dour bunch—you know, that group of humorless, black-cloaked figures hectoring Hester Prynne.

But in Hall's book Calvin is far more important than Rousseau or later thinkers such as Karl Marx. Hall hearkens back to John Adams, who revered Calvin as a harbinger of religious and civil liberty. To properly understand Calvin, his biographer argues, one must compare him not to his successors but to his predecessors, the most important of whom is, of course, St. Augustine. Like Augustine, Calvin addressed the drama of the individual soul, susceptible to sin but capable of redemption through faith in God's grace. In other words, Calvin led the Reformation, opposing the doctrine of good works that had corrupted Catholicism and substituting the notion of justification by faith. The soul's sincerity, not brownie points, secured salvation.

Calvin's emphasis on the dignity and integrity of the individual soul, which became a challenge to the very idea of hierarchy and monarchy, attracted Adams and other American Founding Fathers. Calvin was no modern democrat to be sure, and he was enough of a theocrat to believe heresy had to be punished—even with death sentences—but any careful examination of his career in Geneva shows a man steeped in the idea that individuals worked together collectively to obey the laws of God and to construct a just civil life.

Calvin pioneered government by council and consistory. He was trained as a lawyer, and he believed everyone—including the monarchs of his day—was subject to the law. To know the law of God and to pattern a society in conformance with divine commandments meant congregationalism, a form of religion that dominated early American life and that still exerts enormous influence today.

Hall does an excellent job rehabilitating Calvin, save for one crucial point: it is rather astonishing that this biographer does not squarely deal with the most troubling aspect of Calvinism for modern minds. There is no chapter on determinism (another term for predestination), and neither predestination nor determinism is indexed. The Calvinist believes in the foreordained: your life has already been decided. You are either one of the elect, the recipient of God's grace, or you are damned.

Put that baldly, the obvious response to a Calvinist is "Why should I bother?" If I have no say in the matter, if good works don't count, all I have to do is wait to see if I have the winning ticket. Why Hall does not address these questions that every skeptic of Calvinism has raised is beyond me. It is not enough to say that Calvin was a good man, that he wrote sociable letters and had a lot of friends, or that the good conduct of his immediate disciples is a kind of justification of the man and his ideas. It is not even enough to say that minds hostile to Calvin's nevertheless gave him much credit. Thomas Jefferson, for example, wanted to move Calvin's Genevan academy to Virginia, so highly did this Deist regard the institution of higher learning that Calvin had established. Only when Jefferson could not obtain public funding for this purchase did he turn to plans for his own University of Virginia.

This is all impressive, yet the modern mind cannot get past the doctrine of predestination. What would Calvin say? This, it seems to me, is what Hall should have told us. Instead he offers platitudes about leadership (this biography is part of the publisher's Leaders in Action series). Do we really need this kind of bromide: "Calvin would learn—as many other leaders have—that success is seldom easy or rapid."

Why doesn't Hall pursue, as a Calvin biographer should, the psychology of Calvinism? The Calvinist did not know if he was one of the elect or the damned. Good works might not save him, but good works were necessary as part of his own effort to convince himself that he deserved election. It was the extraordinary drama of not knowing one's ultimate fate that drove Calvinists to create just and equitable societies for themselves and for others. In other words, at every turn what the individual did was up to him. This is a hugely liberating psychology that did indeed lead (ironically) to a sense of selfhood that ultimately doomed Calvinism. And yet, without Calvin it is difficult to see how the secular notion of individual liberty could have flourished.

The modern connection to Calvinism reminds me of T. S. Eliot's statement in "Tradition and the Individual Talent": "Some one said: 'The dead writers are remote from us because we *know* so much more than they did.' Precisely, and they are that which we know."

I wish Hall had shown that we are all fated to be Calvinists, whether we know it or not.

CAN A biographer, Mormon or not, use words like "revelation" without quotation marks? As a "believing historian," what other choice can Richard Lyman Bushman make? Unlike Robert Remini, a non-Mormon author of a recent life of Joseph Smith, Bushman does not write about Smith's "alleged" visions. To do so would be to imply a degree of skepticism and refute the very idea that there can be such a figure as a "believing historian."

"Believing historian" may seem a contradiction in terms. History is not about belief but evidence. But biography is also about a specific person and his world, and thus the genre evokes events as the subject saw them. Joseph Smith understood that his story was incredible. If an angel had appeared to another man and provided golden plates which the man was instructed to translate from the "reform Egyptian" into a new bible, *The Book of Mormon*, Smith said he would not have believed it.

Smith was in his early twenties when he experienced his encounter with the angel Moroni. Poorly educated, he was nevertheless placed in charge of sacred texts that no one else could touch, let alone read, on pain of death. So the angel admonished Joseph, as Mormons call him. Joseph, as Bushman also calls him, never claimed he was dictating to his amanuenses the literal word of God. He was doing the best he could.

Such is the Joseph Smith, rough as a rolling stone, that Bushman brilliantly portrays in *Joseph Smith: Rough Stone Rolling* (2005).

Often called a prophet, Smith was, more properly speaking, a revelator. He simply told people what God and his angels said to him. To be sure, *The Book of Mormon* reflects Smith's autobiography and the Second Great Awakening that Robert Remini explored so well as he situated Smith in the context of Jacksonian America.

Bushman is aware of cultural context, but his work builds on more than eighteen other biographies—most important Fawn Brodie's *No Man Knows My History: The Life of Joseph Smith*, published in 1945 and revised in 1970. While Brodie was not a believing historian, she made it difficult to dismiss Joseph Smith as delusional or a charlatan. In her careful analysis, *The Book of Mormon* could not be rejected as a mere potpourri of pseudobiblical stories.

It is Bushman's treatment of *The Book of Mormon* that makes this biography a stunning accomplishment. Once again he begins with Brodie, a Mormon who broke with her church. She saw the text differently from critics who called it "chloroform in print" (Mark Twain) and "a yeasty fermentation, formless, aimless and inconceivably absurd" (Bernard DeVoto). On the contrary, Brodie replied, "Its structure shows elaborate design, its narrative is spun coherently, and it demonstrates throughout a unity of purpose."

Bushman reports these various opinions but provides his own captivating interpretation. He calls *The Book of Mormon* an "elaborate framed tale of Mormon telling about a succession of prophets telling about their encounters with God. Read in the twenty-first century, the book seems almost postmodern in its self-conscious attention to the production of the text."

Such sentences seem aimed at English departments looking for a new text to mine. Certainly Bushman feels that *The Book of Mormon* has never been accorded its rightful place in American literature. His aim is not to gain Mormon converts but to show how *The Book of Mormon* is a legitimate literary work in its own right, in the same sense the Bible is: "Although the book is above all a religious history of prophesying, preaching, faithfulness, and apostasy, Mormon evokes an entire world."

Bushman acknowledges that proponents of the text "face an uphill battle in resisting this onslaught" of critics who have termed it fictitious and deemed any defense of the book's authenticity hopeless. Yet he draws on the research of Mormons and non-Mormons alike to show that *The Book of Mormon* cannot be explained away as a novel masquerading as scripture.

So why were Mormons persecuted? Why was Joseph Smith assassinated? Why does the church he founded not only endure but thrive? On the one hand, *The Book of Mormon* "challenges biblical authority," even suggesting that the good book may contain errors. Smith's contemporaries viewed him as a spiritual and political threat (he ran for the presidency), with a fanatical church and a private army that menaced American institutions. On the other hand, *The Book of Mormon* as a new revelation, a reformist Christian text, attracted converts dissatisfied with conventional Christian denominations and longing for the return of revelation. Although Bushman does not quite put it this way, *The Book of Mormon* is a work of both affirmation and dissent.

More than that, *The Book of Mormon* has a universalist message; the "American story does not control the narrative," Bushman writes. It does not celebrate democracy, the biographer insists, but "endlessly expounds the master biblical narrative—the history of Israel." The text proposes, in Bushman's words, "a new purpose for America: becoming a realm of righteousness rather than an empire of liberty."

If I have focused on Bushman's interpretation of *The Book of Mormon*, it is because he brings his discussion back to biography—its power and its limitations:

> Biographical analysis runs the risk of making creative works little more than a mirror of the author's life. As one critic puts it, "the book is far grander, much broader, and its internal logic and power go well beyond the life of Joseph Smith."

By delineating the boundaries of biography so sensitively, Bushman has paradoxically enhanced its authority.

NEAR THE beginning of her 2003 biography of *Saint Thérèse of Lisieux* (1873–1897), Kathryn Harrison notes that there have been "countless biographies" of the young Frenchwoman who seems, even before her birth, to have been destined to reinvigorate the modern world with the idea of self-sacrifice and sainthood.

Why, then, another biography? Because it is Kathryn Harrison who wants to write it. Harrison is the author of a controversial memoir, *The Kiss*, a searing account of her own early passions and conflicts, a woman's coming-of-age story that would prepare her— we are expected to infer—to write the life of another young woman who wrote a memoir of her life as well as letters and poetry that were consciously designed to advance her renown. Harrison draws no parallels between her life and her subject's; instead she is the kind of biographer who bears down on her story with an intensity and flair that constitute the only justifications a writer needs.

Harrison's notes and bibliography show that she has done her homework, but it is the quality of her language that distinguishes her book. And this is surely the raison d'être of the Penguin Lives series: choosing the right biographer to rejuvenate a shopworn subject, and in this case to fashion a surprisingly riveting story out of what might otherwise seem foreign and even repelling to the modern reader.

Harrison is quite aware that modern lives are inimical to the idea of hagiography. Thus Zélie, Thérèse's mother, claimed that her daughter sang along with her while Thérèse was still in her womb. "If this is maternal fancy—and a contemporary audience does insist on psychology before marvels—still it betrays something important: even before Thérèse was born, Zélie was besotted with her last child." Hagiography demands marvels; biography relies on psychology. Harrison, however, stands betwixt the two, refusing to choose. She does not say the contemporary audience is right, but she does not say it is wrong either.

When six-year-old Thérèse has a vision of a man resembling her father, only bent over, she later interprets the apparition as God's warning her of her father's impending decline into mental confusion. "A prophecy understood only after its subject has come to pass might be more projection than prediction. But Thérèse's fear of losing her King, the man on which she based her idea of God, was real," the biographer adds. Each time Harrison senses the secular reader scoffing at the saint's supernatural experiences, she concedes the point but at the same time shows how the supernatural and the psychological may be only different ways of explaining experiences that are authentic to the subject.

When it comes to sex, however, Harrison is thoroughly secular. She quotes the adolescent Thérèse's statement that she "burned with the desire to snatch [sinners] from the eternal flames." Thérèse's chosen sinner is Henri Pranzini, a "tall and handsome adventurer" and also a killer of three women. Along with her sister, Thérèse prays for the condemned murderer in a fashion the biographer calls "a triumph of sexual repression." This prayer campaign comes at a time when Thérèse judges herself to be entering "the most danger-ous age for young girls," a phrase the biographer takes as an "oblique reference to sexual awakening." Certainly Thérèse's efforts to starve herself and to deny all pleasures of the body support the biogra-pher's interpretation. But Harrison is careful not to translate all the language of religion into evidence of sexual repression. On the con-trary, even the Pranzini episode is viewed as part of Thérèse's "life-long mission of substitutive suffering."

Thérèse's appeal lies in the way she reenacts the life of Christ in late nineteenth-century France, taking on the sins of the world, ministering to anyone no matter how disagreeable, and suppressing in her own behavior any urge to triumph over others. Her pride is in her humility; her commitment stems from the desire to be "in-cessantly consumed" by her faith in Christ as her personal savior. Sometimes the biographer becomes irritated with her subject, but she is never out of sympathy with her.

When Thérèse is inducted into the Carmelite convent at the ex-traordinarily early age of fifteen (she and her father traveled to Rome, where she personally petitioned the pope for this unprecedented privilege), Harrison notes, the young woman laughed in delight when snow began to fall during the ceremony:

"What thoughtfulness on the part of Jesus!" she exclaimed of the "little miracle," devoting paragraphs of her notebooks to this "incomprehensible condescension" from Jesus, in a voice at once girlishly naive and infuriatingly self-important. Thérèse does give her readers ample occasion to note the inescapable—the divisive and yet potentially transcendent—subjectivity of human experience. "The monastery garden was white like me!" Thérèse marveled. She received the snow as a gift from her bridegroom, and so for her it was.

The reference to Thérèse's "readers" becomes an important theme in the second half of the biography, for the saint consciously shaped her life and her long dying from tuberculosis into an exemplary story that her whole family worked long and hard to help her realize. Even as she experienced excruciating agony on her deathbed, Thérèse went over the details of her autobiography with her sister (also a nun) and gave permission for her book to be edited after her death. Another sister, a devotee of the new art of photography, took pictures of the dying Thérèse. Later, pieces of her bed and other possessions were splintered into relics sent to the faithful around the world. The campaign for sainthood truly began almost from the day she was born, with three of her sisters joining her in the same monastery—and joining in her ambitions.

Called the Little Flower, Thérèse has a shrine in Royal Oak, Michigan, which is where Harrison fittingly ends her biography: There on November 4, 1999, fifty thousand people filed past Thérèse's ornate casket. This display of her remains was the first stop on an eight-year worldwide tour. Part of this saint's appeal is that she made her suffering so accessible to the multitudes. It is odd to say so, but Thérèse was very modern—and also very medieval—in creating so many souvenirs of her suffering.

Renaissance and Seventeenth-Century Biography

In *English Biography in the Seventeenth Century: A Critical Survey* (2005), Allen Pritchard provides a compelling assessment of the lit-

erature in the century before Boswell and Johnson came to dominate the discussion of biography in English literature. The author
demonstrates that biography was already an established genre in the
seventeenth century, though it often came disguised in the form of
sermons and prefaces to authors' collected works. Readers will be
startled to discover that biographies dealt not merely with the lives
of saints, political figures, and others prominent in the upper classes
but also with the middle class and with women, some of whom were
quite learned and had an impact on their communities. Moreover,
biography as a genre not only preceded the novel but also influenced
the structure of the first eighteenth-century novels, which were life
narratives. Pritchard includes chapters on the seventeenth century's
greatest biographers: Izaak Walton, Thomas Fuller, Anthony Wood,
John Aubrey, and Roger North. An impeccable and accessible work
of scholarship, this study makes a fundamental contribution to the
literature on the development of biography as a genre.

A much earlier but still valuable survey is Donald A. Stauffer's
English Biography Before 1700 (1930). He assesses outstanding examples in the development of biography and summarizes works typify-
ing different kinds of biography. Stauffer has chapters on the medieval period (saints' lives and royal chronicles), the Renaissance
(emphasizing More's history of Richard III), ecclesiastical biography,
Izaak Walton, intimate biography (the sense of personal presence and
private life in Cavendish's Wolsey and Roper's More), and autobiography. More is viewed as infusing the royal chronicle with a dramatic
grasp of human personality; Walton's biographies unite the exemplary thrust of saints' lives and ecclesiastical history with an anecdotal
emphasis and respect for primary documents. A final chapter analyzes comments on biographical method in the biographies surveyed.
The bibliography has a subject and author index of early English biographies and a list of the reference works Stauffer has consulted.

William Nelson, in *Fact or Fiction: The Dilemma of the Renaissance Storyteller* (1973), traces the development of the criterion of
truth in Renaissance poetry, fiction, and nonfiction that gradually
evolved from notions of antiquity, which did not condemn "history

or biography if it included that which was not true." The first chapter demonstrates the "slow and uneven process . . . by which fiction came to be separated from the category of history." Subsequent chapters concentrate on how writers came to understand the truth of fiction, of its special claims to knowledge, while acknowledging the existence of a separate, factually verifiable history. Although not a study of biography per se, Nelson's comments on Renaissance narrative help define biography's place in sixteenth- and seventeenth-century literature.

In a study that complements Nelson, *Biographical Truth: The Representation of Historical Persons in Tudor-Stuart Writing* (1984), Judith H. Anderson explains how biographers such as Roper, More, Walton, and Bacon drew upon fact and imagination to create fully realized characters while recognizing the differences between fiction and history. She argues that "truth of fact" and "truth of fiction" (phrases borrowed from Virginia Woolf) can complement each other, though the biographer's employment of both results in considerable ambiguity akin to certain contemporary fiction by writers such as E. L. Doctorow. Anderson contrasts the way historical figures are treated in drama (primarily Shakespeare's *Henry VIII*) and in narrative lives, and since several of her chapters explore the way different biographers treat the same figures (Richard III, Henry VII, Henry VIII, Cardinal Wolsey), she is able to demonstrate the great variety and depth of early biographical writing.

English Biography in the Seventeenth Century: Selected Short Lives (1951), edited by Vivian de Sola Pinto, is a useful anthology. It includes lives of George Herbert (by Izaak Walton), John, Earl of Rochester (by Gilbert Burnet), Isaac Barrow (by Abraham Hill), and Lancelot Andrewes, Robert Boyle, Thomas Hobbes, Andrew Marvell, and John Milton (all by John Aubrey). Pinto's introduction discusses biography in antiquity, which developed three types of the genre: the "ethical," the "royal or court," and the life of the "saint or sage." The seventeenth century contributed an increasing interest in intimate detail, and, sparked by the development of science, biography exhibited an empirical, inductive approach to individual lives while maintaining the ethical and encomiastic impulse originated by the Greeks and the Romans. Notes, chronological table, and select bibliography make this a good introduction to seventeenth-century biography.

In *Seventeenth Century Prose: Five Lectures* (1960), F. P. Wilson provides a survey of seventeenth-century biography charting changes in the genre and its subjects, noting that at the beginning of the century Shakespeare (a "mere dramatist and poet") was not thought worthy of a biography. Walton and other biographers employed "invented conversations" (as did the ancients) but eventually learned to record the table talk of important figures and include it in biographies such as Aubrey's that began to revel in detailed descriptions of their subjects' manners. This accumulating interest in the uniqueness of personality contributed enormously to Johnson's theory of biography and Boswell's practice of it.

Reviews

Most reviewers of biography tell you what they think of the subject, or just summarize the subject's life in a knowing way, and then make a few comments on the book they are supposed to be reviewing. Reviewers like to exercise their own authority over the subject even though much of that authority is gained from reading the biographies they are reviewing. Most reviewers don't seem able or willing to examine the choices biographers make and the narratives they write.

Both reviewers and their editors are lazy. I suppose they would defend their practices by saying that readers need to know about the subject as much as about the biography. But I would say that the summary part of the review, explaining who the subject is, can be dispatched in a paragraph, after which the merits of the biography ought to be assessed—how it stacks up as a biography, its relationship to other biographies on the same subject, and (ideally) what contribution a particular biography makes to the genre.

That may sound like a tall order, especially if a reviewer has no more than, say, nine hundred words. But I do it every week in the *New York Sun*. Plenty of biographers and scholars are equipped to write such reviews, yet organs such as the *New York Times* often choose reviewers who are ignorant of the subject and of biography, or are obviously hostile to the genre itself and regard reviewing biography as a chore.

Some reviewers of fiction, of course, are just as lazy, retelling the story of the novel without dealing with its form or style. But biography, it seems to me, has been especially poorly served, and the biographer's craft, let alone his art, seems to elude all but a handful of reviewers.

For example, I've read several reviews of Sally Cline's biography of Zelda Fitzgerald, and most of them are worthless because they clearly haven't looked at Milford or at Kendall Taylor's recent book. Well, to do that takes time. Even in the *London Review of Books*, which gives the reviewer more space, Nina Auerbach wrote a review that does not even mention Taylor's book. Clearly Auerbach hasn't read it and wouldn't take the time to do so. Until there are reviewers who take that time, biography will continue to receive ignorant evaluations.

Rolland, Romain (1866–1944)

This Nobel Prize–winning novelist wrote biographies of Michelangelo, Handel, Tolstoy, Gandhi, and Beethoven. His work is distinguished by an intense bond with his subjects. It is Rolland's lyrical style that makes him stand out as a biographer. Biography, in his view, was a way to extend his own creative sensibility.

FURTHER READING: For an introduction to Rolland, see Harold March, *Romain Rolland* (1971). For a more advanced discussion, see R. A. Francis, *Romain Rolland* (1999).

Romanticism and Biography

The period of Romanticism (approximately 1789–1832), ending just before the accession of Queen Victoria in 1837, has also been tied to the development of biography, especially in England. Coleridge wrote on the subject of biography in his journal, *The Friend*, and Robert Southey is renowned today much more for his biography of Admiral Nelson than for his poetry. The obvious connection between Romanticism and biography is, of course, the concentration on the self. Goethe's novels like *Wilhelm Meister* created intense interest in the creative individual's growth, also stimulated by Jean-Jacques Rousseau's *Confessions*. Thomas DeQuincey's *Confessions of an English Opium Eater* also brought a new candor to self-examination while William Hazlitt's reminiscences of the Lake poets, especially Coleridge, recreated in vivid detail the mannerisms and talk of his subject—as did Thomas Carlyle's memoirs of Coleridge and other contemporaries. And yet the nineteenth century experienced a disjunction between biography and the other literary arts. Biographers, by and large, attempted nothing like the candor and intensity to be found in Romantic poetry. As Romanticism gave way to Victorianism, the biographer tended to suppress knowledge about his subject's failings, sexual experience, and other aspects of intimacy that Boswell had done so much to promote as the proper province of biography.

Royal Biography

A. J. P. Taylor's *The Habsburg Monarchy* (1948), Antonia Fraser's *Mary, Queen of Scots* (1969), *Edward VIII* by Philip Ziegler, and *George III: A Personal History* by Christopher Hibbert are representative of the genre. In each case, impeccable research is accompanied by a lively and penetrating style. Earlier biographies of royals, such as Lytton Strachey's *Queen Victoria*, remain wonderful examples of style and wit but have been superseded in terms of biographers' access to archival material.

David Cannadine has published one of the best essays on the genre in *The Invention of Tradition* (1983), edited by Eric Hobsbawm and Terence Ranger. A much earlier study, still valuable for its exploration of how historians and biographers have treated the monarchy, is Herbert Butterfield's *George III and the Historians*.

CRITIQUE: Princess Diana has had an enormous impact on how biographers now view the monarchy. Sarah Bradford's simply titled *Diana* (2006) is meant to surpass earlier productions of the Diana industry, as her portentous prologue announces: "By the time of her death in August 1997, she was an icon and a royal rebel, a glamorous figure both worshipped and reviled. . . ." While Buckingham Palace staked out stories about the unstable princess, Fleet Street frothed up other tales about an uncaring and remote royal family. No stranger to hyperbole herself, Bradford continues:

> No one who was in London during that time, or who watched the run-up to the funeral on television, will ever forget the experience or the irrational, dangerous emotions which the death of Diana had stirred in the British people. For the Royal Family its recent history could be seen as pre-Diana and post-Diana, such was the impact this young woman had upon the ancient institution and the people's attitudes towards it.

Diana made her case, her biographer claims, through her "luminous presence and undoubted gifts of empathy with the suffering." Moreover she was not a troubled princess in search of herself but rather a royal in command of her role:

> She groomed her sons to be in touch with the age: she had a clear view of how William should set about his royal task when the time came. Her own approach to what she saw as her job was utterly professional and could not have been carried out by a woman suffering the psychological problems attributed to her.

Wait a minute! It is one thing to accord Diana her due: she was, as Bradford reports, a student of icons, especially Marilyn Monroe, who battled the studios the way Diana assailed the monarchy. But Diana also evinced, in Sally Bedell Smith's words, "borderline behavior." Like Marilyn, Diana was "obsessed with finding her identity, harbored a terror of solitude, and suffered from crushing despair."

To maintain a view of Diana in charge, Bradford describes a princess who could be brutal with her staff and with others devious, manipulative, and suspicious. Call Bradford's effort an overcorrection. Seeking to avoid the sentimentality, the wallowing in victimhood, and the crass psychologizing of earlier biographies, the biographer chooses to create a pro-active Diana.

But Bradford seems almost willful in disregarding evidence that weakens her brief. For example, she attributes much of the talk of Diana's mental illness to her enemies at court. But it was Diana herself who began to reveal the shocking nature of her instability—not just the bulimia but acts of self-mutilation to her arms and legs as well as several suicide attempts.

Much of the disturbing news about Diana's psyche was funneled through friendly channels to Andrew Morton (*Diana: Her True Story* [1992]), who remains in many ways still her best biographer. Sally Bedell Smith (*Diana in Search of Herself* [1999]), Anne Edwards (*Ever After: Diana and the Life She Led* [1999]), and others have paid tribute to Morton's groundbreaking book; indeed, virtually all the important Diana biographers have consulted him. Morton's shocking revelations of Diana's disturbed mentality are all the more powerful because he was her sympathetic conduit—her champion, really.

Morton is usefully augmented by books such as Anthony Holden's *The Tarnished Crown* (1993), in which Diana's behavior is measured against the history of the monarchy. A biography yet to be written might take more seriously than Bradford's what it means to be an icon and how the icon views herself as part of a constellation of avatars.

Bradford unfortunately stumbles because she does not know what to make of the Monroe analogy. The biographer reports, for example, that one of Diana's friends (unidentified in the notes) wanted to send her a "fantastic documentary" about Monroe but did not do so because "it was not good stuff for Diana to be looking at." Diana was vulnerable and had "suicidal tendencies," the friend explained.

What does Bradford make of this story? Nothing, except to point out that both Diana and Marilyn died at the age of thirty-six. Monroe's story is disturbing because in the end all the icon had to offer was herself—that extraordinary empathy that Bradford admires in Diana and that was so much a factor in Monroe's own rise and demise. What comes through in Monroe's films, for example—now that the hoopla about her sexuality is no longer the only aspect of her that Hollywood is selling—is her extraordinary generosity, the way she tells that nebbish Roger Sherman (Tom Ewell) in *The Seven Year Itch*, "You're just elegant."

Monroe put all she had into such roles, and came up empty. Similarly, depression followed Diana's efforts to connect with the world at large. Too much a demand is made on such figures, especially when like Diana and Marilyn they are unsure of their own identities. As one of Diana's friends said, at thirty-six Diana was no closer to understanding herself than she had been at twenty.

Diana used to insist on Marilyn's intelligence. She was right, of course. But intelligence was not enough. And perhaps that's why Diana's friend did not want to send that documentary to her. To identify so intensely with Marilyn Monroe was indeed dangerous, and any biographer who fails to explore that risk puts her biography of Diana in peril.

EVEN WHEN Diana is not the ostensible subject, she casts a shadow on biographies of earlier royal figures. Subtitled *The Scandalous Affair That Nearly Ended a Monarchy*, Jane Robins's *The Trial of Queen Caroline* is as much history as it is biography, forsaking extensive character analysis for the plotting of fast-breaking events and sudden twists of fate. By the end of her narrative, however, the two main characters, George IV and the queen he abjured—not to mention a colorful supporting cast, including the manic-depressive Whig politician Henry Brougham and the radical firebrand journalist William Cobbett—are arrayed with a vividness that is like sitting transfixed before the tube as a world-changing episode enfolds an audience keenly aware of its own interest in the outcome.

It is a commonplace observation that with the advent of cable television networks and 24/7 news coverage, the world is—as William Wordsworth wrote two hundred years ago—"too much with us." That Wordsworth could make such a statement, however, ought to be regarded as a challenge to our conventional notions about how our world has diverged from Caroline's, the world of 1820 when a prince wanted to divorce his princess and everyone speculated about the rights and wrongs surrounding the conflicted couple. Sound familiar?

It is to Jane Robins's credit that she does not draw the parallel—perhaps because it is so obvious, and perhaps because through means of narrative economy and understatement she obliges the reader to make comparisons between then and now. This brilliant strategy heightens the focus on George and Caroline, the former an obese bigamist and the latter a plump adulteress—though Robins wisely avoids such labels since it is her aim to tantalize her readers into entertaining conjectures such as: Was Caroline unfaithful to her prince? Or was she merely careless with the attentions she paid to her male servants and courtiers, indulging in intimate gestures in public that did not necessarily mean she was even more intimate with them in private?

Robins builds up considerable sympathy for Caroline, the same sympathy the British public felt for this royal who liked to consort with commoners and rejected protocol. She wanted to be the people's queen and thought she had the opportunity to be one when George III died in 1820, and she returned to England after a long exile—driven abroad by her husband, who had taken one look at her (he refused to meet her before the marriage), essayed an act or two of sexual intercourse, and then shunned her for the rest of her life.

Such behavior earned George IV a bad press. He was disliked for his conspicuous extravagance and what would today be called "womanizing." Even worse, he had secretly married his mistress, Maria Fitzherbert, a Roman Catholic, before his nuptials with Caroline, thus jeopardizing his position as the next Protestant king and defender of his nation's established church. Finding her prince to be no prince, Caroline agreed to leave Britain even while insisting on her prerogatives as a royal. When George III died, the prince decided it was time to try Caroline for adultery (a capital crime) and rid himself of her forever. Against the advice of her advocate, Henry Brougham, Caroline returned, believing not only that the case against her could not be proven but that the British people would not stand for such an insult to their queen.

Caroline was right. A time when the circulation of the London *Times* was only ten thousand might not seem, as Robins notes, an age when public opinion could be accounted a major political force. But six or seven people might read one issue of a newspaper. And broadsides and all manner of cheap publications inundated the countryside, where they were read (often aloud) to groups of avid Caroline junkies. About the only people who did not plump for Caroline were the Tories and certain stuffy Whig ladies. The women of England, Robins suggests, were outraged that a husband—royal or not—could so demean his spouse. This was not, however, a feminist issue: the populace backed Caroline precisely because George had not honored the traditional way of respecting a wife.

Then radicals like William Cobbett made Caroline their weapon against the unruly monarchy George exemplified. Here Jane Robins departs from Flora Fraser's *The Unruly Queen: The Life of Queen Caroline* (1996). Fraser says in no uncertain terms that Caroline was guilty of adultery. The shrewd Robins never puts it so baldly. Fraser may be right, but as the brilliant Henry Brougham put it to the House of Lords (charged with trying Queen Caroline), the most damning testimony against her came from individual witnesses who could provide no corroboration.

Given the public's hostility toward George IV, and the prosecution's inability to produce the "smoking gun" (someone who had witnessed Caroline having sex outside of marriage), the Tory administration was forced to withdraw its charges against Caroline. Then she made a fatal error: she tried to barge her way into George's coronation. The public turned against her because no matter how offensive they found George, he was still their king. Her actions were deemed undignified.

Caroline died shortly thereafter (probably of stomach cancer) and recouped a good deal of favorable public sentiment. Throughout her trial eminent figures like Wellington feared there might be a revolt in the army, splitting into pro-Caroline and pro-George factions, or even a nationwide upheaval. Such fears were exaggerated, but Robins is right to evoke the tense atmosphere of the time and the sense of foreboding that the country might forsake reform for revolution.

As a work of both history and biography Robins's effort is excellent. As a study of the media and the shaping of public opinion, her work is perhaps even more valuable. And for sheer pleasure in reading a well-wrought narrative, it would be hard to top this book.

Sainte-Beuve, Charles-Augustin (1804–1869)

Sainte-Beuve's literary portraits exerted a wide-ranging influence on the study of literature and the role of biography in understanding an author's work. He believed in the importance of intuitive sympathy, his ability to read an author's character. Whereas Hippolyte Taine and other nineteenth-century critics explored the cultures out of which writers emerged, Sainte-Beuve tended to exult the individual creative personality. Writers like Proust reacted negatively to the critic's views even as Sainte-Beuve's work influenced him. Indeed, Proust's great novel is surely, in part, a product of Sainte-Beuve's probing of the artist's personality. What else is Proust's work but an investigation of the creative mind, anchoring the writer's perceptions in the places and events his sensibility transforms?

FURTHER READING: Francis Steegmuller, ed., *Sainte Beuve: Selected Essays* (1964); Emerson R. Marks, ed., *Literary Criticism of Sainte-Beuve* (1971); Harold Nicolson, *Sainte-Beuve* (1978); Peter France and William St. Clair, ed., *Mapping Lives: The Uses of Biography* (2002); Lewis Freeman Mott, *Sainte-Beuve* (2006).

Sales

An extraordinary number of good subjects get turned down because some editor or publisher doubts the biography will sell. And of course they are usually right. With a few notable exceptions, no literary biography sells more than ten thousand copies, and most sell far less than that. I don't know any literary biographer who has ever made back his or her advance. I'm sure there are a few, but I could name some very important authors who have never seen a royalty check after the advance.

The Sontag biography that my wife and I wrote has not been reprinted in paperback, and there are no plans to do so. Paperback sales are traditionally about half or less of the initial hardcover print run. Evidently five thousand or so copies of a paperback did not seem worthwhile to Norton, even to help recover the advance. The firm expected to make back some of its investment from foreign sales. And two foreign publishers have published the Sontag biography, in Spanish and Portuguese. It is surprising that publishers in France, Germany, and Italy, for example, have not bought the biography. Sontag's publisher, Roger Straus of Farrar, Straus and Giroux, who vehemently opposed the biography, probably had something to do with Norton's inability to secure foreign sales. He accused Norton of deliberately trying to offend him by publishing an unauthorized biography of one of his star authors. When Norton refused to cancel the biography, Straus canceled the book contract of an editor at Norton whose novel Farrar, Straus was supposed to publish. Straus had many important relationships with foreign publishers; indeed, his firm made much of its profit doing business with foreign publishers—publishing their titles in the United States and selling them Farrar, Straus titles for their foreign markets.

Advances may be inflated when publishers bid against one another for a promising book. A kind of self-delusion takes over: because so many publishers covet the book, it is worth jacking up the bids. As soon as publishers buy the biography, however, they succumb to buyer's remorse, wondering how on earth they will generate enough sales to justify the large advance.

Biographies are tough to pitch to publishers, even though biography continues to be a popular genre that is frequently reviewed. Publishers want something new—but not really, because they say readers are not familiar enough with the "new" subject. Agents are no better since they, like publishers, immediately think of terms of the kinds of biographies that have sold in the past. In truth, a biographer simply must have faith in himself and hope that a publisher will eventually be found.

SEE ALSO Advances.

Sartre, Jean-Paul (1905–1980)

Sartre made his reputation as a biographer with *Saint Genet* (1952, translated into English in 1963) and *The Family Idiot*, a three-volume biography of Flaubert (1971–1972), translated into English between 1981 and 1993. Sartre's main theme in these works is the writer's effort to subvert convention. Artists become for the philosopher Sartre exemplary figures, creating and testing their individuality against the tremendous pressure of modern life to conform to societal values.

Sartre's novel *Nausea* (1938, translated into English in 1949) takes a biographer as its subject.

SEE ALSO Biographers in Fiction.

FURTHER READING: Douglas Collins's *Sartre as Biographer* (1980) and Michael Scriven, *Sartre's Existential Biographies* (1984).

Strachey, Lytton (1880–1932)

One of the major figures in modern biography, Strachey has elicited a wide range of contradictory opinion. Critics have lauded his overturning of Victorian pieties, his exquisite sense of form, and his turns of phrase that have made biography into a serious art form. He made modern biography less didactic, solemn, and rhetorical while exercising discriminating powers of selection, detachment, design, and brevity. To the rather stodgy form of biography, Strachey brought the powers of the novelist, especially in the creation of character and vivid scenes. Indeed, some commentators see Strachey as making the biographer the hero in a way that supplants his subjects.

At the same time his skeptical, debunking tone has elicited considerable disapproval, and even his deft handling of psychology became in the hands of his imitators a rather crude labeling of personalities. Strachey himself has been condemned for his shallow irony. As Charles Smyth put it in *The Criterion* ("Historical Biography and Mr. Strachey," vol. 8, 1929, pp. 647–660), Strachey opposes his subjects with a "snigger."

Writing about "History and the Biographer" in the *Yale Review* (vol. 22, 1933, pp. 549–558), Wallace Notestein commented: Strachey makes discovering motive "an easy game," yet nothing in biography is "more hazardous," since motives can be as elusive to the subject as to the biographer.

FURTHER READING: Michael Holroyd, *Lytton Strachey: The New Biography* (1995); *The Letters of Lytton Strachey* (2005).

Suetonius (C.70 A.D.–130 A.D.)

Best known for his *The Lives of the Twelve Caesars*, Suetonius is revered by biographers because of his keen insight into the private lives of public figures, including physical descriptions, family background, personal behavior, and scandal. Like Plutarch, only more so, Suetonius enjoyed a good anecdote. He did not stint documenting, for example, of Tiberius's debaucheries. Unlike Plutarch, Suetonius arranged his narrative by topic, not chronology, and he made much more use of gossip, hearsay, and rumor. His topics included ancestry and family, public career, and physical description, and he treated his subjects comprehensively, warts and all.

FURTHER READING: Barry Baldwin, *Suetonius* (1983) and Michael Grant, *The Twelve Caesars* (1975); and Andrew Wallace-Hadrell, *Suetonius: The Scholar and His Caesars* (1984).

SEE ALSO Plutarch.

Symons, A. J. A. (1900–1941)

Best known for his experimental biography *The Quest for Corvo* (1934), Symons exemplified the modern desire to revive biography as a literary genre comparable in its style to the novel. The biographer had to be more than a recorder of fact. Imaginative insight and a compelling structure were both essential.

FURTHER READING: Symons's important writings about biography are collected in *Essays and Biographies* (1969), edited by Julian Symons, who also published *A. J. A. Symons: His Life and Speculations* in 1950.

SEE ALSO Innovative Biographies for a description of *The Quest for Corvo*.

Unauthorized Biography

Unauthorized biography is written in a completely independent fashion—that is, the unauthorized biographer has not sought permission from his subject's estate or the subject himself. Unauthorized biographers are often attacked for having limited access to their subjects and an ax to grind. On the other hand, the unauthorized biographer is often much more forthcoming than the authorized biographer can be. An unauthorized biography can in fact provide a degree of independence and insight that the more cautious and constrained authorized biography lacks.

CRITIQUE: Some biographers make themselves; others are adopted. Suzanne Marrs belongs to the latter category, which means that her work has been given the imprimatur of the Welty establishment, a confederacy of academics and literary figures gathered round the shrine of St. Eudora.

I give her that honorific because no American writer in living memory has been so adored. As Marrs acknowledges, Welty projected an image of gentle integrity and humane good humor that made her seem a paragon. She received nearly forty honorary degrees (maybe more; Marrs is not sure), which get their own appendix in this biography. No anthology of American literature can do without a Welty story such as that comic classic "Why I Live at the P.O." Only William Faulkner ranks higher in the pantheon of Southern literature.

Welty put the finishing touches to her consecration in her charming and best-selling *One Writer's Beginnings* (1984). Marrs notes that Welty hoped to head off biographers with this memoir, as John Updike has so far successfully done with *Self-Consciousness*. Certainly Welty made it hard for any biographer to probe deeper without seeming to be a spoilsport.

But in *Writing a Woman's Life* (1988), the critic and biographer Carolyn Heilbrun questioned Welty's autobiography, wondering where was the woman who had made a literary career? Where were the ambition, the irony, and bitterness that mark—at least to some extent—all writers' lives? The sanctification had reached such a level in the early 1990s that a blaspheming biographer was bound to desecrate the temple.

I must now declare an interest: I encouraged Ann Waldron to write the first biography of Welty, published as *Eudora: A Writer's Life* (1998). Waldron, a native Southerner and author of acclaimed biographies of Caroline Gordon and Hodding Carter, did not have full access to her subject's papers and was shunned by the Welty establishment. Marrs dismisses Waldron in a sentence, suggesting the biographer's attempt to "humanize the mythic 'Miss Eudora'" resulted in creating "an equally reductive image: the charming and successful ugly duckling." But what are Marrs's own bona fides?

A Welty scholar, she explains that she became her subject's friend during the last fifteen years of Welty's life. Even though she knew Welty opposed not only Waldron but any other writer attempting a Welty biography, why did Marrs ask Welty's permission to write her biography, and why did Welty "promptly" grant the request?

Silence from Marrs. Might Waldron's biography, which appeared in the year Marrs got her go-ahead, have had something to do with Welty's volte-face? What Marrs dare not acknowledge (what would the Welty establishment say?) is that her book would have been inconceivable without Waldron's valiant first effort.

And what did Marrs discover when she was awarded complete access to the Welty sanctuary? Welty had conserved a huge amount of material—strange doings for a biographobe. Surely this hoard should have been burned: Henry James made quite a pyre out of his papers. Instead the only sacred texts Marrs was not permitted to handle were certain family letters held back until twenty years after Welty's death.

Do all these behind-the-scenes revelations about the biography world matter? I think they do, because they affect the biographer, her sources, and the milieu in which her book will be enshrined. Marrs's book comes ready-made with a blurb from a Welty high priest, the novelist Reynolds Price.

This is not a bad book, though Marrs suffers from the bloat that often afflicts authorized biographers. She has relics, and she wants to show all of them. She also feels the need to comment when no comment is necessary. Thus she reports that baby Eudora played with dolls and made up stories about them. "The future story writer was at an early age engaging her imagination." Ah, I see.

Then there are moments when Marrs might comment but thinks she is only conveying amusing information. She notes, for example, that twelve-year-old Eudora created for her brother Edward's entertainment her own book, complete with blurbs:

HEAR WHAT THE CRITICS SAY ABOUT IT!
ANDREW VOLSTEAD—"Never heard of it."
WAYNE B. WHELER—"I haven't read it."
JOHN ROACH STRATTON—"I know nothing about it."

Marrs then describes Eudora in the eighth grade. But hold on! Here Welty is expressing a satirical nature reminiscent of the juvenile Jane Austen, one of Welty's favorite writers. What struck me is that like other ambitious writers—Susan Sontag comes to mind—Welty always wanted to be a writer. And she didn't just want to write; she wanted to take her place in that world of publishing and of writers and critics.

Spending so much of her life in Jackson, Mississippi, Welty made it look like the world came to her. In fact she was out there hustling like any other writer, enjoying her trips to New York City, pursuing novelist Elizabeth Bowen in London, and in general keeping her eye on the main chance.

Waldron shows us such truths in a pointed fashion. Marrs, on the other hand, provides more facts and a much more intimate view of Welty's love life. For Weltyans this biography is indispensable. But they must take into account its provenance, or they will not be getting the whole story.

HERE IS another example of the tensions between unauthorized and authorized biography: *Gellhorn: A Twentieth Century Life* by Caroline Moorehead (2003). "The first major biography of Martha Gellhorn," Moorehead's publisher announces. So there is at least one minor biography? I hope readers will ask. In fact there are two: *Nothing Ever Happens to the Brave* (1990) and *Beautiful Exile* (2001)—both written by me, though I do not consider them minor. The first made Gellhorn furious; the second provoked a press campaign by her friends in Britain to discredit me. Perhaps this explains why I am not included in Moorehead's "sources and select bibliography." She has been authorized by Gellhorn's estate, and that means I have become the nonbiographer.

Martha Gellhorn is rightly described in the publisher's copy as having pursued a "heroic career as a reporter [which] brought her to the front lines of virtually every significant international conflict between the Spanish Civil War and the end of the Cold War." She was also Ernest Hemingway's third wife, the only one to walk out on him, and a fine writer of novellas, which Knopf published together in a fat volume a decade ago.

I learned a good deal more about Gellhorn from Moorehead—chiefly how she viewed her own life in letters that only her authorized biographer has been allowed to read. Gellhorn was more critical of herself than I had imagined, freely acknowledging that she put all her skill into reporting. She had a great eye and ear, but she had no gift for analysis. I knew that Gellhorn could write only about what she had seen and heard, and that she was no thinker, but I did not realize how she herself came to the same conclusion after futile efforts to complete books about the Spanish Civil War, Cuba, and Vietnam.

What is new in this biography? How does Moorehead handle her sources? How does her book accord with my understanding of biography as a genre?

First, Moorehead has had the kind of unlimited access to the evidence and interviewees that every biographer seeks. I was delighted to see descriptions of Gellhorn's austere London flat, virtually a mirror of her astringent mind, to discover that she was very pleased with her long and narrow feet and had Ferragamo make shoes especially for her, and that "new words made her laugh with sudden delight." From Plutarch to Boswell and beyond, biographers have given us these little details and anecdotes that make their subjects live again.

There is one source, however, that Moorehead studiously avoids. In her only reference to me, the biographer repeats Gellhorn's charge that my work is riddled with errors. Moorehead need not have trusted my book. By using almost any of the internet search engines, she could have found my archive at the University of Tulsa, open to any researcher who wants to examine the notes, correspondence, and tape-recorded interviews from my two biographies of Martha Gellhorn. I eagerly read Moorehead to see what I had got wrong, but was disappointed. Her biography only confirms what I wrote in a published letter to *The Guardian*—that the charges had no merit. I even wrote to one of Gellhorn's closest friends, the biographer Victoria Glendinning, who replied that she doubted I had made errors and assured me that Martha was just mad at me.

When Martha got mad, she lost all perspective. She was mad at her own native land and lived most of her life away from it. She was mad at the Palestinians and would not brook a single word of criticism of Israelis. She loved the Spanish Republic and never wrote one word about how its loyalists committed atrocities or how the Stalinists eliminated all elements of the left that did not hew to Moscow's line. She was a partisan in every sense of the word and was even proud of denouncing journalists who talked about that "objectivity shit." There was right and there was wrong, and there was nothing in between.

Moorehead sees this side of Martha—but only selectively. This is one of the most anti-American books I have ever read. Moorehead repeats without comment every hysterical charge Gellhorn makes against the United States. The biographer is dismayed only when Gellhorn does not give equal consideration to the Palestinians or to the Germans, whom Gellhorn did not believe would ever create a democratic country.

As a biographer, I'm rather shocked at how little attention Moorehead devotes to Gellhorn's St. Louis background. True enough, you will find the relationship between Martha and her mother Edna is sensitively told, but Edna's work as a reformer in St. Louis and how that reforming spirit energized Martha is not portrayed. Martha's namesake and grandmother, a provocative social reformer in St. Louis, is not even mentioned! Gellhorn conducted a lifelong campaign to distance herself from St. Louis and hurt her mother terribly by giving no credit to the city's progressive ethos, and Moorehead writes in the same vein—as if she were writing not a biography but completing Gellhorn's autobiography.

In general this biography is out of tune with what, for all her anti-Americanism, made Gellhorn an American figure, and out of sync with her almost desperate effort not to sound like an American. Thus I was astounded at Moorehead's reference to Gellhorn's "accent as unmistakeably still of the American Midwest." No American friend of Gellhorn's I interviewed saw any trace of her St. Louis intonation. On television she sounded like a posh confection of British/Eastern seaboard talk. Perhaps she saved the Midwestern "drawl" to entertain her British friends.

Still, Moorehead does deliver the news—with much to say about Gellhorn's lovers, from Bertrand de Jouvenel (seduced at sixteen by Colette) to Ernest Hemingway to General James Gavin, and many more. Crossed off the lover list, however, is H. G. Wells, primarily because Gellhorn denied the affair and was "scrupulous," Moorehead asserts, about identifying her lovers. Maybe so, but H. G. said they did make love, and having done my own extensive research on this randy writer for a biography of Rebecca West, I see no reason to dispute his account.

Has Moorehead's work changed the basic shape and significance of Martha Gellhorn's life as I described it? I don't think so. And for that I'm grateful.

SEE ALSO Authorized Biography.

FURTHER READING: Michael Millgate, *Testamentary Acts* (1992); Ian Hamilton, *Keepers of the Flame* (1994); Denis Brian, *Fair Game: What Biographers Don't Tell You* (1994); Carl Rollyson, *Reading Biography* (2004), *Essays in Biography* (2004), and *A Higher Form of Cannibalism: Adventures in the Art and Politics of Biography* (2005).

Vasari, Giorgio (1511–1574)

Vasari occupies an important place in the history of both biography and Western art. An artist himself, he knew some of the biographical subjects he wrote about in his *Lives*. Like many of the greatest biographers, he was writing memoirs as well as studies of his subjects. Vasari provides wonderful anecdotes about Michelangelo and Donatello, for example, sometimes even noting their very words and habits.

No one is comparable to Vasari in the English language writing before the eighteenth century. His integration of art criticism and biography is not rivaled before the nineteenth century. He made his share of mistakes—attributing some works wrongly to certain artists—but his effort to establish a documentary record is impressive. He conducted many interviews and consulted a wide range of documents, including chronicles, histories, letters, other biographies, and official records.

Vasari is important as well because of his sense of history, defining the idea of a Renaissance, which Italian artists had done so much to advance. His chief limitation was his idea that art progresses. Impressed with an ability to render perspective and the development of other realist techniques, Vasari tended to downgrade art of the medieval period, judging it by the standards of his own age rather than by the period in which the art was created. Modern art historians have rejected this idea that art progresses, seeing other values in pre-Renaissance art that should be judged on its own terms.

Vasari's depiction of Michelangelo, in particular, elevated the artist into a kind of heroic individual, a view that otherwise was not fully developed until the nineteenth-century Romantics.

FURTHER READING: T. S. R. Boase, *Giorgio Vasari: The Man and the Book* (1979) and Leon Satkowski, *Giorgio Vasari: Architect and Courtier* (1993).

Walton, Izaak (1593–1683)

Best known for his life of John Donne, Walton emphasized not the poet but the man of piety. He practiced a somewhat modified form of the hagiographic religious biography, publishing several biographies of churchmen: *The Life of Sir Henry Wotton* (1651), *The Life of Mr. Richard Hooker* (1665), *The Life of George Herbert* (1670), and *The Life of Dr. Sanderson* (1678). The biographies were meant to be appended to collections of their writings. These were lives to revere and learn from, not examples of biography as a full exploration of human character.

Nevertheless Walton holds an important place in the history of biography because he infused his writing with great feeling and memories of subjects who had become his friends. Passages in his work are nearly novelistic, so intense is his aim to create empathy for his subjects. He also includes scenes and anecdotes that still appeal to the modern reader. Rather than simply documenting and praising lives, he portrayed them with an immediacy that is rare in the biographies of his time.

Woolf, Virginia (1882–1941)

Biographers should disclose all facets of their subjects and avoid all forms of censorship, Woolf wrote, for only in that way can biographies produce "the creative fact; the fertile fact; the fact that suggests and engenders." Although Woolf wrote perceptively about biography in essays such as "The Art of Biography" and in her novels, her own practice as a biographer is undistinguished. When she wrote about her friend Roger Fry, her tone was subdued. She succumbed, in fact, to the biographer's malady: an excessive concern that she not offend the memory of her subject and his family. Thus she violated her own precepts.

SEE ALSO Biographers in Fiction for a discussion of Woolf's *Orlando*, a fictional treatment of biography.

Works Cited

Ackroyd, Peter. *Dickens* (1990).

Alkon, Paul. "Boswellian Time." *Studies in Burke and His Time*, vol. 14, 1973.

Alpern, Sara, Joyce Antler, Elisabeth Isabel Perry, and Ingrid Winther Scobie, eds. *The Challenge of Feminist Biography: Writing the Lives of Modern American Women* (1992).

Altick, Richard D. *Lives and Leters: A History of Literary Biography in England and America* (1966).

Anderson, Judith H. *Biographical Truth: The Representation of Historical Persons in Tudor-Stuart Writing* (1984).

Atlas, James. "Choosing a Life." *New York Times*, January 13, 1991.

Backscheider, Paula. *Reflection on Biography* (1999).

Bailey, Blake. *A Tragic Honesty: The Life and Work of Richard Yates* (2003).

Bainbridge, Beryl. *According to Queeney* (1991).

Baldwin, Barry. *Suetonius* (1983).

Barnes, Julian. *Flaubert's Parrot* (1985).

Barzun, Jacques. "Biography and Criticism—A Misalliance Disputed." *Critical Inquiry*, March 1975.

Bate, Walter Jackson. *Samuel Johnson* (1977).

Battigelli, Ann. *Margaret Cavendish and the Exiles of the Mind* (1998).

Benjamin, Walter. "The Work of Art in the Age of Mechanical Reproduction." *Illuminations*, ed. Hannah Arendt (1969).

Berthoud, Roger. *The Life of Henry Moore* (1987).

Blackburn, Julia. *Daisy Bates in the Desert: A Woman's Life Among the Aborigines* (1994).

Boase, T. S. R. *Giorgio Vasari: The Man and the Book* (1979).

Bosco, Ronald, and Joel Myerson. *The Emerson Brothers: A Fraternal Biography in Letters* (2005).

Bradford, Gamaliel. *Bare Souls* (1924).

Bradford, Sarah. *Diana* (2006).

Brands, H. W. *Woodrow Wilson* (2003).

Brenman-Gibson, Margaret. *Clifford Odets: American Playwright. The Years from 1906 to 1940* (1982).

Brian, Denis. *Fair Game: What Biographers Don't Tell You* (1994).

Brinkley, Douglas, and Julie Fenster. *Parish Priest: Father Michael McGivney and American Catholicism* (2006).

Brodie, Fawn. *No Man Knows My History: The Life of Joseph Smith* (1945, revised 1970).

———. *Thomas Jefferson: An Intimate History* (1964).

Bromwich, David. "Some Uses of Biography." In *A Choice of Inheritance: Self and Community from Edmund Burke to Robert Frost* (1989).

Bushman, Richard Lyman. *Joseph Smith: Rough Stone Rolling* (2005).

Butterfield, Herbert. *George III and the Historians* (1959).

Byatt, A. S. *Possession* (1990).

Cannadine, David. *The Invention of Tradition* (1983).

Capaldi, Nicholas. *John Stuart Mill: A Biography* (2004).

Carrère, Emmanuelle. *I Am Alive and You Are Dead: A Journey into the Mind of Philip K. Dick* (2004).

Churchwell, Sarah. *The Many Lives of Marilyn Monroe* (2005).

Clifford, James L., ed. *Biography as an Art: Selected Criticism 1560–1960* (1962).

Clifford, James L. "Hanging Up Looking Glasses at Odd Corners": Ethnobiographical Prospects." *Studies in Biography*, 1978.

Clinch, Nancy. *The Kennedy Neurosis* (1973).

Cockshut, A. O. J. *Truth to Life: The Art of Biography in the Nineteenth Century* (1974).

Cody, John. *After Great Pain: The Inner Life of Emily Dickinson* (1971).

Coe, Jonathan. *Like a Fiery Elephant: The Story of B. S. Johnson* (2004).

Collingwood, R. G. *The Idea of History* (1946).

Collins, Douglas. *Sartre as Biographer* (1980).

Conradi, Peter. *Iris Murdoch: A Life* (2001).

Coren, Michael. *The Man Who Was G. K. Chesterton* (1989).

Cox, Patricia. *Biography in Late Antiquity* (1983).

Cross, Amanda. *The Players Come Again* (1990).

Cross, Wilbur. *An Outline of Biography from Plutarch to Strachey* (1924).

Dorey, T. A., ed. *Latin Biography* (1967).

Dowling, William C. "Boswell and the Problem of Biography." *Harvard Studies in English*, vol. 8, 1978.

Dudley, Dorothy. *Forgotten Frontiers: Dreiser and the Land of the Free* (1932).

Dunaway, David King. "The Oral Biography." *Biography*, Summer 1991.

Dunn, Waldo H. *English Biography* (1916).

Edel, Leon. *The Psychological Novel* (1955).

———. *Literary Biography* (1957).

———. "The Figure Under the Carpet." *Telling Lives,* ed. Marc Pachter (1979).

———. *Stuff of Sleep and Dreams* (1982).

———. *Writing Lives* (1984).

———. *Henry James* (1985).

Edwards, Anne. *Ever After: Diana and the Life She Led* (1999).

Elias, Robert H. *Theodore Dreiser: Apostle of Nature* (1948).

Ellmann, Richard. *James Joyce* (1959).

———. *Golden Codgers: Biographical Speculations* (1973).

———. "Freud and Literary Biography," *Freud and the Humanities,* ed. Peregrine Horden (1985).

Empson, William. *Using Biography* (1984).

Epstein, William H. *Contesting the Subject: Essays in Postmodern Theory and Practice of Biography and Biographical Criticism* (1991).

Erikson, Erik. *Young Man Luther: A Study in Psychoanalysis and History* (1958).

———. *Children and Society,* Second Edition (1963).

———. *Identity: Youth and Crisis* (1968).

———. "On the Nature of Psycho-Historical Evidence: In Search of Gandhi." *Daedalus* 97 (Summer 1968).

———. *Gandhi's Truth: On the Origins of Militant Nonviolence* (1969).

———. *Dimensions of a New Identity* (1974).

Faulkner, William. *Absalom, Absalom!* (1936).

———. *Go Down, Moses* (1942).

Felman, Shoshan, and Dori Laub. *Testimony: Crises of Witnessing in Literature, Psychoanalysis and History* (1992).

Ffinch, Michael. *G. K. Chesterton* (1986).

Field, Andrew. *Nabokov: His Life in Part* (1977).

Fish, Stanley. "Biography and Intention." *Contesting the Subject: Essays in Postmodern Theory and Practice of Biography and Biographical Criticism,* ed. William H. Epstein (1991).

———. "Just Published: Minutiae Without Meaning." *New York Times,* September 7, 1999.

Fleming, Candace. *Ben Franklin's Almanac: Being a True Account of the Good Gentleman's Life* (2003).

France, Peter, and William St. Clair, eds. *Mapping Lives: The Uses of Biography* (2002).

Fraser, Antonia. *Mary, Queen of Scots* (1969).

Fraser, Flora. *The Unruly Queen: The Life of Queen Caroline* (1996).

Freedman, Russell. *Eleanor Roosevelt: A Life of Discovery* (1993).

———. *The Wright Brothers: How They Invented the Airplane* (1994).

———. *Martha Graham: A Dancer's Life* (1998).

Freud, Sigmund. *Leonardo da Vinci and a Memory of His Childhood* (1910).

Freud, Sigmund, and William C. Bullitt. *Thomas Woodrow Wilson: A Psychological Study* (1967).

Frisch, Michael. *A Shared Authority: Essays on the Craft and Meaning of Oral and Public History* (1990).

Fromm, Gloria, ed. *Essaying Biography: A Celebration of Leon Edel* (1986).

Fumaroli, Marc. "From 'Lives' to Biography: The Twilight of Parnassus." *Diogenes*, Fall 1987.

Garraty, John A. *The Nature of Biography* (1957).

Garrett, George. "Literary Biography in Our Time." *Sewanee Review*, Summer 1984.

Geary, Joseph. *Spiral* (2003).

George, Alexander and Juliette. *Woodrow Wilson and Colonel House: A Personality Study* (1956).

Giankaris, C. J. *Plutarch* (1970).

Giddens, Gary. *Bing Crosby: A Pocketful of Dreams, The Early Years, 1903–1940* (2001).

Gindin, James. *The English Climate: An Excursion into a Biography of John Galsworthy* (1979).

Girard, Linda Walvoord. "Series Thinking and the Art of Biography for Children." *Children's Literature Association Quarterly*, Winter 1989.

Gitelson, Celia. *Biography* (1991).

Gittings, Robert. *The Nature of Biography* (1978).

Glover, Jane. *Mozart's Women: The Man, the Music, and the Loves in His Life* (2006).

Gluck, Sherna Berger, and Daphne Patai, eds. *Women's Words: The Feminist Practice of Oral History* (1991).

Golding, William. *The Paper Men* (1984).

Goldman, Albert. *The Lives of John Lennon* (1988).

Grant, Douglass. *Margaret the First: A Biography of Margaret Cavendish, Duchess of Newcastle* (1957).

Grant, Michael. *The Twelve Caesars* (1975).

Grayling, A. C. *The Quarrel of the Age: The Life and Times of William Hazlitt* (2001).

Grushow, Ira. "Biography as Literature." *Southern Humanities Review*, Spring 1980.

Guiles, Fred Lawrence. *Norma Jean: The Life of Marilyn Monroe* (1970).

Guralnick, Peter. *Last Train to Memphis: The Rise of Elvis Presley* (1994).

———. *Careless Love: The Unmaking of Elvis Presley* (1999).

Gurevich, Aron. *Medieval Popular Culture: Problems of Belief and Perception* (1988).

Gutman, Robert. *Mozart: A Cultural Biography* (1999).

Hall, David W. *A Heart Promptly Offered: The Revolutionary Leadership of John Calvin* (2006).

Halperin, John. *Novelists in Their Youth* (1990).

Hamilton, Ian. *In Search of J. D. Salinger* (1988).

———. *Keepers of the Flame* (1994).

Handlin, Oscar. *Truth in History* (1979).

Harris, Mark. *Saul Bellow: Drumlin Woodchuck* (1980).

Harrison, Kathryn. *Saint Thérèse of Lisieux* (2003).

Hart, Francis. R. *Scott as Romantic Biographer* (1971).

Heffernan, Thomas J. *Sacred Biography: Saints and Their Biographers in the Middle Ages* (1988).

Heilbrun, Carolyn. *Writing a Woman's Life* (1988).

———. *Women's Lives: The View from the Threshold* (1999).

Hibbert, Christopher. *George III: A Personal History* (2000).

———. *Disraeli: The Victorian Dandy Who Became Prime Minister* (2006).

Hildeshimer, Wolfgang. *Marbot: A Biography* (1983).

Hilles, Frederick W., ed. *New Light on Dr. Johnson: Essays on the Occasion of his 250th Birthday* (1967).

Hintz, Evelyn J. "A Speculative Introduction: Life-Writing as Drama." *Mosaic*, Fall 1987.

Hoberman, Ruth. *Modernizing Lives: Experiments in English Biography 1918–1939* (1987).

Holden, Anthony. *The Tarnished Crown: Diana and the House of Windsor* (1993).

Holmes, Richard. *Footsteps* (1985).

———. *Coleridge: Early Visions* (1990).

———. *Dr. Johnson and Mr. Savage* (1994).

Homberger, Eric, and John Charmley. *The Troubled Face of Biography* (1988).

Honan, Park. *Author's Lives* (1990).

James, Henry. *The Aspern Papers* (1888).

———. "The Real Right Thing" (1898).

Johnson, Diane. *Lesser Lives* (1972).

Johnson, Edgar. *One Mighty Torrent: The Drama of Biography* (1937).

Johnson, Samuel. *Lives of the Poets* (1781).

Jungk, Peter Stephan. *The Perfect American* (2005).

Kaplan, Fred. *Thomas Carlyle: A Biography* (1983).

Kelley, Kitty. *His Way: The Unauthorized Biography of Frank Sinatra* (1986).

Kendall, Paul Murray. *The Art of Biography* (1965).

Keynes, Geoffrey. *John Evelyn* (1937).

Langer, Elinor. *Josephine Herbst: The Story She Could Never Tell* (1984).

Lees, Francis Noel. "The Keys Are at the Palace: A Note on Criticism and Biography." *Literary Criticism and Historical Understanding. Selected Papers from the English Institute*, ed. Phillip Damon (1967).

Le Guin, Charles A. "The Language of Portraiture." *Biography* 6 (1983).

Leibowitz, Herbert A. *Fabricating Lives: Explorations in American Autobiography* (1991).

Lewis, Roger. *Anthony Burgess: A Biography* (2004).

Lingeman, Richard. *Theodore Dreiser: An American Journey* (abridged edition, 1993).

Lively, Penelope. *According to Mark* (1984).

Lochhead, Marion. *John Gibson Lockhart* (1954).

Longaker, Mark. *English Biography in the Eighteenth Century* (1931).

Loving, Jerome. *The Last Titan: A Life of Theodore Dreiser* (2005).

Lurie, Alison. *The Truth About Lorin Jones* (1988).

McGinley, Bernard. *Joyce's Lives: Uses and Abuses of the Biografiend* (1996).

McGreevey, James. *The Confession* (2006).

Mailer, Norman. *Marilyn* (1972).

———. *The Executioner's Song* (1979).

Malamud, Bernard. *Dubin's Lives* (1979).

Malcolm, Janet. *The Silent Woman* (1994).

Mann, Thomas. *Doctor Faustus* (1948).

Markus, Julia. *J. Anthony Froude: The Last Great Undiscovered Victorian* (2005).

Marrs, Suzanne. *Eudora Welty: A Biography* (2005).

Marshall, Gerald W. "John Evelyn and the Construction of the Scientific Self." In *The Restoration Mind* (1935).

Maugham, W. Somerset. *Cakes and Ale, or The Skeleton in the Cupboard* (1930).

Maurois, André. *Aspects of Biography* (1929).

May, Georges. "'His Life, His Works': Some Observations on Literary Biography." *Diogenes*, Fall 1987.

Mazlish, Bruce. *James and John Stuart Mill: Father and Son in the Nineteenth Century* (1975).

Meade, Marion. *Buster Keaton: Cut to the Chase: A Biography* (1995).

Meyers, Jeffrey, ed. *The Biographer's Art: New Essays* (1989).

Milford, Nancy. *Zelda* (1970).

Millgate, Michael. *Testamentary Acts: Browning, Tennyson, James, Hardy* (1992).

Millhauser, Steven. *Edwin Mullhouse: The Life and Death of an American Writer, 1943–1954, by Jeffrey Cartwright* (1972).

Mitchell, Roger. *Clear Pond: The Reconstruction of a Life* (1991).

Momigliano, Arnaldo. *The Development of Greek Biography* (1971).

Moorehead, Caroline. *Gellhorn: A Twentieth-Century Life* (2006).

———. *Selected Letters of Martha Gellhorn* (2006).

Morris, Edmund. *Dutch: A Memoir* (1999).

———. *Beethoven: The Universal Composer* (2005).

Morton, Andrew. *Diana: Her True Story* (1992).

Nabokov, Vladimir. *The Real Life of Sebastian Knight* (1941).

Nadel, Bruce Ira, ed. *Victorian Biography: A Collection of Essays from the Period* (1986).

Nagourney, Peter. "The Basic Assumptions of Literary Biography." *Biography* Spring 1978.

Nelson, William. *Fact or Fiction: The Dilemma of the Renaissance Storyteller* (1973).

Nettles, Elsa. "Henry James and the Art of Biography." *South Atlantic Bulletin*, November 1978.

Nicolson, Harold. *Some People* (1927).

———. *The Development of English Biography* (1928).

Niven, Penelope. *Carl Sandburg* (1991).

———. *Carl Sandburg: Adventures of Poet* (2003).

Nolin, Bertil. *Georg Brandes* (1976).

Noonan, Peggy. *John Paul the Great: Remembering a Spiritual Father* (2006).

Notestein, Wallace. "History and the Biographer. *Yale Review*, vol. 22, 1933.

Novarr, David. *The Lines of Life: Theories of Biography, 1880–1970* (1986).

Oates, Joyce Carol. "The Sacred Marriage." In *Marriages and Infidelities* (1972).

O'Brien, Patrick. "Is Political Biography a Good Thing?" *Biography*, Winter 1996.

Oliviera, Carmen. *Rare and Commonplace Flowers: The Story of Elizabeth Bishop and Lota de Macedo Soares* (2002).

O'Neill, Edward. *A History of American Biography, 1800–1935* (1935).

Perks, Robert, and Alistair Thompson, eds. *The Oral History Reader* (1998).

Peters, Margot. "Group Biographies: Challenges and Methods." *New Directions in Biography*, ed. Anthony M. Friedman (1981).

Petrie, Dennis W. *Ultimately Fiction: Design in Modern American Literary Biography* (1981).

Pimlott, Ben. *Frustrate Their Knavish Tricks: Writings on Biography, History, and Politics* (1995).

Pinto, Vivian de Sola. *English Biography in the Seventeenth Century: Selected Short Lives* (1951).

Piper, David. "The Development of the British Literary Portrait Up to Samuel Johnson." *Proceedings of the British Academy*, vol. 54, 1968.

Powell, Anthony. *John Aubrey and His Friends* (1948).

Powers, Lyall, ed. *Leon Edel and Literary Art* (1988).

Pritchard, Allan. *English Biography in the Seventeenth Century: A Critical Survey* (2005).

Reed, Joseph W., Jr. *English Biography in the Early Nineteenth Century, 1831–1838* (1966).

Reid, B. L. *Necessary Lives: Biographical Reflections* (1990).

Remini, Robert. *Joseph Smith* (2002).

Rhiel, Mary, and David Suchoff, eds. *The Seductions of Biography* (1996).

Robins, Jane. *The Trial of Queen Caroline* (2006).

Rollyson, Carl. *Marilyn Monroe: A Life of the Actress* (1986).

———. *Lillian Hellman: Her Legend and Her Legacy* (1988).
———. *Nothing Ever Happens to the Brave: The Story of Martha Gellhorn* (1990).
———. *Biography: An Annotated Bibliography* (1991).
———. *The Lives of Norman Mailer: A Biography* (1991).
———. *Picasso* (1993).
———. *Rebecca West: A Saga of the Century* (1996).
——— and Lisa Paddock. *Susan Sontag: The Making of an Icon* (2000).
———. *Beautiful Exile: The Life of Martha Gellhorn* (2004).
———. *Reading Biography* (2004).
———. *Biography Before Boswell* (2005).
———. *Essays in Biography* (2005).
———. *Female Icons: Marilyn Monroe to Susan Sontag* (2005).
———. *A Higher Form of Cannibalism: Adventures in the Art and Politics of Biography* (2005).
———. *Lives of the Novelists* (2005).
———. *To Be a Woman: The Life of Jill Craigie* (2005).
Ronell, Avital. *Dictations: On Haunted Writing* (1986).
Rose, Phyllis. *Parallel Lives: Five Victorian Marriages* (1983).
———. "Fact and Fiction in Biography." In *Writing of Women: Essays in a Renaissance* (1985).
Rushton, Julian. *Mozart* (2006).
Russell, D. A. *Plutarch* (1973).
Sadie, Stanley. *Mozart: The Early Years, 1756–1781* (2005).
Salwak, Dale, ed. *The Literary Biography* (1996).
Sartre, Jean-Paul. *Nausea* (1938).
———. *Saint Genet* (1952).
———. *The Family Idiot: Gustave Flaubert, 1821–1857* (1981).
Satkowski, Leon. *Giorgio Vasari: Architect and Courtier* (1993).
Scardigli, Barbara, ed. *Essays on Plutarch's Lives* (1995).
Scriven, Michael. *Sartre's Existential Biographies* (1984).
Serafin, Steven, ed. *American Literary Biographers. First Series* (1991).
———. *American Literary Biographers. Second Series* (1991).
———. *Eighteenth Century British Literary Biographers* (1994).
———. *Nineteenth Century British Literary Biographers* (1994).
Shelston, Alan. *Biography* (1977).
Sisman, Adam. *Boswell's Presumptuous Task* (2001).
Smith, Sally Bedell. *Diana in Search of Herself: Portrait of a Troubled Princess* (1999).
Smythe, Charles. "Historical Biography and Mr. Strachey." *The Criterion*, vol. 8, 1929.
Solomon, Maynard. *Mozart: A Life* (1995).
Spacks, Patricia Meyer. *Gossip* (1985).

Stahl, Jerry. *I, Fatty* (2005).

Stannard, David E. *Shrinking History: On Freud and the Failure of Psychohistory* (1980).

Stauffer, Donald A. *English Biography Before 1700* (1930).

———. *Late Nineteenth and Early Twentieth Century British Literary Biographers* (1995).

Stone, Lawrence. "Prosopography." *Daedalus*, Winter 1971.

Strachey, Lytton. *Eminent Victorians* (1918).

———. *Queen Victoria* (1921).

———. *Portraits in Miniature and Other Essays* (1931).

Stuart, Duane Reid. *Epochs of Greek and Roman Biography* (1967).

Sussman, Peter Y. *Decca: The Letters of Jessica Mitford* (2006).

Swanberg, W. A. *Dreiser* (1965).

Symons, A. J. A. *The Quest for Corvo* (1934).

Taylor, A. J. P. *The Habsburg Monarchy* (1948).

Terkel, Studs. *Hard Times: An Oral History of the Great Depression* (1977).

Thayer, William Roscoe. *The Art of Biography* (1920).

Thomson, David. *Warren Beatty and Desert Eyes: A Life and a Story* (1987).

Tillyard, E. M. W., and C. S. Lewis. *The Personal Heresy: A Controversy* (1939).

Tims, Hilton. *Erich Maria Remarque: The Last Romantic* (2003).

Tosches, Nick. *King of the Jews* (2005).

"Tough Talk: A Conversation with Peter Manso." *Provincetown Annual,* Summer 1987.

Tripp, C. A. *The Intimate World of Abraham Lincoln* (2005).

Updike, John. "Two Cheers for Biography." *New York Review of Books,* April 3, 2000.

Uphaus, Robert. *William Hazlitt* (1985).

Vesterman, William. "Johnson and the *Life of Savage*." *ELH,* vol. 36, 1969.

Vine, Barbara. *The Blood Doctor* (2003).

Waldron, Ann. *Claude Monet: First Impressions* (1991).

———. *Francisco Goya* (1992).

———. *Eudora: A Writer's Life* (1998).

Walter, James, and Raija Nugent, eds. *Biographers at Work* (1984).

Wardman, Alan. *Plutarch's Lives* (1974).

Wellek, Rene. *A History of Modern Criticism* (1965).

Welty, Eudora. *One Writer's Beginnings* (1984).

Wendorf, Richard. *Articulate Images: The Sister Arts from Hogarth to Tennyson* (1983).

Wheeler, David, ed. *Domestick Privacies: Samuel Johnson and the Art of Biography* (1987).

White, Newman. "The Development, Use and Abuse of Interpretation in Biography." In *English Institute Essays* (1943).

White, Richard, Jr. *Kingfish: The Reign of Huey P. Long* (2006).

Whittemore, Reed. *Whole Lives: The Shapers of Modern Biography* (1988).

———. *Pure Lives* (1989).

Wilson, Arthur M. "The Humanistic Bases of Biographical Interpretation." *English Institute Annual* (1942).

Wilson, F. P. *Seventeenth-Century Prose: Five Lectures* (1960).

Wilson, John Scott. "Popular History and Biography." *Handbook of American Popular Culture,* ed. M. Thomas Inge (1989).

Woolf, Virginia. *Jacob's Room* (1922).

———. *Orlando* (1922).

———. *Flush: A Biography* (1933).

———. "The Art of Biography." In *The Death of the Moth and Other Essays* (1942).

Worthen, John. *D. H. Lawrence: The Early Years, 1885–1912* (1991).

Young-Breuhl, Elizabeth. In "The Complexities and Rewards of Biography Should Be Better Appreciated on Campuses." *Chronicle of Higher Education,* January 10, 1990.

Ziegler, Philip. *Edward VIII* (1991).

Index

A NOTE ON THE AUTHOR

Carl Rollyson has written biographies of Rebecca West, Norman Mailer, Martha Gellhorn, Lillian Hellman, Marilyn Monroe, and (with Lisa Paddock) Susan Sontag. He has also written or edited a number of literary studies and reference works, among them *Reading Susan Sontag, Herman Melville A to Z*, and *A Critical Survey of Long Fiction*. He has been a Fulbright Fellow and is now professor of English at Baruch College of the City University of New York. He lives in Cape May County, New Jersey.